TEST YOUR SELF AND THOSE YOU LOVE

TEST YOUR SELF AND THOSE YOU LOVE

Evaluate Your Mental Health and Reclaim Joy

WILLIAM GLADSTONE AND NELL GIBBON

Waterside Productions

Printed in the United States of America

First Printing, 2020

ISBN-13: 978-1-949001-62-4 print edition
ISBN-13: 978-1-949001-63-1 ebook edition

Waterside Productions
2055 Oxford Ave
Cardiff, CA 92007
www.waterside.com

TABLE OF CONTENTS

Acknowledgements · vii

Introduction · ix
- How Do I Use This Book? · x
- History of The NASA Mental Health Test, from William Gladstone · · · · · · · · · · · · xii

Part 1: Your First Consultation · 1

Chapter 1: Your First Consultation; This is Where & How We Begin · · · · · · · · · · · · · · · · · 3

Chapter 2: The Seven Characteristics of Human Behavior Healthcare Providers Care About · · · · · · · 6

Chapter 3: The Five Stages of Emotional Wellbeing · 12

Part II: Test Your Emotional Wellbeing · 19

Chapter 4: Take The NASA Test · 21

Part III: Self-Assessments for Every Life Stage · 43

Chapter 5: What's My Personality Type? · 45

Chapter 6: What Life Events Are Really Stressing You Out? · 61

Chapter 7: A Clinical Look at Depression · 65

Chapter 8: How Bad is My Anxiety? · 86

Chapter 9: Bully or Bullied? Assessments to See if You're One or the Other · · · · · · · · · · · · · · 98

Chapter 10: Spotting Potentially Violent Behavior & Gun Violence · · · · · · · · · · · · · · · 104

Chapter 11: Do I Have an Eating Disorder or Disordered Eating? · · · · · · · · · · · · · · · · 108

Chapter 12: Do I Drink Too Much Alcohol? · 113

Chapter 13: Do I Have a Drug Problem? ·118

Chapter 14: How's Your Love Life? Take Our Relationship & Marriage Assessment · · · · · · · · · · · 125

Chapter 15: Are You in an Unhealthy Relationship? A Chapter on Abuse · · · · · · · · · · · 134

Chapter 16: Do I Have the Baby Blues? Testing Your Mood During Pregnancy and Postpartum · · · · 141

Chapter 17: On Post Traumatic Stress Disorder With a Special Section for Armed
Forces Members and First Responders · 153

Chapter 18: On Aging, Test for Vitality & Your Risk for Alzheimer's · · · · · · · · · · · · · · 160

Chapter 19: The Importance of a Spiritual Intake · 169

Part IV: Getting The Help You Need and Deserve · 175

Getting The Help You Need and Deserve · 177
- Where Do I Go for Help and What Should I Expect? · 177
- A Brief Explanation of the Most Popular Types of Clinical Treatments · · · · · · · · · 178
- How Do I Afford Therapy? · 179

- How Do I Make Time for Therapy? · 180
- Can You Recommend Self-Care Tips? · 180
- How Should I Intervene When I Think Someone Needs Help? · · · · · · · · · · · · 183

Part V · 187
Conclusion: In the End Adversity Makes Us Stronger · · · · · · · · · · · · · · · · · 189
Appendix A: Resource Directory · 191
Appendix B: Book Recommendations · 197
Appendix C: Hotlines · 205
Notes · 207

ACKNOWLEDGEMENTS

The authors would like to acknowledge the contributions of the many mental health professionals who made this book possible. First, we would like to thank Dr. Douglas H. Powell of Harvard University Health Services. Dr. Powell developed the Theory of the Five States of Adaptability (which we renamed The Five Stages of Wellbeing for this current edition) in conjunction with his research as a NASA consultant and Harvard University-affiliated psychologist.

We were inspired by Dr. Powell's work to create our modernized version of The NASA Test, which tests one's overall wellbeing and ability to cope in the face of stressful live events or circumstances. We have modified Dr. Powell's theory to the needs of the general public and have developed our own thoughts concerning the nature and treatment of mental illness and emotional wellbeing. The NASA Test and the remainder of this book are entirely the responsibility of the authors.

We would also like to thank the many other researchers, psychologists, and psychiatrists who have generously allowed their tests to be adapted and reproduced for this book. We are grateful for their skill, dedication, and diligence in devising practical testing instruments for the benefit of all.

Finally, we have relied on our own backgrounds and experience as a clinical psychotherapist and a professional anthropologist in presenting this material in a sensitive and useful manner. In putting together our unique package of tests and information, we have attempted to be faithful to the spirit of the material we have selected.

Introduction: A Letter to Our Readers

According to a recently published study in PSYCHOLOGICAL MEDICINE, depression and mental health disorders are increasing rapidly throughout America[1] (most likely the rest of the world as well though the study was only based on data for Americans). Suicide rates, opioid addiction and mass gun violence have never been higher or more prevalent.

The annual suicide rate in America now exceeds fifty thousand with more than one million annual attempts each year.[2] More than one hundred people die every day in America due to gun violence.[3] Almost twenty million Americans suffer from drug addiction.[4] More than seventy thousand Americans die annually from drug overdoses.[5] We must find a way to change these disturbing trends. This book TEST YOUR SELF AND THOSE YOU LOVE: Evaluate Your Mental Health and Reclaim Joy is dedicated to helping end the mental health crisis in America and throughout the world.

We believe self-knowledge is one of the key ingredients a person must possess in order to thrive. TEST YOUR SELF AND THOSE YOU LOVE is a book based on the premise that education in itself is an intervention. This book provides you with crucial mental health information. When used correctly, it acts as an early warning system so you can take control over your own psychological wellbeing and perhaps encourage someone you care about to do the same. Too often people wait too long before they get the help they need and deserve, and a tragedy occurs or they lose precious time — time they can never get back — feeling depressed, or anxious, sick or sad. This DOES NOT have to be the case. We believe happiness is your birthright. We believe powerful psycho-educational tools should be available to anyone who has access to the Internet, bookstore or public library.

Thankfully, having mental health challenges is no longer a stigma to the extent it was forty years ago, when the first version of this book was published. Americans now openly recognize that most people will be impacted by a mental health challenge or a serious addiction, or they will have to help a family member deal with one. Health care professionals have an obligation to encourage individuals to take responsibility for their own mental, emotional, physical and spiritual health. And, in order to prevent local and national tragedies, we as concerned Americans citizens must do a better job teaching others how to gauge the behavior of loved ones, friends, colleagues, students, employees and community members. We must all work together to quickly help and effectively treat someone who exhibits troubling mental health symptoms.

Although we do not encourage readers to psychoanalyze the mental health of friends, family members or coworkers by taking matters into their own hands, we want everyone to familiarize themselves with the symptoms of major mental illnesses and addiction. Knowing what to look for is a fundamental part of the prevention and intervention process. In most cases, you do not need to be confrontational, but if you see something, say something – as the Sandy Hook Promise organization advises all of us to do. Perhaps gently leaving a copy of this book with someone you're concerned about will serve as the catalyst that will encourage them to seek help.

Remember, TEST YOUR SELF AND THOSE YOU LOVE doesn't replace a visit to a trained health-care professional, but it hopefully does spur someone to see a provider. Only that provider can properly evaluate the situation and recommend a treatment plan. So please, always seek the advice of a trained professional if you have any questions or need further guidance.

TEST YOURSELF AND THOSE YOU LOVE now contains over 30 clinically proven mental health assessments – covering a variety of situations from pregnancy to your personality type – while still featuring The NASA Mental Health Test which has been carefully modernized for your needs without losing any of its effectiveness. Many of the tests contained in this definitive guide aren't just thought provoking, they're fun and easy to score. And the best part is you can enjoy taking them from the comfort of your own home, office, agency or dorm room.

As a highly trained psychotherapist, journalist and social activist, Nell Daly has dedicated her life's work to helping people master stress and overcome personal challenges so they can live lives filled with more joy and purpose. William Gladstone — as a Harvard University trained cultural anthropologist, author, film maker and book publisher — has examined the nature of stress on individuals and groups for many decades. Together they have rewritten Mr. Gladstone's best-selling *Psychology Today* Book of the Month Club "featured selection" which has already sold more than 250,000 copies.

The original NASA TEST, the assessment that centers our book, was developed by Dr. Douglas. H. Powell while he was employed by NASA. NASA invested hundreds of thousands of dollars developing this original test which was used to select the first astronauts for America's space program. Dr. Powell then adapted the test for use by Harvard University psychologists to spot signs of mental illness and to prevent suicides among Harvard students and graduate students. Mr. Gladstone, working alongside Dr. Powell, created a version suitable for self-testing which you now have unique access to in this book.

Nell has handpicked the other thirty-plus assessments and carefully added directions and guidance on how to take and score them. Where necessary, she provides background based on twenty thousand plus hours of patient interventions. Nell has treated every type of patient and problem – her advice can be trusted.

We encourage you to take this test and share it with those you love. We advise you to complete the other assessments that are applicable to your life. You'll quickly learn more about how you're feeling right now and what you need to do to feel better.

No matter who you are or where you find yourself in life at this moment TEST YOUR SELF AND THOSE YOU LOVE offers you guidance and entertainment. We hope this book helps you individually and those you love. One never knows how important a book or kindness can be to others. Be good to yourself and those around you and let's create a world that is full of joy, creativity, free from suffering and full of meaning.

All the best,
William Gladstone and Nell Daly

How to Use This Book

We've designed this book to make it easy and entertaining to assess your own mental health. Remember, you're unique and have your own particular strengths and weaknesses. Our goal is to help you get a sense of how well you're coping and if there are any other pressing issues you or someone you care about should address.

The book is divided into four parts.

Part 1 serves as a foundation for the rest of the book. It provides some light easy-to-read psycho-education for the reader to learn from Nell's experience in mental instability: poor diet (gut health), toxins in the environment, an increase in violence in our society, disconnection from each other due to reliance on technology, past trauma, etc.

Nell discusses how symptoms are messengers and our ability to cope (or not) under stress is a strong indicator of a person's mental health status and strength. Nell introduces the *Five Stages of Emotional Wellbeing* and then we round out the chapter by going through The Seven Characteristics of Human Behavior that clinical psychologists look at when they assess you as a patient—setting the stage for Part 2.

In **Part 2** of the book, Bill introduces the most comprehensive exam in the book—a one of a kind test modified from a questionnaire developed by NASA that measures a person's overall wellbeing. Again, this distinctive *Test of Adaptability*—which we renamed The NASA Test—was inspired by a Harvard-affiliated psychologist and the work he did for NASA screening future astronauts.

Adaptability, as it turns out, is an indicator of both your mental health status and strength. Put another way, how resilient you are in the face of adversity determines in large part the quality and trajectory of your life. Your results from The NASA Test will tell you your baseline. Before implementing a treatment plan, health care providers need to determine your baseline. Now with The NASA Test, you can determine it, too.

We then follow the test up with a section dedicated to helping readers interpret their results which should be used as a jumping off point, not to self-diagnose or replace medical care by a licensed provider.

In **Part 3** of *Test Your Self*, you'll find a compilation of carefully selected instructive self-assessments and personality tests. These tests assess common issues many of us face, both personally and in our families, during certain life stages. For example, we have a test that determines if you may be at risk for suicide (with a specific subtest for teenagers), suffering with an eating disorder, a test that measures drinking habits, calculates your stress levels and looks into the health of your marriage. We've included questionnaires on postpartum depression, PTSD, memory loss and stress, just to name a few.

One of the most profound surveys in this chapter gauges a person's anger management style and levels of impulse control. This is in conjunction with work that Sandy Hook Promise is currently doing; teaching people what the warning signs are of someone who might be at risk of committing a public shooting. This will be extremely useful to parents and school administrators who are worried about a student who is becoming socially isolated.

We have ordered the tests chronologically according to life phases. The tests come with a detailed set of directions and an explanation of what the assessment tests for. The tests can range from 10 to 50 questions and they're all easy to score with segments at the end that help readers properly evaluate and understand their results. In this section you'll see pop outs with "Quick Stats" and at the end each chapter we provide you with tips. Look for "What Will Help You."

Part 4 answers any lingering questions the reader may have about next steps. We talk about how to get help and what to expect when you do get help. We give suggestions about how to intervene when you think someone you know or care about might be in trouble. We briefly discuss a variety of modern and proven treatment modalities: nutrition tips, information on meditation and psycho-spiritual practices, the value of belonging to a community organization, the power of relational therapy and how we all need more sleep and more hydration in our lives. Lastly we provide lots of practical ways you can improve the quality of your life and the lives of those around you starting today.

In our **Appendix** section, we provide an extensive current resource guide corresponding to each chapter / mental disorder or social issue presented in the book.

Ultimately this book is designed to help readers learn about mental health in a very personal way. It's designed to help readers decide if they should or shouldn't seek further treatment; for many this is a difficult decision to make. It's a guide meant for families to use in times of crisis. It doesn't replace medical care. It supplements your wellbeing regime with information.

We encourage people to take these tests because they have been proven effective—sometimes just seeing the scores spurs change – and often individuals discover their own strengths and weaknesses. We urge readers to dive into the last section of the book and explore new treatments and pathways to self-care. You may want to share this book with friends, family, and others. In helping others, you help yourself.

The History of The NASA Test

In the words of William Gladstone…

"I met Dr. Powell when I was a graduate student at Harvard University in 1976 studying medical anthropology. Dr. Powell had just arrived from NASA where he had been one of the head psychologists selecting astronauts for America's Space Program. He was then subsequently hired by Harvard to assist with Harvard's mental health services for undergraduates, graduates, faculty and employees. At that time the primary concern at Harvard was the relatively high rate of undergraduates committing suicide.

I sat in on a lecture Dr. Powell gave where he distributed a seven page document to the graduate student fellows attending an Adams House dinner. Dr. Powell explained that while at NASA he had developed a behavioral based test of adaptability that he had used to measure the mental fitness of those intending to become astronauts. It was important that such candidates showed not just mental toughness but adaptability since they would be facing conditions in space travel for which they could not be truly prepared for in advance.

I was immediately fascinated by the psychological test that he had created. I started checking off symptoms that applied to my own mental state and observed that almost every other graduate student in attendance was doing the same.

Dr. Powell spent the next forty-five minutes explaining how to use the test and how to spot signs of mental illness among our undergraduate charges. I was seriously impressed with how simple and easy the test was! I also quickly recognized that this was a test that could save lives.

After the lecture, I introduced myself to Dr. Powell and explained to him my interest in medical anthropology and that as an anthropologist I was impressed with his approach to measuring mental health. **Dr. Powell had unintentionally or not developed in his work with NASA a measuring tool that could be applied cross culturally to any population and any nationality.**

This was profound.

I met with Dr. Powell the following month and presented to him, in greater detail, my vision for a popular book based on his NASA TEST OF ADAPTABILITY. Dr. Powell felt this was an excellent idea and encouraged me to develop a full outline with sample chapters that he approved. We quickly found a book publisher.

When the book was finished Dr. Powell was pleased with the work, but unfortunately had to recuse himself as being listed as a co-author as advised by the head of Harvard's Psychology department (he was under some pressure to publish an academic book, not a work in the field of popular psychology. Dr. Powell removed his name from the book but gave me his blessing with the hope that the book would help many people.

As it turned out Dr. Powell was granted his wish. The original edition of How to Test Your Mental Health sold in excess of 250,000 copies and was chosen by Psychology Today as a featured selection in the Psychology Today book club."

PART I

Chapter 1: Your First Consultation; This is Where & How We Begin

Nell Gibbon

"I have no idea where to begin."

Without fail, these are the first words patients ever say to me.

When they come into my office for that initial session, they're usually overwhelmed, highly symptomatic and worried about how they're going to unpack their emotions for me in just sixty minutes.

Sitting across from them, I smile softly knowing it's on me to make them feel comfortable. "Don't worry," I say in a calm but encouraging tone, "Start wherever you like. We'll eventually make sense of your story."

It usually doesn't take long for someone who desperately wants psychic relief to spill what's plaguing their heart, mind and soul. Most of the time, whatever they're trying to resolve or let go of, has been bottled up and it's a relief to get it all out to someone who is objective. People, in general, wait too long to get help. The truth is many of us waste an enormous amount of time feeling stuck and sick when we don't really have to.

As they grab for tissues and fidget nervously on my couch, new patients go on to tell me how and why they feel depressed, anxious, confused, broken hearted, disassociated, angry, betrayed, in love, in lust, lost and exhausted. I listen attentively and look for clues. I read their affect. I try to determine if they may be suffering with something listed in the DSM-5 (the traditional and widely accepted manual mental health workers use for diagnostic purposes and billing codes), or if what's bringing them into therapy is something more external: a divorce, a miscarriage, or a recent move that's left them feeling isolated and empty.

After they finish "unpacking" their story, (and this often takes more than just one session), we take a collective deep breath and exhale; pieces of their life metaphorically askew on the coffee table between us.

"Do you want to know what I think?" I typically ask, breaking the inevitable silence that settles over the room.

"Yes, of course," they say. They are in my office, in the end, for some direction and advice.

If I think it won't cause further harm, I let them know what, in my clinical opinion, is going on. I've always felt it's unethical to treat someone for something without telling them a "diagnosis," (if I see one), even though many of us were trained to not disclose our true feelings unless asked. In my opinion, early stage therapy – at its best – should be infused with what we call psychoeducation.

Psychoeducation refers to the process of providing information to those seeking or receiving mental health services. Yes, much of a therapist's or psychiatrist's job entails helping people understand if they have a problem, what caused the problem, and mapping out a path towards healing.

We're clearly in the middle of a mental health crisis in this country. Bill and I are well aware that private treatment is, in many cases, a luxury because not everyone can afford therapy and not everyone feels comfortable seeking help. Our intention with *Test Your Self* is to remove a barrier to treatment. We wrote this book to give the general public inexpensive access to quality psycho-education, the exact same kind I give in my office, and to give clinicians better tools to evaluate and determine a patient's baseline.

Nothing can or should ever take the place of getting a thorough mental health evaluation from a trained health care professional. However, *Test Your Self* can help anyone jumpstart their healing process. The simple battery of tests, anyone can take from the privacy of their own home, will teach people more about their personality type, wellbeing, relationships and any common mental health issue listed in the book.

The NASA Test, when taken correctly, provides anyone with a solid baseline of their mental health status and the chapters leading up to it – *The Seven Characteristics of Human Behavior that Healthcare Providers Care About* and *The Five Stages of Emotional Wellbeing* – are jam packed with psychological information you'll find useful at any stage of life. And, because we couldn't stop there, each chapter has loads of tips to guide our readers towards next healthcare steps, just in case you or someone you love feels like the assessment or content of any given chapter deeply resonated with them. Please note, even if an assessment that you take doesn't show you have a cause for concern, a healthcare provider should be consulted if you think there is a mental health issue that needs attention.

What Causes Mental Health Problems?

People, understandably, want to know what causes their mental health problems, or unwanted negative symptoms. There is rarely ever just one cause. We're all pots of simmering water but sometimes, when you add a combination of new ingredients, we boil over. Perhaps, for example, you suffer with chronic exhaustion and low-grade depression that you haven't been able to shake since you were diagnosed with thyroid disease five years ago. And currently you're having trouble getting pregnant *and* you were just downsized at your job. Individually, none of these things seem from the outside like they would be insurmountable. Yet, when taken together, all of these things hitting at once can cause someone to become highly symptomatic, or in this case more severely depressed or anxious.

Overall, "mental illnesses," or simply being human beings with complex moods, are generally caused by three main factors: psychological triggers, environmental exposure (during prenatal, childhood or adulthood) and genetics. Unfortunately, some of us are born more naturally predisposed to developing certain mood disorders or personality traits that don't always aid our wellbeing.

Take into account that mental/social factors can contribute to the symptoms of mental, emotional, and physical stress. Find where the wounds are and teach people to heal themselves from the inside out.

Your Symptoms Are Messengers

Your pain, your problems, what quietly knocks at your soul – as writer Elizabeth Lesser says – needs to be paid attention to, not dismissed. Those symptoms are warning you that something isn't right either inside of you or outside of you. You're being asked to slow down and listen to what your body and mind and emotional state is trying to tell you. You're being asked to take care of yourself better, to change the way you're living, to transform. Your symptoms are the gateway from which you can identify what needs to be dealt with in your life or in your body, so you can continually step into your full potential.

I can't tell you how many times someone has come into my office and asked me point blank "to make all their anxiety go away." They're always surprised by my answer.

In a world that loves instant gratification, we're always looking for a way to eradicate any uncomfortable pain we feel. But the truth is, fighting through what the uncomfortable is trying to teach us makes us grow, and makes us change the things in our lives that need to be changed. Sometimes we need to feel the pressure of uncomfortable feelings to shift into a more authentic life.

First, figure out what's causing you to feel so anxious and then work on healing that part of your body or your life. Your pain is the messenger. Consult a professional if this is too difficult on your own.

Perhaps anxiety is an abusive marriage, or a gut damaged by artificial sweeteners, or too much alcohol. Perhaps anxiety is saying change jobs, or get more sleep, or finally talk about the death of a loved one. It's not that there isn't a time and a place for psychiatric medication, but we must resist the urge "to fix" our feelings quickly so we can learn what those feelings are trying to tell us. We must fight the urge to believe we are "broken" to begin with and in desperate need of "fixing." There is a big difference between "fixing" and adapting.

The Importance of Being Adaptable

There are a few fundamental truths about people. One was this: people who are in good emotional, spiritual and physical health have a better chance of handling stressful life events than someone who isn't. People who are "well" adapt when life throws them curve balls. The opposite is also true; people who don't take care of their emotional, physical and spiritual health have a very difficult time handling stressful life events. People who are "unwell" generally crumble under stress.

The NASA Test was built to assess whether space candidates were well enough to adapt in space. The results of the test provided a baseline for a candidate's mental health status. It has now become a fantastic scientific tool for anyone to use who wants to know how well he or she is doing, in terms of their mental health and their ability to adapt.

The next chapter has carefully broken down the abstract notion of adaptability into seven concrete and observable aspects. Taken as a whole, these seven characteristics alongside the five elements of well-being offer a very tangible picture of a person's health.

Going Forward

Think of this book as something you can do before a consultation or as an extension of your first consultation; it's psychoeducational gold. Again, you should always seek an accurate diagnosis from a mental health professional, but this book provides an overview of common mental illnesses, stressful events you might experience in any life stage, and self-assessments for each topic to get you thinking more deeply about your own behaviors, attitudes and mental health.

Suggested steps can be taken to further educate yourself and/or receive the help you, or a loved one, deserve. Talking to someone and educating yourself about mental health is essential to bettering yourself. You can speak to a religious figure (minister, rabbi, priest), school therapist, trusted adult, friend, doctor, clinical therapist, psychologist or alternative healer to help guide you – or someone you love – back on the right track to healing, recovering and thriving.

CHAPTER 2: THE SEVEN CHARACTERISTICS OF HUMAN BEHAVIOR HEALTHCARE PROVIDERS CARE ABOUT

The Seven Characteristics of Human Behavior

Our model of *The Five Stages of Emotional Wellbeing* is based on seven characteristics of your life that doctors and therapists universally use to evaluate new clients or patients. Each characteristic refers to a definable area of behavior or what's sometimes called "aspect of your life" that is distinct and observable.

1) Your Anxiety/Stress Levels
2) Your Mood
3) Your Thoughts
4) Your Level of Activity
5) Your Ability to Organize Thoughts & Routines (Self Discipline)
6) The Quality of Your Interpersonal Relationships
7) The Status of Your Physical Wellbeing (Physical Health)

In real life, of course, there is plenty of crossover among these seven characteristics with changes in one characteristic often associated with and dependent upon changes in another. For example, a change in Mood (#2), might either provoke or be the result of a change in a romantic relationship, which obviously falls under the characteristic of Interpersonal Relationships (#6) or the Status of Your Physical Wellbeing (#7). Because one characteristic can clearly affect the others, we always pay close attention to all seven characteristics throughout this book.

After we assess how you're doing in each characteristic by asking you lots of questions, we put all of the scores together and look at the whole picture. Those scores will give us a clearer picture of your overall mental health. We can then fit you into one of the Five Stages of Emotional Wellbeing. Put more simply, we're going to ask you questions to assess each of these seven areas of your life and then your score will tell you what stage of emotional wellbeing you fall into: a highly functional stage, a normal stressed out stage, showing some clear signs that you're having trouble coping stage, that you're in a highly dysfunctional state or that your behavior is alarming.

We are going to figure out how you're personally doing by using different pieces of evidence. So, think of building your psychological profile like you would a legal case. A single piece of incriminating evidence, such as a motive, is not necessarily significant unless associated with other types of evidence – access to the murder weapon, lack of an alibi, opportunity to perform the act, and so forth. When several different strands of evidence are taken together and align with each other, then and only then can a strong case be made for reaching a conclusion.

The same holds true when we're trying to paint a picture of someone's mental health. A single disturbed behavior pattern for characteristic #7, Physical, associated with a majority of normal behavior patterns would not necessarily indicate a pattern of highly dysfunctional behavior. But highly dysfunctional behavior patterns for all seven characteristics would be very strong indicators that a mental imbalance is present, and needs to be addressed.

LET'S CLEARLY DEFINE EACH ASPECT FOR YOU

Although the names of the seven characteristics are common words, please do not assume that you understand exactly what they mean. Yes, these are everyday words but mental health professionals use them in a slightly different way. We want to provide you some more detail before you take our *Test of Adaptability*. Please read the following definitions and examples.

Characteristic #1: Your Anxiety/Stress Levels

Stress refers to the levels of anxiety you feel on a daily basis. Therapists and doctors want to know how much your stress and anxiety levels interfere with your ability to function during the day.

We all know what anxiety feels like but just in case you need a little refresher, here are a list of common symptoms: agitation, fingernail biting, sweating, rapid breathing, a sense of physical tightness, and nervousness. Sometimes anxiety can make you feel nauseous, easily overwhelmed and even depressed (because you're so anxious all the time). So when we start asking you questions about your anxiety and stress levels were also touching on your Mood (#2) and your Physical Wellbeing (#7).

It's important to remember, as we look at stress, certain amounts of anxiety or stress in everyday life is both inevitable and necessary. To feel nervous or anxious on, let's say, a first date, when attending an important business conference, or right before delivering a school speech is common. In fact, feeling stress and anxiety plays a vital role in many tasks. It motivates us and often times, if channeled correctly, improves "our game." This is considered positive stress.

Common examples of negative stress or anxiety that should be treated are: if a person wakes up feeling panicky for weeks, has trouble riding on the subway because they're afraid of a terrorist attack or being closed in, or feels persistently nauseous all day at work, constantly worried they're going to make a mistake. Chronic states of moderate anxiety to severe stress are not healthy for the mind or the body.

Characteristics #2: Your Mood

Mood refers to how a person feels. Everyone experiences different moods at different times. There are irritable moods and pleasant moods. There are moods of happiness, sadness, optimism, pessimism, or numbness. As such, a mood is a relative term that depends in large part on your general personality type, your temperament and the circumstances in which you find yourself. For example, what's an optimistic mood for a cynic may resemble a pessimistic mood for a wide-eyed idealist.

In evaluating your own mood, it's best to judge by your own experience of emotions and not by stereotyped images of joy or sadness presented in films, television and of course – social media! Moods usually have a direct cause and are of short or moderate duration. Failing an examination, not getting an expected raise at work, losing a baseball game after making a crucial error – these are the kinds of events that provoke moods of sadness, irritability, or depression, depending on individual circumstances. This is normal and to be expected.

It would be considered abnormal if such events created a depressed mood that lasted days or even weeks and was not in accordance with more positive experiences that took place after the initial disappointment. In cases of severe mental disorder, a mood of depression or emotional numbness may so overwhelm an individual that he or she is incapable of responding to his or her environment at all.

We want to point out that: **a good guide toward evaluating your pattern and experience of moods is to look at your sense of humor**. A person who is not suffering from mental problems does not lose his or her sense of humor for long, even in the midst of intense feelings of anger, frustration, or sadness. This person is able to step back and laugh at himself or herself and not take life too seriously. Someone with a good sense of humor is also able to appreciate the feelings of others and to allow, through playful jokes and other affectionately intended overtures, to change other people's moods for the better.

If you or someone you know loses their sense of humor for a long period of time, is bitingly sarcastic or is constantly using self-deprecation as a defense—this would certainly be a red flag. These behaviors would be an indication that, in terms of mood experiences, an individual is suffering from some form of mental stress, at the very least. Obviously, if someone isn't able to feel amiable, again, for an extended period of time, a medical evaluation would be recommended.

Characteristic #3: Your Thoughts

We need to know the quality of a person's thoughts: what they're thinking about, how often and are the thoughts mostly negative or positive. Thought behavior is classified in different ways. For the purpose of this book and the test we developed it's important you understand the following types of thoughts: intrusive thinking, ruminating and circular thinking, organized vs. disorganized thinking, and positive vs. negative thinking. Let us explain what we mean in plain language by explaining types of thought patterns that therapists and mental health providers care about.

Intrusive Thinking

Have you ever had the thought that you might spontaneously hurt someone you don't know and wonder *"where did that thought come from?"* Let us start out by saying that some level of intrusive thinking is totally normal.

For example, oftentimes patients come into Nell's office and describe the sensation of standing on the subway platform and all of the sudden they imagine pushing someone in front of the train. Or, many postpartum mothers for example, have intrusive thoughts about hurting their infants. Usually these thoughts are followed by an extreme sense of guilt and fear; fear they're turning into the type of person who might commit a crime. We just want to note here that fear and guilt are actually healthy signs when it comes to intrusive thinking. Less extreme versions of intrusive thinking usually occur when a person is in mourning. They can be flooded with memories of the deceased or missing loved one at the most random times.

Oftentimes just teaching people the concept of intrusive thinking helps alleviate the anxiety they're feeling over not being able to control these thoughts. However, if the thoughts are persistent and interfering with your daily life (remember that's the golden rule we use to determine if something is really a problem or not), or if they are enticed by the thoughts and not bothered by them, further investigation is recommended.

Ruminating or Circular Thinking

We all ruminate from time to time. We all obsess over things that are stressing us out like: a romantic relationship, finances, our children, and our careers. Usually when we ruminate we're trying to figure something out or change something that occurred, something from our past that we now feel we have no control over.

Ruminating or circular thinking becomes a problem when that one thought pattern consumes all of our mental energy and we stop accomplishing daily life tasks that need to get done. Ruminating can be addictive. People who ruminate often suffer from symptoms of depression, anxiety and OCD (obsessive compulsive disorder).

Organized vs. Disorganized Thinking

Have you ever had a hard time following a person's story? They seem "all over the map" or reference people without explaining who they are? These red flags are generally signs of someone who is a disorganized thinker, which is different than someone who has trouble staying on task. It's important to note here that disorganized thinking doesn't necessarily mean a person has ADD or ADHD however it can be a symptom. Organized thinking is described as the ability to start a line of reasoning and to bring it to a conclusion without other thoughts interfering. In other words you're able to have a thought, plan an action and follow through with what needs to get done – without lots of mental noise potentially slowing you down.

Negative Thinking vs. Positive Thinking

The quality of your thoughts really matters. They dictate how you feel about yourself and your life. Unfortunately, we all know what negative thinking is because we all do it – but how much a person does it and what the mental tape says obviously varies from person to person. There have been thousands of studies and books written on the power of negative and positive thinking. For the purpose of this book we're going to keep going back to one question when assessing any of the seven characteristics: if something is interfering with your life, it's probably a problem.

If negative self-talk rules your inner monologue and contributes to low self-esteem, low motivation, and poor moods than it's a problem that needs to be addressed.

However, a word of caution in evaluating thought behavior when you take our *Test of Adaptability*; most people at some time in their life experience all the different forms of thought behaviors described above. The key to evaluating your level of thought behavior is to focus on your most common daily and weekly patterns, not the occasional exceptions.

Characteristic #4: Your Level of Activity

Activity refers to what a person is interested in, how much they accomplish on a daily basis and the level of enthusiasm they have for their chosen activities. Therapists look at a person's drive and energy levels to do activities as a way to evaluate how they're doing and feeling. Activity includes work, play, hobbies, fitness routines, and any task or project that engages both mind and body.

The activity of a healthy person is characterized by an interest in different kinds of activities and a sense of competence in many areas of both personal and group activities. The ability to take risks, to be mediocre in some areas, and to try again after failing is characteristic of a healthy pattern of activities. Under normal circumstances, an individual is able to engage both in continuous activities, such as working on an assembly line for several hours without stopping, and in uneven activities, such as preparing a meal that requires measuring and adding different ingredients while helping their children with their homework.

When an activity becomes compulsive or ritualistic and doesn't give a person a sense of joy or satisfaction, it may indicate a problem. Sometimes people stop doing certain activities because they are no longer challenging, but if that isn't the case, and a person has become unenthusiastic about doing something they once love—they need to be evaluated.

Some key questions to ask yourself that may help you determine how well you're doing with the character trait: are you active or do you think you're relatively inactive compared to others? Are you often hyperactive without really accomplishing anything? Do you do only things that are "important," never taking time off to play or rest or do something silly or inconsequential? Do you follow a rigid set of activities with infrequent changes?

Characteristic #5: Your Ability to Organize Thoughts & Routines (Self Discipline)

Organizational refers to your capacity to plan and carry out whatever you wish to do—and the things that simply need to get done—which make you a highly functioning and responsible member of society. In other words, how much self-discipline or control do you have over your thoughts and behaviors?

Organizational control and how self-disciplined we are shows up in many aspects of our lives: eating habits, work habits, self-care habits, relationship habits, even thinking habits (as we briefly talked about above) just to name a few. This characteristic has a lot to do with what mental health providers call executive functioning—our ability to accomplish tasks and meet goals.

To further clarify what we mean when we talk about this characteristic is a short list of questions we might ask a new patient.

1) Do you have the self-discipline to control your thinking enough to finish tasks on schedule and without difficulty?
2) Do you overextend your abilities in an attempt to do more than you comfortably can in the time at your disposal?
3) Do you need constant encouragement from others to keep at a difficult or tedious job, or are you able to set your own pace and motivate yourself?
4) Do you need a perfect work environment, or are you able to handle ambiguity and disturbances without becoming unsettled?
5) Do you learn from experience or act impulsively, not really examining the pros and cons of different problem-solving strategies?
6) Do you suffer with impulse control?
7) Do you look to gratify a desire before asking yourself if it's good or bad for your wellbeing?

8) How do you handle unexpected events that suddenly force you to change your schedule?

9) Do you have the ability to adapt quickly and maintain your mood or do you start to get super anxious, overly frustrated or angry?

It's easy to be highly functioning, considerate, and in control when you feel good about your life or when your life is going really well. It's how you behave when you feel disappointed, depressed, anxious or stressed that often indicates a more true measurement of your organizational skills, self-discipline and self-control.

Characteristic #6: The Quality of Your Interpersonal Relationships

The aspect of Interpersonal Relationships refers to the quality of your relationships with parents, colleagues, co-workers, neighbors, friends, and members of your community. Mental health providers are highly trained to assess the quality of a patient or client's interpersonal relationships.

We want to make sure that a person forms close bonds with others, sustains healthy short term and long-term stable relationships, works well in groups but also isn't overly dependent on others. We like to see a person exist inter-dependently as opposed to co-dependently with the people closest to them. We also like to see that a patient isn't either avoiding closeness with others or constantly involved in volatile situations with friends and / or romantic partners.

Characteristic #7: Your Physical Wellbeing

In this book, physical wellbeing refers to how well a person feels physically: the presence or absence of bodily symptoms or diseases. It should go without saying that a person's physical wellbeing is very important to assess when you're looking at someone's overall mental health because **physical illness affects mental health and vice versa.**

Common ways in which mental problems may manifest themselves physically include changes in eating and sleeping patterns, gastrointestinal disorders, skin blemishes, headaches, insomnia, or a change in alcohol use. And common ways that physically problems can cause mental health issues are poor gut health or hormonal imbalances that interfere with cognition (brain functioning) and moods.

Chapter 3: The Five Stages of Emotional Wellbeing

The NASA Test was invented to help those running the space program choose astronauts; NASA needed some way of figuring which candidates were emotionally, mentally and physically strong enough to handle going into space. Now The NASA Test it will help you determine, from the comfort of your own home, where you fall on a scale that measures wellbeing. Here is an explanation as to what each stage means.

When you walk into a therapist or doctor's office to an assessment on how you're doing—physically, emotionally and mentally—they begin by asking you lots of questions and listening to your answers, picking up on verbal and nonverbal cues.

How much are your problems (for example, your moods, your finances, your drug use, your physical illness, your recent breakup) affecting your ability to function? We should all ask ourselves this question on a regular basis; the answer immediately helps us determine which parts of our lives need to be cleaned up, changed or healed.

Where one falls on the scale isn't what we call a fixed state; how we function as humans fluctuates from day to day. We can easily flow from one stage of the scale to the other depending on a whole host of internal and external circumstances. In other words, our health changes over time and is a reflection of one's immediate life situation.

When The NASA Test was first developed, they used slightly different words to describe each stage and some of those words we wouldn't find acceptable now. For instance, the test labeled people as neurotic, a term that was popular to use at the time when describing someone who we now might consider overly anxious. We took the liberty of modernizing the language on The NASA Test, so the clinical terminology would be easily understood and resonate with our readers. Talking about mental illness is a trigger for many. There are so many misconceptions around it.

All terms in this chapter should also be seen as relative. For example, there's no such thing as a 'typical person' who fits exactly into every medical or psychological model. These labels reflect working hypotheses. At best, they're generalizations and abstractions that psychologists have been able to develop over time. They enable us to diagnosis people so we can make better use of available medical resources. With that being said, these labels do hold some power and should not be used casually. In American society calling someone *anxious,* or *mentally ill, or low functioning* can be a severe injury and far more harmful to an individual's wellbeing than the symptoms upon which the diagnosis is based.

Please remember, there's no hierarchy of human worth or perfection. If you fall under the 'anxious' category rather than the 'highly adaptive' category, this does not mean you're inferior or less aware. This may simply be a reflection of your current social circumstances, a difficult family situation, a difficult childhood, a stressful job, financial problems, a loss of religious or spiritual beliefs, or more likely a combination of all of these things.

Everyone has problems. Everyone has defenses. Everyone engages in behavior from time to time that could be called atypical or maladaptive. The objective when taking The NASA Test, and any of the tests that follow, is not to determine whether you're "crazy" or "sick" or "disturbed." The assessments will help you recognize which stress and problems you currently face in your life that are impairing your ability to cope effectively. Think of this as your roadmap to better health.

What the Five Stages Really Mean

Stage One: Highly Adaptive

How shall we define *highly adaptive* behavior? The idea of *highly adaptive* is so influenced by cultural values that an objective cross-cultural or universal definition is truly impossible to draw. However, according to most in the field of human psychology, a degree of *high adaptation* is met when an individual demonstrates the ability to get along well with others and works to achieve predetermined goals, while at the same time finding enjoyment and fulfillment in the privileges and responsibilities that our culture encourages.

A *highly adaptive* person is able to make decisions and not merely react. He or she is able to accept what's thrown at them and roll with it. They're resilient and aren't afraid to pivot and adapt in order to move forward. His or her life is, for the most part, an integrated whole, and a failure in one area of their lives does not devalue his or her entire identity.

We would generally describe these people as capable doers with a good sense of perspective. They handle loss or stress with appropriate measure. They participate fully in all three areas of life – work, love and play – even if at times they must focus on one more than the other to feel fulfilled or due to practical reasons outside their control. They have a solid feeling of who they are, what they do, and why they do it.

Examples of how a *highly adaptive* person might behave:

- They're adept at self-regulating their moods and stress management.
- They have a good sense of humor even when they experience adversity.
- Bad or anxious moods don't last long.
- They're able to retain and process information easily.
- They're productive thinkers; their thoughts help carry out their plans.
- They don't obsess too much, let negative thoughts take over and refrain as much as possible from circular thinking.
- They approach activities with enthusiasm.
- They can handle continuous activity or stop-and-start types of activity.
- They can carry out plans and find solutions to multi-step problems.
- They have the capacity to be intimate with others; they can be a friend and have friends.
- They feel and are physically well.

Stage Two: Adaptive

If *highly adaptive* is an ideal state of wellbeing, what we call *adaptive* is where most of us will fall after taking The NASA Test.

I'm always hesitant to use the word *typical* or "normal" to describe any one person's behavior or personality type. There really is no *typical* or "normal" we should all be aspiring when it comes to mental health. However, it's important to teach people to see themselves and their reactions to stressful situations – and their own sense of wellbeing – in relation to others. Put another way, as pack animals we use each other as guideposts or barometers; starting from birth, observing what's appropriate and inappropriate behavior is how we learn to be social creatures that live in community with one another.

When a person is functioning in an *adaptive* way, they may complain of stress but their symptoms often take care of themselves when external pressures are removed. In other words, their temporary symptoms are not indicators of a brewing serious mental disorder.

In general, those who are functioning in a *adaptive* way are coping normally to abnormal stress and strain. Such abnormal stresses might be the following: school exams, deadlines pressures at work, the breakup or loss of an important interpersonal relationship, economic loss, tragic world events or the untimely death of a loved one. Under such circumstances, you can expect your ability to adapt to be slightly or moderately impaired.

Broadly speaking, someone who is *adaptive* is coping effectively given their circumstances and personality type; they aren't in an emotional, spiritual, financial or physical place in their life to fully enjoy everything about it, but they're coping enough, enjoying opportunities that come their way without presenting with, let's say, a persistent depression or obsessive compulsive anxiety disorder.

They're people who despite their stress will probably still carry out day-to-day normal responsibilities. At times, their reactions or performance may vary according to other factors, such as mood and physical well-being, but they aren't at the point at which their stress levels prohibits them from engaging in work and carrying out obligations.

Examples of how an *adaptive* person might behave:

- Their stress has a cause (i.e., exams, disrupted personal relations, a pending operation).
- Their stress may sometimes inhibit their work.
- They may sometimes be moody or intolerant of others.
- They have the ability to use humor to relieve tension.
- They may obsesses over their problems but not to the point of completely interfering with work, love and play.
- They may feel overwhelmed and nervous about taking risk or failing at new things but they still try.
- They may sometimes fall back on ritualistic behavior and ridged schedules in order to cope with stressful events or with the more chaotic parts of life.
- Their anxiety often stimulates them to take action.
- They can have anxiety about pleasing others or gaining approval.
- They sometimes manipulate others to seek attention.
- They can be, at times, overly emotional or irritable with others depending on their stress levels.
- Their ability to take care of themselves physically fluctuates depending on their stress levels.
- They can feel tension, periods of exhaustion and don't look their best all the time.
- They may use drugs or alcohol to cope with stress in a way that *only sometimes* interferes with their daily functioning.

Stage Three: Somewhat Adaptive

Stage three is summed up with this phrase: *constant emergency behavior in the absence of real emergencies.* People who fall into the *somewhat adaptive* category seem to healthcare providers, colleagues, friends and loved ones as if they're constantly under pressure regardless of external realities. Living on high alert, they tend to have major problems in at least one sphere of their life (work, play or love) and they find it necessary to "act out" all the time in order to reduce their stress levels.

They're still able to accomplish most tasks, and at least go through the motions of normal social and professional life, fulfilling duties and obligations to friends, family and co-workers. However, the major difference is they do not enjoy the challenges, and even though they find themselves getting along okay, they are typically anxious and depressed and they would prefer to restrict their activities and back away from any demands that might be made upon them.

In stage three, a person's mood is an important indicator of lessened adaptability. Depression or anxiety may last for weeks, instead of days and even in the face of pleasant events. They may act irrationally, lash out, cry excessively or deny their problems. They aren't capable of experiencing moments of true calm, or of feeling perfectly relaxed. When they aren't volatile, they may shift into ambivalence questioning their ability to feel love, affection, hate, or any strong emotion for another.

Examples of how a *somewhat adaptive* person might behave:

- They show signs of stress with no apparent cause (anxious for no reason).
- They're having trouble functioning at work.
- They may suffer with signs of panic or anxiety disorder symptoms.
- They may suffer with any number of disorders listed in the DSM-5.
- Their dark moods last for longer periods than before.
- They have strong emotional reactions and expressions without apparent cause.
- They may lack a sense of personal awareness.
- They may have mild, ongoing fears and phobias.
- They often have a hostile sense of humor.
- They may have blocked emotions resulting in a flat affect.
- They tend to overanalyze and constantly question their decisions and emotions.
- They may experience sexual side effects due to their mental state.
- They may be hyperactive with no particular purpose.
- They may be lethargic.
- They may be occasionally impulsive and / or have a limited capacity for self-insight and change.
- Their OCD and rituals interfere with work, play and love.
- Their interpersonal relationships feel and seem unstable; they cling to those they don't really care for or push people away because they're unable to compromise.
- They often use drugs and alcohol to "feel better" or "forget" their problems.
- They have many fluctuations in their physical wellbeing, including gastrointestinal problems, headaches or acne.

Stage Four: Low Functioning

Stage four is an intensification of stage three behavior and symptoms. A person who falls into this stage is not functioning well, and their inability to function has become consistent and predictable to everyone around them. Instead of maladaptive behaviors lasting a few weeks, their episodes of un-wellness last for extended periods of time. And unlike stage three, unwanted symptoms or negative behaviors—which get better or worse depending on life circumstances—stage four symptoms and behaviors continue in spite of environmental circumstances improving or opportunities to behave differently.

Even when loved ones, colleagues or friends treat the *low functioning* person in an ideal fashion they still exhibit disruptive or destructive behavior. They do not have the ability or awareness to take advantage of opportunities to grow. Also, in stage four, the person begins to make organizational adjustments to accommodate their problem behavior. They can't really cope so they often abandon responsibilities, by quitting jobs or taking extended unexplained periods of time off from work. They tend to abandon family responsibilities or leave what feels like chaos in their wake.

Their *low functioning* behavior is further removed from any real external cause of stress. Instead, they have internalized stressful situations to the point that they occur spontaneously and are almost unrelated to what actually goes on in their interactions with persons or things. They become angry for apparently no reason. They perceive threats where they do no exist. They react to what they think others want to do or say and not to what they actually do or say. They expect and often cause co-workers, school friends, or others with whom they come into contact with to alter their procedures to accommodate their needs. In this stage, at least two of the three areas of life (work, love and play) are seriously impaired. They may be unable to organize their behavior or control their thoughts.

Perhaps the greatest difference between stage three and stage four behavior is that in stage four *low functioning* individuals feel totally consumed with stress or appear paralyzed in the face of stress. They have reached the end of the coping line, so to speak, and they can no longer rely on their abilities, friends, interests and positive strengths to get them through a crisis. If in stage three an individual is still able to help himself or herself, in stage four this has become increasingly difficult or nearly impossible. They often need a formal intervention or the aid of a professional.

Examples of how a *low functioning* person might behave:

- They have periods of nearly unbearable anxiety with no obvious cause.
- Their background moods often affect their ability to work, love and play.
- They have ongoing depressed, unhappy states (or possible suicide attempts); no amount of support or reassurance helps.
- They may get "high" on ideas or plans, but they have problems finishing tasks or following through to complete the project at hand.
- Their phobias and fears affect their judgment and productivity.
- They exhibit self-destructive, risk-taking behavior.
- They distort reality.
- They are suspicious, continually over interpreting insignificant pieces of information.
- They have great difficulty making even simple decisions.
- Their activities are usually solitary, they engage in them seriously, and they give no particular sensation of pleasure or sense of accomplishment.

- Obsessive rituals have taken over their life.
- They often display impulsive behavior that disrupts their plans or relationships, and they don't learn from their mistakes or experiences.
- They show continued withdrawal or aggression towards friends and peers, resulting in abandonment.
- They have extreme dependency on others and a strong need to manipulate others.
- They have chronic psychosomatic problems – ulcers, colitis, insomnia, migraines, absence of menses, anorexia, chronic overeating – in the absence of a clear-cut cause.
- They are involved in chronic solitary drug or alcohol abuse, as a coping mechanism or in order to self-medicate.

Stage Five: Alarming Behavior

When a person is classified as stage five, according to The NASA Test, they're suffering with a major mental illness (or emotional distress) and they should be treated as soon as possible. Stage five behavior is the lowest functioning stage and friends, loved ones and medical care providers should be worried about their safety. People in stage five can usually no longer function adequately as members of society. Their inner conflicts consume all of their available energy, and they have exhausted their strengths and positive resources for coping.

It should be noted that within stage five there is a wide a range of behavior variation. Severe cases require institutionalization. Milder cases may be treated on a outpatient basis.

General attributes of *alarming behavior* and symptoms include disrupted living patterns in all three areas of life (work, love and play), an inability to care for oneself, and gross distortions of reality or hallucinations. There's nothing stable about their lives. There are frequent and major breakdowns in all areas of life. There is not, as commonly exists in stage four, one saving area of competence and fulfillment that enables the individual to survive and cope.

Those in stage five no longer see certain aspects of the world as those around them do, and they have a difficult time articulating what they see and what they feel. As a result, a common symptom or the *alarming behavior* stage is chronic, severe conflict with parents, friends, school, and / or the law. They're unable to adapt to the needs of others. They live in a world of their own and when others impinge on their freedoms, they can no longer coordinate their behaviors to work with others.

People who exhibit *alarming behavior* may be diagnosed as actively psychotic or suicidal, in a bi-polar swing (either manic or severely depressed), paranoid or schizophrenic. They can't seem to control their impulses. In stage five, one's mood and behaviors bring a total halt to one's ability to work, love or play. In stage five, a person's compulsions and obsessive thinking interfere *completely* with daily life.

They may be an active drug addict, who is in the throws of denial, or is at risk of overdosing. They may be fixated on conspiracy theories or they may be active in an organization that promotes hate based on race, class, gender, national ties or socioeconomic status. They may have withdrawn into a subgroup or fixated on pubic acts violence. In essence, stage five individuals aren't coping and can be dangerous to themselves or others.

Examples of how someone who falls into the *alarming behavior* stage might behave:

- You have continued obsessive thoughts.

- You have gross perceptual distortions (i.e., you do not see, hear or feel what others do).
- You are frequently engaged in compulsive, ritualistic activity.
- You have very little self-control; you are easily influences by external suggestion or internal feelings.
- Work is nearly impossible.
- They are involved in disturbing, impulsive behavior.
- They live in a world of their own, unable to relate realistically to others.
- They are involved in frequent sociopathic behavior (e.g., habitual lying, cheating, stealing and physical attacks).
- They may display what's called out of the ordinary physical posturing (i.e., body movements that appear strange).
- They typically have many unaddressed physical problems or live a very unhealthy lifestyle.

Conclusion

Now that you have a basic understanding of *The Five Stages of Emotional Wellbeing* we use in conjunction with The NASA Test and during standard diagnostic sessions, feel free to take The NASA Test again in order to verify your results. Remember, you can take the test at any time during any life stage to get a sense of how you're doing. Or, you can give the test to anyone you're concerned about currently always keeping in mind that a mental health self-assessment isn't an substitute for a true evaluation and diagnosis from a qualified medical provider.

PART II:

TEST YOUR EMOTIONAL WELLBEING

CHAPTER 4: TAKE THE NASA TEST

See How You Cope with Stress & Learn Where You Fall on Their Well Being Scale

"We are made of star stuff."
– Carl Sagan, American astronomer

Keep in mind that emotional wellbeing varies throughout different times in your life and there are degrees of functioning. Sometimes we cope really well with life, sometimes we're very stressed out and symptomatic.

You can take this test again at a future date just so you can increase the reliability of your test scores.

Now for the fun part, let's find out how well you cope with stress and how resilient you already are! Remember *The Seven Characteristics of Human Behavior* that we talked about in Chapter 3. Below are 7 checklists that correspond to each of those behaviors.

1) Read the question at the top of each page and then check off the statements you agree with being as honest with yourself as you can.
2) Then, follow the directions at the end on how to score the test.
3) Using our scoring system, your total score will be used to rank your emotional wellbeing from **highly adaptive** to **alarming behavior** (that calls for immediate medical attention).

<u>Please note:</u>

*An example is provided after the first checklist to help you calculate your score in case you get confused.

Don't be alarmed if your behavior includes symptoms from any of the five different stages of emotional wellbeing. Given the complex and varied nature of human emotional wellbeing, this is quite possible. The charts are devised to take into account these contradictions. Remember emotional wellness and "unwellness" or dis-ease is on a continuum.

Characteristic #1: Your Anxiety / Stress Level

> **DIRECTIONS:** Do you have these typical behaviors and symptoms? For each characteristic, check the box if it applies to you.

- ☐ You're stressed about something that is happening right now or something that has happened in the past.
- ☐ You can do something that helps you to relieve the stress you feel.

☐ You have clear-cut signs of stress and/or anxiety (agitation, rapid breathing, sweating)

☐ Your anxiety may sometimes inhibit your ability to work.

☐ You are often defendant on strong defenses (such as extreme isolation, persistent anger, grandiose thinking) to make your anxious feelings bearable.

☐ You have periods of nearly unbearable anxiety with no obvious cause or understanding.

☐ Your anxiety feels unbearable to deal with without medication.

☐ Your anxiety inhibits your work most of the time.

☐ Your anxiety is only relieved by fantastical thinking (distortions, hallucinations, grossly inappropriate plans).

Characteristic #2: Your Mood

☐ Your mood swings have a specific cause.

☐ You usually have a sense of humor.

☐ Your moods can be intense, but they pass within a short time.

☐ You are often easily upset, or you are often moody, or intolerant of others.

☐ You use explosive humor as a stress reliever.

☐ Your moods often last for long periods.

☐ You have periodic hysterical behavior.

☐ You have strong emotional expressions, often without apparent reason.

☐ You often use a hostile sense of humor (sarcasm, etc.).

☐ You have mild ongoing fears and phobias.

☐ You take unnecessary risks to overcome your fears.

☐ You have specific blocked or flattened emotions (e.g., love, hate).

☐ Your background moods often affect your ability to work, love, and play.

☐ You often have ongoing depressed, unhappy states.

☐ You have made suicide attempts, or you have frequent thoughts about suicide.

☐ You can get "high" on ideas but you have problems following through.

☐ You have self-destructive, risk-taking behaviors.

☐ You often have periods of hysterical behavior (tantrums, emotional outbursts, or destructive behavior).

☐ You experience delusions, thought disorders or hallucinations.

☐ You have severe states of depression, are often unreachable; you shut down on your work or romantic partners.

Characteristic #3: Your Thoughts

☐ You are able to gather and process information easily.

☐ Your thoughts, whatever they are, don't upset you for long.

☐ Your thoughts usually help you to carry out your plans.

☐ Your thoughts are intensely, narrowly focused on your task or problem.

☐ Your experience some anxiety relief through your thoughts (e.g., daydreaming, or sexual fantasies).

☐ You often block out all but important information.

☐ You have a tendency to analyze rather than experience your feelings.

☐ You often question your ability to feel important emotions.

☐ You often experience obsessive worrying or negative self-talk.

☐ You often have chronic distortions of reality.

☐ You are often alert to an unspecified danger.

☐ You often screen out or miss important thoughts that disrupt your living.

☐ You have repetitive or bothersome thoughts that disrupt your daily life.

☐ Your thoughts often stop you from experiencing strong feelings (e.g., love, anger).

☐ You have difficulty making decisions.

☐ You continually obsess.

☐ You have gross perceptual distortions (i.e., visual or auditory hallucinations).

Characteristic #4: Your Level of Activity

☐ You have enthusiasm and interest in doing and participating, and you have a sense of competence.

☐ You can take risks and be resilient; you can dare to be mediocre, or even fail and try again.

☐ You can handle either continuous ongoing activity or stop-and-start types of activity.

☐ According to your temperament, you usually have lots of activity or little activity.

☐ You often have anxiety about new risks, or you often feel overloaded.

☐ You often use ritualistic words and behavior when you're being put to the test (e.g., say the same mantra to yourself over and over again, wear the same socks for a big event).

☐ You are often hyperactive with no particular purpose or result.

☐ You require much inspiration or feedback in order to work adequately.

☐ You are usually unable to take risks.

☐ You generally avoid new activities.

☐ The way you used to relieve stress no longer works.

☐ You take no pleasure in your accomplishments, your activities are often solitary, and you feel a sense of pain and anxiety if they aren't completed.

☐ You are frequently engaged in compulsive, ritualistic, activities.

☐ You have extreme difficulty in changing your patterns of activity.

Characteristic #5: Organization of Thoughts & Routines (Self-Discipline)

☐ You are able to sit still and accomplish tasks for the necessary periods of time they require to finish.

☐ You can work in the absence of inspiration or feedback.

☐ You can plan and carry out solutions to multi-step problems.

- ☐ You are able to learn from your own experience.
- ☐ You are free to act differently under varying circumstances.
- ☐ Your anxiety often stimulates you to take action.
- ☐ You often find yourself lying or cheating when you are under pressure.
- ☐ You are becoming increasingly rigid: you require clear-cut guidelines, or you need perfect conditions in order to function.
- ☐ You regularly feel that you are being overextended.
- ☐ Unpredictable events are often able to disrupt or to negatively influence your performance.
- ☐ You are involved in *occasional* impulsive behaviors.
- ☐ Your personal rituals often interfere with your work (e.g. sharpening pencils).
- ☐ You have a limited capacity for self-insight and for change.
- ☐ Your behavior is often mechanical.
- ☐ Unexpected minor events often cause you to stop working or enjoying fun activities.
- ☐ In order to function, you often find yourself performing obsessive rituals.
- ☐ You often display impulsive behavior that disrupts your plans; you don't learn from your mistakes or experience.
- ☐ You have very little self-control; you are easily influenced by outside suggestion or by inner feelings.
- ☐ Your feelings generally make it impossible to work.
- ☐ You are often *regularly* involved in disturbing, impulsive behavior.

Characteristic #6: Quality of Your Interpersonal Relationships

- ☐ You can be a friend and you can have friends.
- ☐ You have an increasing capacity for intimacy with others.
- ☐ When you withdraw emotionally or become aggressive, it usually has a clear cause, and it soon passes.
- ☐ You use your upset feelings to seek attention from others or to manipulate others.
- ☐ You are often anxious to please others.
- ☐ You are often unwilling or unable to "play."
- ☐ You are often overly emotional when it comes to your interpersonal relationships.
- ☐ You are often irritable with others.
- ☐ You often find yourself interacting with others in a compulsive or inappropriate manner.
- ☐ You must always get your own way; you are unable to compromise.
- ☐ You can be scapegoated by others, or you can be a bully.
- ☐ You often prematurely initiate one-to-one relationships that you later regret.
- ☐ You have stormy or deteriorating friendships, and you often hold grudges.
- ☐ You generally need constant outside support or approval.
- ☐ You often experience feelings of low self-esteem.
- ☐ You are often somewhat antisocial in your behavior, or you feel alienated.
- ☐ You are extremely dependent on others, or you have a strong need to manipulate others.

☐ You often hold extreme grudges against other people.

☐ You live in a world of your own, unable to relate to others.

☐ You are frequently involved in antisocial behavior (e.g., lying, cheating, stealing, or physical attacks).

Characteristic #7: Your Physical Health

☐ You have stable patterns of eating, good digestion, healthy skin, and normal breathing, sleeping, and weight.

☐ You recover relatively quickly from an illness or an accident.

☐ You have a sense of physical wellbeing.

☐ You have many fluctuations in eating and sleeping patterns, or changes in weight, minor gastrointestinal (GI) problems, and blemishes.

☐ You often feel tense, tired, or exhausted.

☐ You intentionally find yourself using drugs or alcohol in order to cope.

☐ You have periodic skin blemishes, GI problems, struggle with obesity, lack of appetite, sleep disturbances, or headaches.

☐ You have physical tics and/or stuttering.

☐ You have many complaints about your health, often with no clearly defined symptoms.

☐ You often use drugs and alcohol or seek medical help to "feel better."

☐ You are involved in episodes of drug abuse, often reinforced by your friends or contacts.

☐ You appear stiff and / or uptight in your physical mannerisms.

☐ You have ongoing psychosomatic problems – ulcers, colitis, insomnia, migraine, absence of menses, anorexia – often without a clear-cut cause.

☐ You medicate yourself with drugs and alcohol, often alone, in order to cope.

☐ You are continually exhausted, without apparent reason.

☐ You display bizarre physical postures.

☐ You have many ongoing physical problems, some without apparent cause.

☐ You have serious addictions (e.g., drugs and alcohol, sexual behavior, eating disorders, gambling).

SCORING:

Scorecard for Characteristic #1: Anxiety / Stress Levels

DIRECTIONS:

1) Refer to the checklist for "Characteristic #1: Your Anxiety / Stress Levels" on the preceding pages.

2) Transfer your checks to the boxes on this page by shading the boxes that correspond. Remember, your behavior may fall into several stages, or what we like to call, scale of emotional well-being. We will explain the outcomes at the end of the chapter.

HIGHLY Adaptive	ADAPTIVE	SOMEWHAT Adaptive	LOW Functioning	ALARMING Behavior
1. ☐				
2. ☐				
	3. ☐			
	4. ☐			
		5. ☐		
		6. ☐		
			7. ☐	
			8. ☐	
				9. ☐
				10. ☐

3) Now, fill in the number of points for each symptom you checked off on the "scorecard." For example, if you have a check mark in **Box #1**, you scored 10 points.

SYMPTOM	POINTS	YOUR SCORE	WORK SPACE
1	10	_____	
2	10	_____	
3	20	_____	
4	20	_____	
5	30	_____	
6	30	_____	
7	40	_____	
8	40	_____	
9	50	_____	
10	50	_____	

4) Add up your score for this characteristic, writing the total in the space provided.

5) Now add the number of symptoms you checked off (this will be a number between 1 and 10) and write this number beneath your total score.

6) Divide the total score by the number of symptoms reported. The result is your score on the **wellbeing scale for your anxiety and stress levels.**

7) Record this number in the box below.

8) Refer to the number in the box, when you have completed all your scoring for each characteristic, so you can calculate your overall mental health adaptability score at the end of the assessment.

$$\frac{\square\square\square\square\square\ \square\square\square\square\square}{\square\square\square\square\square\square\ \square\square\ \square\square\square\square\square\square\square\square} = \text{---} = \boxed{}$$

For example, if you checked Stress / Anxiety symptoms 1, 2, 3, 6, and 9, you would proceed thus: a total score of 120 divided by 5 symptoms equals a Stress /Anxiety point score of 24.

$$\frac{\square\square\square\square\square\ \square\square\square\square\square}{\square\square\square\square\square\square\ \square\square\ \square\square\square\square\square\square\square\square} = \frac{120}{5} = 24$$

You have just finished the first of seven mini-charts.
The procedure for the next six is the same.

Scorecard for Characteristic #2: Your Mood

DIRECTIONS:

1) Refer to the checklist for "Characteristic #2: Your Mood" on the preceding pages.
2) Transfer your checks to the boxes on this page by shading the boxes that correspond. Remember, your behavior may fall into several stages, or what we like to call, scale of emotional well-being. We will explain the outcomes at the end of the chapter.

HIGHLY Adaptive	ADPATIVE	SOMEWHAT Adaptive	LOW Functioning	ALARMING Behavior
1. ☐				
2. ☐				
3. ☐				
	4. ☐			
	5. ☐			
		6. ☐		
		7. ☐		
		8. ☐		
		9. ☐		
		10. ☐		
		11. ☐		
		12. ☐		
			13. ☐	
			14. ☐	
			15. ☐	
			16. ☐	
			17. ☐	
			18. ☐	
				19. ☐
				20. ☐

3) Below, fill in the number of points for each symptom you checked off on the "scorecard." For example, if you have a check mark in **Box #1**, you scored 10 points.

SYMPTOM	POINTS	YOUR SCORE	WORK SPACE
1	10	_____	
2	10	_____	
3	10	_____	
4	20	_____	
5	20	_____	

6	30	_____
7	30	_____
8	30	_____
9	30	_____
10	30	_____
11	30	_____
12	30	_____
13	40	_____
14	40	_____
15	40	_____
16	40	_____
17	40	_____
18	40	_____
19	50	_____
20	50	_____

4) Add up your score for this characteristic, writing the total in the space provided.

5) Now add the number of symptoms you checked off (this will be a number between 1 and 20) and write this number beneath your total score.

6) Divide the total score by the number of symptoms reported. The result is your score on the **wellbeing scale for your moods.**

7) Record this number in the box below.

8) Refer to the number in the box, when you have completed all your scoring for each characteristic, so you can calculate your overall mental health adaptability score at the end of the assessment.

$$\frac{\square\square\square\square\square\ \square\square\square\square\square}{\square\square\square\square\square\square\ \square\square\ \square\square\square\square\square\square\square\square\square} = \frac{\quad}{\quad} = \boxed{}$$

Scorecard for Characteristic #3: Your Thoughts

DIRECTIONS:

1) Refer to the checklist for "Characteristic #3: Your Thoughts" on the preceding pages.

2) Transfer your checks to the boxes on this page by shading the boxes that correspond. Remember, your behavior may fall into several stages, or what we like to call, scale of emotional well-being. We will explain the outcomes at the end of the chapter.

HIGHLY Adaptive	ADAPTIVE	SOMEWHAT Adaptive	LOW Functioning	ALARMING Behavior
1. ☐				
2. ☐				
3. ☐	4. ☐			
	5. ☐			
	6. ☐	7. ☐		
		8. ☐		
		9. ☐	10. ☐	
			11. ☐	
			12. ☐	
			13. ☐	
			14. ☐	
			15. ☐	
				16. ☐
				17. ☐

3) Below, fill in the number of points for each symptom you checked off on the "scorecard." For example, if you have a check mark in **Box #1**, you scored 10 points.

SYMPTOM	POINTS	YOUR SCORE	WORK SPACE
1	10	_____	
2	10	_____	
3	10	_____	
4	20	_____	
5	20	_____	
6	20	_____	

7	30	_____
8	30	_____
9	30	_____
10	40	_____
11	40	_____
12	40	_____
13	40	_____
14	40	_____
15	40	_____
16	50	_____
17	50	_____

4) Add up your score for this characteristic, writing the total in the space provided.

5) Now add the number of symptoms you checked off (this will be a number between 1 and 17) and write this number beneath your total score.

6) Divide the total score by the number of symptoms reported. The result is your score on the **wellbeing scale for your thoughts.**

7) Record this number in the box below.

8) Refer to the number in the box, when you have completed all your scoring for each characteristic, so you can calculate your overall mental health adaptability score at the end of the assessment.

$$\frac{\square\square\square\square\square\ \square\square\square\square\square}{\square\square\square\square\square\square\ \square\square\ \square\square\square\square\square\square\square\square\square} = -\!- = \boxed{}$$

Scorecard for Characteristic #4: Your Level of Activity

DIRECTIONS:

1) Refer to the checklist for "Characteristic #4: Your Level of Activity" on the preceding pages.

2) Transfer your checks to the boxes on this page by shading the boxes that correspond. Remember, your behavior may fall into several stages, or what we like to call, scale of emotional well-being. We will explain the outcomes at the end of the chapter.

HIGHLY Adaptive	ADAPTIVE	SOMEWHAT Adaptive	LOW Functioning	ALARMING Behavior
1. ☐				
2. ☐				
3. ☐				
	4. ☐			
	5. ☐			
	6. ☐			
		7. ☐		
		8. ☐		
		9. ☐		
			10. ☐	
			11. ☐	
			12. ☐	
				13. ☐
				14. ☐

3) Below, fill in the number of points for each symptom you checked off on the "scorecard." For example, if you have a check mark in **Box #1**, you scored 10 points.

SYMPTOM	POINTS	YOUR SCORE	WORK SPACE
1	10	_____	
2	10	_____	
3	10	_____	
4	20	_____	
5	20	_____	
6	20	_____	
7	30	_____	
8	30	_____	
9	30	_____	
10	40	_____	
11	40	_____	

12	40	_____
13	50	_____
14	50	_____

4) Add up your score for this characteristic, writing the total in the space provided.

5) Now add the number of symptoms you checked off (this will be a number between 1 and 14) and write this number beneath your total score.

6) Divide the total score by the number of symptoms reported. The result is your score on the **wellbeing scale for your level of activity.**

7) Record this number in the box below.

8) Refer to the number in the box, when you have completed all your scoring for each characteristic, so you can calculate your overall mental health adaptability score at the end of the assessment.

$$\frac{\Box\Box\Box\Box\Box\ \Box\Box\Box\Box\Box}{\Box\Box\Box\Box\Box\Box\ \Box\Box\ \Box\Box\Box\Box\Box\Box\Box\Box} = \frac{\quad}{\quad} = \boxed{}$$

Scorecard for Characteristic #5: Organization of Thoughts & Routines (Self – Discipline)

DIRECTIONS:

1) Refer to the checklist for "Characteristic #5: Organization of Thoughts & Routines" on the preceding pages.

2) Transfer your checks to the boxes on this page by shading the boxes that correspond. Remember, your behavior may fall into several stages, or what we like to call, scale of emotional well-being. We will explain the outcomes at the end of the chapter.

HIGHLY Adaptive	ADAPTIVE	SOMEWHAT Adaptive	LOW Functioning	ALARMING Behavior
1. ☐				
2. ☐				
3. ☐				
4. ☐				
5. ☐				
	6. ☐			
	7. ☐			
		8. ☐		
		9. ☐		
		10. ☐		
		11. ☐		
		12. ☐		
		13. ☐		
			14. ☐	
			15. ☐	
			16. ☐	
			17. ☐	
				18. ☐
				19. ☐
				20. ☐

3) Below, fill in the number of points for each symptom you checked off on the "scorecard." For example, if you have a check mark in **Box #1**, you scored 10 points.

SYMPTOM	POINTS	YOUR SCORE	WORK SPACE
1	10	_____	
2	10	_____	
3	10	_____	
4	10	_____	

5	10	_____
6	20	_____
7	20	_____
8	30	_____
9	30	_____
10	30	_____
11	30	_____
12	30	_____
13	30	_____
14	40	_____
15	40	_____
16	40	_____
17	40	_____
18	50	_____
19	50	_____
20	50	_____

4) Add up your score for this characteristic, writing the total in the space provided.

5) Now add the number of symptoms you checked off (this will be a number between 1 and 20) and write this number beneath your total score.

6) Divide the total score by the number of symptoms reported. The result is your score on the **wellbeing scale for your organization of thoughts and routines characteristic.**

7) Record this number in the box below.

8) Refer to the number in the box, when you have completed all your scoring for each characteristic, so you can calculate your overall mental health adaptability score at the end of the assessment.

$$\frac{\square\square\square\square\square\ \square\square\square\square}{\square\square\square\square\square\square\ \square\square\ \square\square\square\square\square\square\square\square} = --- = \boxed{}$$

Scorecard for Characteristic #6: The Quality of Your Interpersonal Relationships

DIRECTIONS:

1) Refer to the checklist for "Characteristic #6: The Quality of Your Interpersonal Relationships" on the preceding pages.

2) Transfer your checks to the boxes on this page by shading the boxes that correspond. Remember, your behavior may fall into several stages, or what we like to call, scale of emotional well-being. We will explain the outcomes at the end of the chapter.

HIGHLY Adaptive	ADAPTIVE	SOMEWHAT Adaptive	LOW Functioning	ALARMING Behavior
1. ☐				
2. ☐				
3. ☐				
	4. ☐			
	5. ☐			
	6. ☐			
	7. ☐			
	8. ☐			
		9. ☐		
		10. ☐		
		11. ☐		
		12. ☐		
		13. ☐		
		14. ☐		
		15. ☐		
		16. ☐		
			17. ☐	
			18. ☐	
				19. ☐
				20. ☐

3. Below, fill in the number of points for each symptom you checked off on the "scorecard." For example, if you have a check mark in **Box #1**, you scored 10 points.

SYMPTOM	POINTS	YOUR SCORE	WORK SPACE
1	10	_____	
2	10	_____	
3	10	_____	
4	20	_____	

5	20	_____
6	20	_____
7	20	_____
8	20	_____
9	30	_____
10	30	_____
11	30	_____
12	30	_____
13	30	_____
14	30	_____
15	30	_____
16	30	_____
17	40	_____
18	40	_____
19	50	_____
20	50	_____

4) Add up your score for this characteristic, writing the total in the space provided.

5) Now add the number of symptoms you checked off (this will be a number between 1 and 20) and write this number beneath your total score.

6) Divide the total score by the number of symptoms reported. The result is your score on the **wellbeing scale for your interpersonal relationships.**

7) Record this number in the box below.

8) Refer to the number in the box, when you have completed all your scoring for each characteristic, so you can calculate your overall mental health adaptability score at the end of the assessment.

$$\frac{\square\square\square\square\square\ \square\square\square\square\square}{\square\square\square\square\square\square\ \square\square\ \square\square\square\square\square\square\square\square} = \overline{\quad} = \boxed{}$$

Scorecard for Characteristic #7: Your Physical Health

DIRECTIONS:

1) Refer to the checklist for "Characteristic #7: Your Physical Health" on the preceding pages.

2) Transfer your checks to the boxes on this page by shading the boxes that correspond. Remember, your behavior may fall into several stages, or what we like to call, scale of emotional well-being. We will explain the outcomes at the end of the chapter.

HIGHLY Adaptive	ADAPTIVE	SOMEWHAT Adaptive	LOW Functioning	ALARMING Behavior
1. ☐				
2. ☐				
3. ☐	4. ☐			
	5. ☐			
	6. ☐	7. ☐		
		8. ☐		
		9. ☐		
		10. ☐		
		11. ☐	12. ☐	
			13. ☐	
			14. ☐	
		15. ☐	16. ☐	
				17. ☐
				18. ☐

3) Below, fill in the number of points for each symptom you checked off on the "scorecard." For example, if you have a check mark in **Box #1**, you scored 10 points.

SYMPTOM	POINTS	YOUR SCORE	WORK SPACE
1	10	_____	
2	10	_____	
3	10	_____	
4	20	_____	
5	20	_____	
6	20	_____	
7	30	_____	
8	30	_____	
9	30	_____	

10	30	_____
11	30	_____
12	40	_____
13	40	_____
14	40	_____
15	40	_____
16	50	_____
17	50	_____
18	50	_____

4) Add up your score for this characteristic, writing the total in the space provided.

5) Now add the number of symptoms you checked off (this will be a number between 1 and 18) and write this number beneath your total score.

6) Divide the total score by the number of symptoms reported. The result is your score on the **wellbeing scale for your physical health.**

7) Record this number in the box below.

8) Refer to the number in the box, when you have completed all your scoring for each characteristic, so you can calculate your overall mental health adaptability score at the end of the assessment.

$$\frac{\square\square\square\square\square \ \square\square\square\square\square}{\square\square\square\square\square\square \ \square\square \ \square\square\square\square\square\square\square\square} = \underline{} = \boxed{}$$

Your Emotional Well-Being Bar Graph

Now that you have computed your total scores for each of the seven aspects, you will be able to fill in the bar graph with a full picture of your mental health. In Chapter 6, we will give you a thorough explanation of what your results mean and tell you what steps you can take to improve your health – starting today.

DIRECTIONS:

1) Go back to each characteristic and input your wellbeing score below (the same number you put in the box at the end of each scorecard).

Characteristic	#1: Anxiety	#2: Mood	#3: Thoughts	#4: Activity	#5: Self-Discipline	#6: Relationships	#7: Physical Health
Score							

2) Now, take that number and plot it on the graph below for an alternative view of your NASA mental health picture.

Mental Health Bar Graph
POINTS

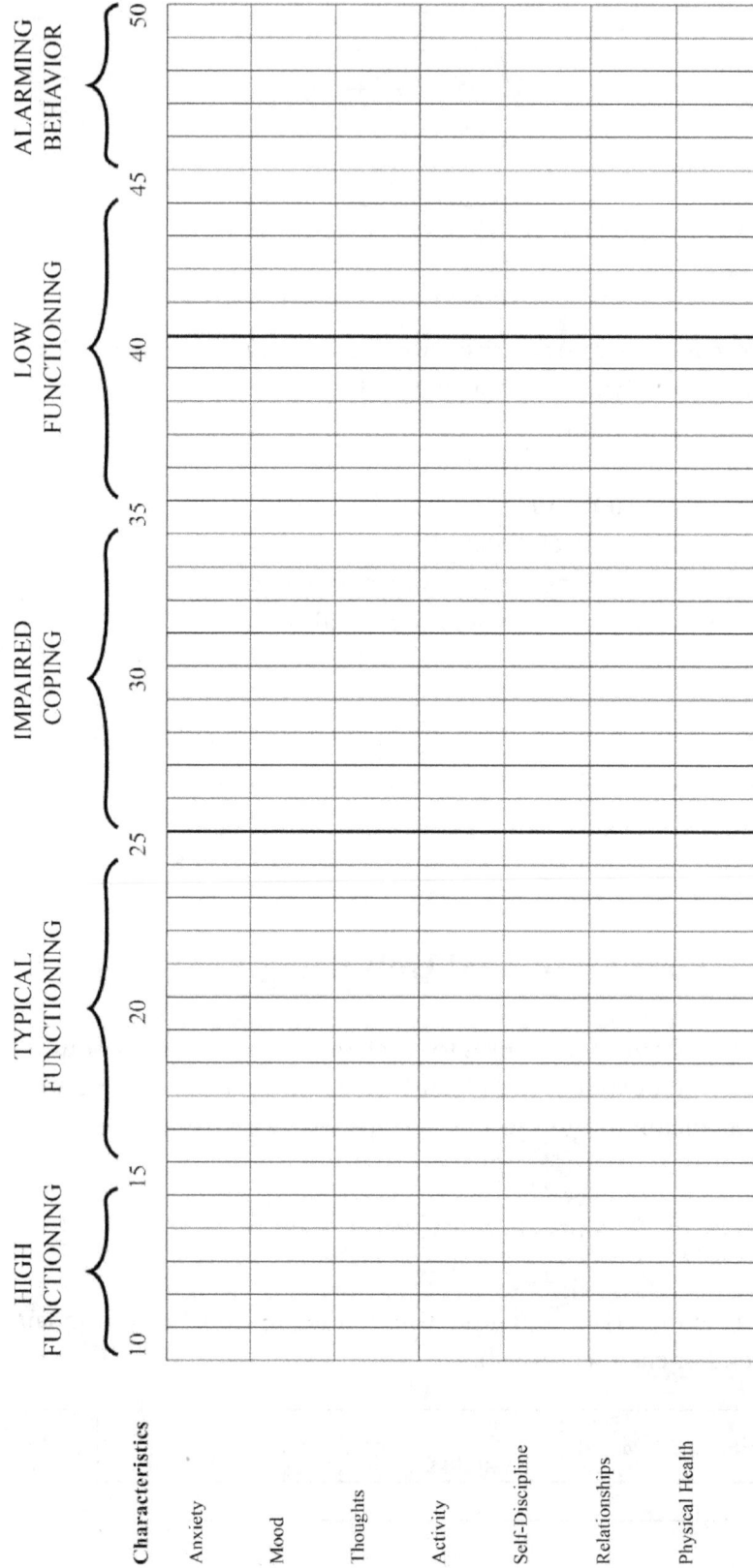

Characteristics	HIGH FUNCTIONING		TYPICAL FUNCTIONING		IMPAIRED COPING		LOW FUNCTIONING		ALARMING BEHAVIOR
	10	15	20	25	30	35	40	45	50
Anxiety									
Mood									
Thoughts									
Activity									
Self-Discipline									
Relationships									
Physical Health									

10-25 Within realm of expected behavior. Normal functioning. May want help with specific problems. Preventive therapy.

26-40 Serious stresses and problems. Professional help may be advisable. Functioning with difficulty.

40-50 Marginal functioning. Seek professional help.

INTERPRETATION:

For general interpretation, your point scores and bar graph can be broken down to one of three possible categories. A score in the *10 to 25-point range* is within the realm of *high functioning and typical functioning*. You may want help with specific problems and might benefit from preventive therapy, but you have no serious mental or emotional problems at this time and you have a high level of mental adaptability.

If you score in the *26 to 35-point range*, you are *functioning, but with difficulty*. For The NASA Test we called this impaired coping. You have serious stresses and problems, and professional help is probably advisable.

A score in the *36 to 45-point range* indicates the level of *low functioning* and is a clear call to seek professional help.

Anything above the *45-point range* indicates the level of *alarming behavior* and is a clear warning that you need psychiatric help and you could be in the middle of a psychiatric emergency.

Once again, remember that your mental health changes over time, as does your physical health. Whatever category of mental adaptability you may be in today is not necessarily a permanent definition of your mental well-being. At the same time, be aware that your mental health might possibly deteriorate rather than improve, if problems are left untreated. A healthy environment or positive intervention might greatly increase your sense of well-being.

SELF-EVALUATION

The bar graph gives you a picture of your overall emotional well-being. It tells you which areas of behavior give you problems, the degree to which they are problems, and the areas in which you are functioning well. Note that very few scores will fall in either the high functioning category of under 10 to 15 points, or the alarming behavior category of 45 points or more. Most scores and most people fall somewhere in between. We all have mental health issues of varying degrees, but we are still able to function.

Depending on your bar graph scores, the state of your mental health may be obvious at a glance or, for borderline cases, you may need a more precise point evaluation. The calculation of an exact point score is possible. Merely add up your point scores for each of the seven characteristics and divide by seven as in the following examples.

Please see the following chapters with self-assessments for what you may be struggling with. For a larger discussion of wellbeing tips see the last section of this book, *Part IV: Getting The Help You Need and Deserve.*

Part III:

Self Assessments for Every Life Stage

Chapter 5: What's My Personality Type?

<u>What makes you who you are?</u>

There's lots of debate in the psychological community over personality assessments.[6] Do they offer any valuable insight into who we are or how we behave? Are they even scientifically valid measurements of a phenomenon that is so complex? The reality is, it's hard to assess something that's constantly shifting; who we present ourselves to be, what our personality is, may very much depend on the context of any given situation. Researchers have also found that our personalities can change drastically over time.[7]

We have collected a variety of personality assessments so you can assess your own personality and come up with your "type." Why? Because first and foremost it's fun! And whether they are "scientifically valid" or not—it will make you think a little more deeply about how you function in the world compared to those around you. Here are the assessments:

1) **The Big Five Personality Assessment.** This is an original assessment we created based on the Big Five Personality Traits (also known as the Five-Factor Model of Personality). Under the Five-Factor Model, you can identify your ranking with each of the big five personality traits. This is a long assessment with an extensive list of statements you can agree with or not.

2) **The Personality Reactions Assessment.** This is another original assessment we created also based on the Big Five Personality Traits. This is a shorter assessment than the previous one, and it will ask you about specific situations rather than statements.

3) **The Colors Personality Test.**[8] This test was created based off The True Colors methodology which states that the colors orange, gold, green, and blue all represent a distinct primary personality type. There are many variations of this test available online. Our assessment was modified from a Colors Personality Test worksheet[9] originally intended for a classroom setting.

Big Five Personality Assessment

DIRECTIONS: Read each statement carefully and indicate your extent of agreement with a checkmark in the proper place.

** Please note: for this test we swapped out the word neuroticism for anxiousness. We are of the clinical opinion that calling anyone a neurotic personality is outdated terminology and isn't a useful present-day interpretation of the assessment.

Extraversion

	Strongly Agree	Agree	Neither Agree Nor Disagree	Disagree	Strongly Disagree
1. keep in the background. (-)					
2. I am the life of the party. (+)					
3. I feel comfortable around people. (+)					
4. I wait for others to lead the way. (-)					
5. I start conversations. (+)					
6. I talk to a lot of different people at parties. (+)					
7. I have little to say. (-)					
8. I find it difficult to approach others. (-)					
9. I don't mind being the center of attention. (+)					
10. I don't talk a lot. (-)					
11. I make friends easily. (+)					
12. I don't like to draw attention to myself. (-)					
13. I take charge. (+)					
14. I am quiet around strangers. (-)					
15. I know how to captivate people. (+)					
16. I often feel uncomfortable around others. (-)					
17. I feel at ease with people. (+)					
18. I bottle up my feelings. (-)					
19. I am skilled in handling social situations. (+)					
20. I am a very private person. (-)					

Agreeableness

	Strongly Agree	Agree	Neither Agree Nor Disagree	Disagree	Strongly Disagree
1. I am interested in people. (+)					
2. I sympathize with others' feelings. (+)					
3. I am hard to get to know. (-)					
4. I take time out for others. (+)					
5. I feel others' emotions. (+)					
6. I am not interested in other people's problems. (-)					
7. I love children. (+)					
8. I am indifferent to the feelings of others. (-)					
9. I am on good terms with nearly everyone. (+)					
10. I show my gratitude. (+)					
11. I feel little concern for others. (-)					
12. I have a good word for everyone. (+)					
13. I think of others first. (+)					
14. I insult people. (-)					
15. I have a soft heart. (+)					
16. I love to help others. (+)					
17. I know how to comfort others. (+)					
18. I make people feel at ease. (+)					
19. I inquire about others' well-being. (+)					
20. I am not really interested in others. (-)					

Conscientiousness

	Strongly Agree	Agree	Neither Agree Nor Disagree	Disagree	Strongly Disagree
1. I am always prepared. (+)					
2. I find it difficult to get down to work. (-)					
3. I follow a schedule. (+)					
4. I often forget to put things back in their proper place. (-)					
5. I do things in a half-way manner. (-)					
6. I get chores done right away. (+)					
7. I do things according to a plan. (+)					
8. I leave a mess in my room. (-)					
9. I continue until everything is perfect. (+)					
10. I am exacting in my work. (+)					
11. I leave my belongings around. (-)					
12. I waste my time. (-)					
13. I like order. (+)					
14. I pay attention to details. (+)					
15. I shirk my duties. (-)					
16. I love order and regularity. (+)					
17. I like to tidy up. (+)					
18. I neglect my duties. (-)					
19. I make plans and stick to them. (+)					
20. I make a mess of things. (-)					

Anxiousness

	Strongly Agree	Agree	Neither Agree Nor Disagree	Disagree	Strongly Disagree
1. I get stressed out easily. (+)					
2. I often feel blue. (+)					
3. I seldom get mad. (-)					
4. I feel threatened easily. (+)					
5. I change my mood a lot. (+)					
6. I am not easily bothered by things. (-)					
7. I get overwhelmed by emotions. (+)					
8. I get caught up in my problems. (+)					
9. I take offense easily. (+)					
10. I seldom feel blue. (-)					
11. I worry about things. (+)					
12. I am easily disturbed. (+)					
13. I grumble about things. (+)					
14. I rarely get irritated. (-)					
15. I panic easily. (+)					
16. I get upset easily. (+)					
17. I have frequent mood swings. (+)					
18. I am relaxed most of the time. (-)					
19. I get irritated easily. (+)					
20. I get angry easily. (+)					

Openness to Experience

	Strongly Agree	Agree	Neither Agree Nor Disagree	Disagree	Strongly Disagree
1. I have difficulty understanding abstract ideas. (-)					
2. I am quick to understand things. (+)					
3. I spend time reflecting on things. (+)					
4. I try to avoid complex people. (-)					
5. I have a rich vocabulary. (+)					
6. I am full of ideas. (+)					
7. I can handle a lot of information. (+)					
8. I have difficulty imagining things. (-)					
9. I love to think up new ways of doing things. (+)					
10. I am good at many things. (+)					
11. I avoid difficult reading material. (-)					
12. I have a vivid imagination. (+)					
13. I have excellent ideas. (+)					
14. I will not probe deeply into a subject. (-)					
15. I carry the conversation to a higher level. (+)					
16. I use difficult words. (+)					
17. I am not interested in abstract ideas. (-)					
18. I avoid difficult reading material. (-)					
19. I do not have a good imagination. (-)					
20. I catch on to things quickly. (+)					

SCORING: Each statement is assigned different values, depending on if it's a (+) statement or a (-) statement. Refer to the tables above to see which statement is which when determining your scores.

Scoring (+) Statements:
1 = Strongly Disagree
2 = Disagree
3 = Neither Agree nor Disagree
4 = Agree
5 = Strongly Agree

Scoring (-) Statements:
5 = Strongly Disagree
4 = Disagree
3 = Neither Agree nor Disagree
2 = Agree
1 = Strongly Agree

Write your scores for each category in the table below. Finally, add up each column and write your total scores.

Statements	Extraversion	Agreeableness	Conscientiousness	Anxiousness	Openness to Experience
Q1					
Q2					
Q3					
Q4					
Q5					
Q6					
Q7					
Q8					
Q9					
Q10					
Q11					
Q12					
Q13					
Q14					
Q15					
Q16					
Q17					
Q18					
Q19					
Q20					
TOTAL					

INTERPRETATION: Scores are interpreted based on each individual category:

Extraversion – Characterized by sociability, an outgoing nature, and a willingness to meet new people. Someone who is very extraverted loves to be active and involved. They get their energy from being with others.

On the flipside, someone who is very introverted loves to keep to themselves and be alone most of the time. It should be noted that introverts can like being social and having a few friends, but they don't get their energy from being with others. They get their energy from being by themselves.

Agreeableness – Characterized by trust, kindness, affection, empathy, and helpfulness. Someone who is very agreeable will aim to see eye to eye with others, resolve conflict, and make peace. They care about what others think and want everyone to get along. On the flipside, someone who is not agreeable won't care about agreeing with people or getting along. They will say what's on their mind. They may be more likely to insult someone or behave rudely if they disagree with a viewpoint.

Conscientiousness – Characterized by thoughtfulness, preparation, schedules and structure. Someone who is very conscientious is detail-oriented and always plans five steps ahead. They like having a routine and knowing what to expect. They may like being in control. On the flipside, someone who is not conscientious may dislike routine and structure. They are more of a free spirit. They may neglect their responsibilities or slack off. They may not manage their time well and can appear ill prepared at work or at school.

Anxiousness – Characterized by someone who exhibits more volatile moods, someone who scores as anxiousness may be or appear to be more emotionally unstable at times than the other personalities. They may have more mood swings and react more harshly when upset. They tend to be sensitive and take things personally. They may be more likely to be sad, or angry or nervous — especially when things don't go according to their plan. On the flipside, someone who doesn't score high in anxiousness may react more calmly and rationally when faced with obstacles. They're in control of their emotions.

Openness to Experience – Characterized by imagination, creativity, insight, and adventure, someone who is open to experiences may be more likely to try new things. They may be more creative or willing to try new things. They tend to be curious. They may be more willing to give people or things second chances. On the flipside, someone who isn't open to experiences is content staying in their comfort zone. They may be more judgmental when it comes to differences of opinion, culture, and world views.

If your score is 80 or above, you *definitely* have the characteristics of someone who has that personality trait.
- For example, if you were interpreting your Conscientiousness subscale, and your score was 91, you would be very conscientiousness.

If your score is 50 to 79, you *moderately* have the characteristics of someone who has that personality trait.
- For example, if you were interpreting your Agreeableness subscale, and your score was 67, you would be moderately agreeable.

If your score is 30 to 49, you *somewhat* have the characteristics of someone who has that personality trait.
- For example, if you were interpreting your Anxiousness subscale, and your score was 32, you would be somewhat anxious.

If your score was 29 or less, you *barely or don't at all* have the characteristics of someone who has that personality trait.

- For example, if you were interpreting your Extraversion subscale, and your score was 14, you would be classified as an introvert. You would not be extroverted.

The Personality Reactions Assessment

DIRECTIONS: Read each statement below. For each question, circle (a) or (b) for the reaction you would *most likely* have if you were in the given scenario.

1) When you strongly disagree with someone, and you know you can never understand their point of view, are you more likely to:
   (a) Tell them you'll have to agree to disagree and try to move on to a better topic
   (b) Say their point-of-view is idiotic, and go on to explain why

2) A project deadline for work or school was moved up. You now have less time than you originally anticipated to get it done:
   (a) You immediate stress about how you're going to finish. You're already panicking.
   (b) You calmly develop a revised plan to get the project done in time.

3) You are invited to go to an art museum with some friends. Art isn't really your thing, but they swear it is the best museum they've been to:
   (a) You tell them you're not going. You already know you won't like anything there.
   (b) You decide to go to see for yourself what it's like. Who knows, you might change your mind about art.

4) You move to a new city and you don't know anyone:
   (a) You get involved in local events and meet new people. You start to make friends.
   (b) You don't go out much and mainly focus on work and your personal hobbies. You prefer to keep to yourself.

5) When you're interested in a subject and want to learn more about it, are you more likely to:
   (a) Read books and do your research on the topic to find everything about it you can find.
   (b) Skim the Wikipedia page article about it.

6) You're getting married. Which ceremony do you prefer:
   (a) A small gathering, with just your closest family and friends.
   (b) A big affair. Everyone you know is invited. You want everyone to be there and see you on your special day.

7) Your old school reunion is coming up. It is unclear what exactly the plans are or where you are all meeting:
   (a) You take control of organizing this event. Leave it up to you to get it done!
   (b) You're sure you'll hear the details about it eventually. No need to think about it now.

8) Two of your friends are having an argument. While in private, one of your friends asks for your thoughts on the matter:

    (a) You don't have an opinion. It's their business, not yours.

    (b) You offer a few possible solutions to help your friends resolve their argument.

9) Your partner tells you they must cancel an upcoming date that you've been really looking forward to because they have a sudden family event and must go see their family:

    (a) You are angry at your partner and very sad that the date was cancelled. You feel jealous of your partner's family.

    (b) You understand they must go. You're not upset or angry at all. You'll wait for their return.

10) You have a huge essay due in a class that is worth a large percentage of your overall grade. Do you:

    (a) Procrastinate for ages and then rush to get it done the night before it's due.

    (b) Start working on outlining, writing the essay, and making revisions weeks before it is due.

SCORING: All questions relate to one of the big five personality traits. You will see which question is matched with which trait below. Assign the appropriate scores based on your answers. Then add up your points for each individual category/subscale.

Extraversion: Questions #4 and #6

Q4:   If you chose Answer A, give yourself **5 points.**
       If you chose Answer B, give yourself **1 point.**

Q6:

       If you chose Answer A, give yourself **1 point.**
       If you chose Answer B, give yourself **5 points.**

Q4 Score: _____
Q6 Score: _____
TOTAL (add up your answers from Q4 and Q6): _____

Agreeableness: Questions #1 and #8

Q1:   If you chose Answer A, give yourself **5 points.**
       If you chose Answer B, give yourself **1 point.**

Q8:

       If you chose Answer A, give yourself **1 point.**
       If you chose Answer B, give yourself **5 points.**

Q1 Score: _____
Q8 Score: _____
TOTAL (add up your answers from Q1 and Q8): _____

Conscientiousness: Questions #7 and #10

Q7:   If you chose Answer A, give yourself **5 points.**
       If you chose Answer B, give yourself **1 point.**

Q10:

If you chose Answer A, give yourself **1 point.**

If you chose Answer B, give yourself **5 points**.

Q7 Score: _____

Q10 Score: _____

TOTAL (add up your answers from Q7 and Q10): _____

Anxiousness: Questions #2 and #9

Q2:   If you chose Answer A, give yourself **5 points.**

If you chose Answer B, give yourself **1 point**.

Q9:

If you chose Answer A, give yourself **5 points.**

If you chose Answer B, give yourself **1 point**.

Q2 Score: _____

Q9 Score: _____

TOTAL (add up your answers from Q2 and Q9): _____

Openness to Experience: Questions #3 and #5

Q3:   If you chose Answer A, give yourself **1 point**.

If you chose Answer B, give yourself **5 points**.

Q5:

If you chose Answer A, give yourself **5 points.**

If you chose Answer B, give yourself **1 point**.

Q3 Score: _____

Q5 Score: _____

TOTAL (add up your answers from Q3 and Q5): _____

INTERPRETATION: Scores are interpreted based on each individual subscale. For personality types refer to the ones explained in the pages above. Again, as mentioned previously, for this test we swapped out the word neuroticism for anxiousness, as we share the clinical opinion that calling anyone a neurotic personality is outdated and isn't a useful present-day interpretation.

If your total score is a 2, you *do not* have the characteristics of someone who has that personality trait.
- For example, if you were interpreting your Extraversion subscale, and your score was 2, you would not be extraverted (you would be introverted).

If your total score is a 6, you *somewhat* have the characteristics of someone who has that personality trait.
- For example, if you were interpreting your Agreeableness subscale, and your score was 6, you would be somewhat agreeable.

If your total score is a 10, you *definitely* have the characteristics of someone who has that personality trait.
- For example, if you were interpreting your Conscientiousness subscale, and your score was 10, you would be very conscientiousness.

Colors Personality Test

DIRECTIONS: Below are 10 incomplete sentences that describe people. Each sentence has four possible endings. On the lines next to each response, rate the responses in order of how you're most likely or least likely to respond, from 1-4. Give four points to the phrase that is "most like you," three points to the phrase that is "next most like you," two points to the next phrase, and one point to the phrase that is "least like you."

1) When I make decisions:

_____ (a) I do it quickly and go with the first impressions.

_____ (b) I think about it, consider the options and then decide.

_____ (c) I listen to my feelings and consider how my decisions will affect others.

_____ (d) I take it seriously and always try to make the right decision.

2) The best way for others to show me they care about me is to:

_____ (a) Do fun things with me.

_____ (b) Give me space to be myself.

_____ (c) Spend time with me doing whatever.

_____ (d) Do what I want to do; not let me down or go back on their word.

3) When I'm with my friends, I like to provide:

_____ (a) The excitement; the fun; the jokes.

_____ (b) Questions; answers; a logical way of looking at things.

_____ (c) Concern for others; a lot of caring.

_____ (d) The planning; a sense of security; a good standard.

4) I like to:

_____ (a) Act on a moment's notice; do risky things.

_____ (b) Provide answers or give thought to people's questions.

_____ (c) Help maintain a sense of harmony and togetherness.

_____ (d) Be responsible, dependable, and helpful to others.

5) One thing I am really good at is:

_____ (a) Acting courageously.

_____ (b) Thinking.

_____ (c) Being sensitive.

_____ (d) Organizing.

6) Friends who know me best would say that I am:

_____ (a) Competitive.

_____ (b) Reserved, thoughtful.

_____ (c) Emotional, friendly

_____ (d) Neat, prepared.

7) My basic approach to life is:

   _____ (a) To take one day at a time and have fun.

   _____ (b) To figure out what life is all about.

   _____ (c) To help others and be happy and succeed.

   _____ (d) To plan for the future and make it as good as possible.

8) When I am feeling discouraged or "down in the dumps":

   _____ (a) I often become rude, mad, or sometimes even mean.

   _____ (b) I withdraw, don't talk very much, and try to think my way out of the problem.

   _____ (c) I feel emotional, am sad, and usually like to talk it over with someone close to me.

   _____ (d) I try to figure out what's causing the problem and fix it.

9) I feel good about myself when:

   _____ (a) I can do things that are difficult.

   _____ (b) I can solve problems or figure things out.

   _____ (c) I can help other people.

   _____ (d) I am appreciated or rewarded for things I do.

10) Family and friends would probably describe me as:

   _____ (a) Charming, a natural leader, clever, someone who is fun to have around.

   _____ (b) Thoughtful, someone who has good ideas, someone who likes to figure out problems.

   _____ (c) Nice, friendly, someone who gets along with others and is helpful to everyone around them.

   _____ (d) Neat, organized, prepared, someone who does tasks quickly and efficiently.

SCORING: Next, read through each of your answers and fill in the table below according to the scores you assigned for each letter in each question. When you're finished, indicate the totals for each column/response.

Question	A	B	C	D
Q1				
Q2				
Q3				
Q4				
Q5				
Q6				
Q7				
Q8				
Q9				
Q10				
Q11				
TOTAL				

Total your columns and place your results in the blanks below.

     (a) Orange   _____

(b) Green _____

(c) Blue _____

(d) Gold _____

The "A" answers apply to the color "Orange."

The "B" answers apply to the color "Green."

The "C" answers apply to the color "Blue."

The "D" answers apply to the color "Gold."

INTERPRETATION: The higher your total, the more your personality is suited to the corresponding color. For example, if your highest number is 35 in the C column, the color your personality matches with the most is Blue. If your second highest number is 26 in the A column, the secondary color your personality matches with is Orange.

What is your first color? _____ What is your second color? _____

How to Interpret Your Color

Each color says something unique about your personality. If you identify with orange the most, you are energetic, spontaneous, and charming. If you identify with gold, you are punctual, organized, and precise. If you identify with green, you are analytical, intuitive, and visionary. If you identify with blue, you are empathic, compassionate, and cooperative.[10] Here's what each color says about you, according to True Colors International:[11]

Blue

If your personality most closely matches up with the color blue, here are some personality traits to describe you. You are:

- Enthusiastic
- Sympatric
- Warm
- Communicative
- Compassionate
- Peaceful
- Authentic
- Imaginative

You like to help other people and work on your relationships. You always want to find a resolution. You are caring and passionate.

Green

If your personality most closely matches up with the color green, you are:

- Analytical
- Inventive

- Logical
- "Big Picture" Thinker
- Abstract
- Independent
- Intelligent

You're an independent thinker. You enjoy challenges, and you enjoy your work. You may always strive to make an informed decision with numbers to back you up, no matter how big or how small that decision is. You take your time and don't act before you're ready to.

Gold

If your personality most closely matches up with the color gold, you are:
- Loyal
- Dependable
- Prepared
- Thorough
- Sensible
- Punctual
- Organized

You want to maintain your organizational habits, handle all the details, and work hard. You prioritize work over enjoying your free time. You love to get work done. You are someone who thinks and plans ahead.

Orange

If your personality most closely matches up with the color orange, you are:
- Witty
- Charming
- Spontaneous
- Impulsive
- Eager
- Physical
- Energetic
- Risk-taker

You are willing to take risks. You are excited and adventurous. You are open to new opportunities. You dislike structure and gravitate towards freedom. You are also competitive, and you may always be striving to be better and improving yourself.

What Will Help You

Now that you know a lot more about your personality, how can you use that knowledge? How can it help you? How can knowing your personality benefit you in your life? There are several reasons why knowing your personality type can be beneficial:

- **Knowing your personality type helps inform you of who you are.** You can learn more about yourself and what your strengths and weaknesses are from knowing your personality type. This can help you when you're trying to decide on a career direction, what personal hobbies you might enjoy, trying to understand why you've always liked or disliked something, when and how you can best recharge or relax, or if you're working with a group of people on a project for school or work – you may need to decide what aspects of the project you can handle, what you may want more support with, and what environment you need for your best performance.
- **Knowing your personality matches up to a defined personality type can help you feel less alone.** Ever wondered why you thought or acted a certain way? Did you think you were the only one? Understanding your personality type reassures you that you're not the only one who reacts a certain way to certain situations. It's comforting to know, for example, that other introverts may have similar struggles. Connecting with like minded personalities gives us a sense of belonging even though we should strive to live and work around all sorts of dynamic people.
- **You may better understand other people and perspectives, which can lead to having better relationships and less conflict overall.** It's clear that personalities are complex. After all, the Myers-Briggs personality test, which is just one assessment, has *16 unique personality types* – that's a lot. Everyone is different. Not everyone has the same views as you! You can see from the brief breakdown of each personality type that people can be so different in how they see and approach the world. This may lead you to think more deeply about the personality types of your family, friends, and loved ones. Do you suddenly feel more empathy or have more patience for them? Knowing personality types helps you set expectations of others which means you more readily handle your interactions with them. Communication will hopefully become much more effective and efficient now.

However, you should be aware that your personality type may not tell you everything you need to know about yourself either. Be cautious of the following:

*Your personality type may not be completely accurate, especially if you have only taken one test, or just a handful of tests. You may be dishonest without realizing it. Remember, research has shown us that our personalities don't always stay the same as we get older and continue to gain life experience. In other words, people do change.

*From a career perspective, **a personality assessment can indicate which jobs you *might* like, but that doesn't mean you're automatically going to like them.** You may be uninterested in some or all of the career suggestions offered. That's okay. Your personality type is not a complete guide to who you are or what you're interested in, it's just a potential guideline based on what people in general with your personality type may enjoy doing.

*You shouldn't tie your personality type to your identity too much.** This may hold you back from trying new activities or meeting new people. As stated above, your personality type may also not be 100% accurate. Don't confine yourself to a box of who exactly you think you should be. Just be.

CHAPTER 6: WHAT LIFE EVENTS ARE REALLY STRESSING YOU OUT?

Identify Stressors you have with the Life / Life Events Change Scale

Have you ever moved and then had a baby a few weeks later? Or dealt with the death of a loved one while you were in the first few months of starting a new job? We all know that the stress from certain life events can cause physical illness as well as emotional problems, so let's see how you're actually doing. Now that you've taken and scored yourself on our *The NASA Test*, in Part 1 of the book we wanted to give you assessments that pertain to specific challenges we all face.

The *"Check Your Stress Test,"* also known as the *Life Change Index Scale*[12], is a great way to measure how change, even positive change, can affect you. This test will help you to quantify the amount and types of changes you've experienced in the past 12 months by citing positive and negative life events. The items in the test fall into two categories: one that reflects your personal lifestyle and choices over which you have some control; and ones that reflect events or occurrences that happen *to you*, choices for which you have less control. Each is rated according to the amount of adjustment needed to cope with them. This scale has been modified and expanded to accommodate many different types of life events.

Check Your Stress: The Life Change Index Scale

> **DIRECTIONS:** To use the scale, circle "yes" or "no" if you have or have not experienced that event in the past year.

1. Death of spouse or long-term partner (100)	YES	NO
2. Divorce (73)	YES	NO
3. Separation from spouse or long-term partner (65)	YES	NO
4. Incarcerated in jail or other institution (63)	YES	NO
5. Death of a close family member or loved one (63)	YES	NO
6. Personal injury or illness (53)	YES	NO

7. Marriage (50)	YES	NO
8. Fired at work, laid off, or dismissed / dropped out of school (47)	YES	NO
9. Marital or partner reconciliation (45)	YES	NO
10. Retirement (45)	YES	NO
11. Family member or loved one with health problems (44)	YES	NO
12. Pregnancy (40)	YES	NO
13. Intimacy issues (e.g., lack of sexual or emotional intimacy) (39)	YES	NO
14. New household member (newborn, adopted child, aging parent) (39)	YES	NO
15. Workplace changes (e.g., merger, reorganization, bankruptcy) (39)	YES	NO
16. Financial stability or instability (e.g., promotion, unemployment) (38)	YES	NO
17. Death of a close friend (37)	YES	NO
18. Career change (e.g., different job, going back to school) (36)	YES	NO
19. Increased problems (or resolved ones) with long-term partner (35)	YES	NO
20. A large mortgage or loan (e.g., $100,000 in student loans) (31)	YES	NO
21. Foreclosure of mortgage or loan (30)	YES	NO
22. New responsibilities at work / school (e.g., promotion, demotion) (29)	YES	NO
23. Child leaving home (e.g., to be independent, to go off to college) (29)	YES	NO
24. Issues with partner's family (e.g., in-laws, siblings) (29)	YES	NO
25. Outstanding personal achievement (28)	YES	NO
26. Partner / family member becomes employed / unemployed (26)	YES	NO
27. Starting or graduating from school/university (26)	YES	NO
28. Changed living conditions (e.g., new home, remodeling) (25)	YES	NO

29. Changed habits (e.g., improving appearance) (24)   YES   NO

30. Work relationship issues (e.g., boss, co-workers) (23)   YES   NO

31. Change in work / school hours or conditions (20)   YES   NO

32. Moving to a new residence (e.g., house, apartment, new state) (20) YES   NO

33. Switching schools/university (20)   YES   NO

34. Changing hobbies (e.g., picking up new skills) (19)   YES   NO

35. Changing religious activities (e.g., practicing a new religion) (19) YES   NO

36. Changing social activities (e.g., clubs, events, sports, meetups) (18) YES   NO

37. A moderate loan or mortgage (e.g., $25,000 in student loans) (17)   YES   NO

38. Changing sleeping habits (e.g., trouble falling or staying asleep) (16) YES   NO

39. Attending more or less events with family or loved ones (15)   YES   NO

40. Changing eating habits (e.g., eating more or less) (15)   YES   NO

41. Vacation / time off (13)   YES   NO

42. Major holidays (12)   YES   NO

43. Minor violations of the law (e.g., speeding, noise violations) (11) YES   NO

TOTAL: _____

SCORING: Add up the scores for the life changes you have experienced within the past year and place the total on the line at the end of the scale.

INTERPRETATION:
If your points equal 1-150: your score indicates no significant problem. You have a manageable level of stress in your life.

If your points equal 150-199: your score indicates in the **Mild Life Crisis Level** with a 35% chance of illness. You need to be aware of the sources of stress in your life.

If your points equal 200-299: your score indicates the **Moderate Life Crisis Level** with a 50% chance of illness. You need to reduce your stress as soon as possible.

If your points equal 400+: your score indicates the **Major Life Crisis Level** with an 80% chance of illness. You need to seriously reevaluate your life and immediately reduce further risks to your health.

Where you surprised by some of the items that were on the list? Where you surprised by your score? This test puts things into perspective and makes you reflect on what triggering events may have caused anticipated or unanticipated stress in your life. Sometimes it's clear a life event will be stressful, like being diagnosed with an illness or losing a job, other times we dismiss things like holidays as being stressful events even though the idea of getting together with family, for some, can emotionally throw off the whole month before that particular holiday.

As Hans Selye, M.D., the father of modern stress research once said, "Complete freedom from stress is death." Some stress is a necessary part of life that cannot be avoided entirely. But, both too little or too much stress can lead to a state of *dis*-stress. It is distress (not stress alone) that sets the stage for mind/body *dis*-ease. Health is a matter of creating and maintaining a delicate balance.

What Will Help You

My best advice, take a hard look at this inventory and circle the life events that are still causing you a moderate or severe amount of stress. Then, rank them from most stressful to least stressful. Now you can see, clearly laid out in front of you, what life stressors you need to tackle. Come up with a written plan for each one. If fighting with your partner or spouse is on the list, seek counseling. If you are under a great deal of financial stress, can you work with a financial planner (or friend who is particularly organized about money) to come up with a budget? Or, if you need to start taking care of your physical health can you come up with a new workout routine and stick to it? Find accountability partners and get moving.

Some of the stressful life events listed above happen to us; they are inherently completely out of our control, like death of a loved one. For resources on how to work with grief and support networks for specific issues please see our *Resources* section at the back of the book.

CHAPTER 7: A CLINICAL LOOK AT DEPRESSION

Being chronically sad is no way to live. Period. Yet, many of us do. In fact, depression is the leading cause of disability in people between the ages 15-44 and it impacts 6.3 million individuals (2.6 percent of the American population) a year. For many people living with clinical depression it feels like a way of life. I should know, I've treated thousands of patients who were suffering with depressive symptoms – many of them insisted they would never get better. This is simply not true. Depression doesn't have to rule your life. With proper education and care living what Nell likes to call *happyish* (a good expectation to have regarding one's mood), recovery is possible.

In this chapter, Nell is going to help you understand the many levels of depression, how it manifests differently in people at specific life stages and what causes it, including some lesser talked about factors like poor gut health, smart phones, our over usage of social media and what happens to our mental health when we completely disconnect from nature. The assessments provided will help you see if you or a loved one possibly has a variation of the disorder. Lastly, we'll explain treatment options. *Please note two things: if you're having suicidal ideation (recurring thoughts of hurting yourself) or you know of someone who is, that's considered a medical emergency. Medical care is necessary. Do not wait. Call your doctor or head to your nearest emergency room now.*

To help you find what specifically is needed, this chapter is in three parts: 1) assessing depression in adults 2) psychoeducation about teen suicide, a silent epidemic in this country and 3) assessing depression in children. Feel free to skip forward to the section that most pertains to your situation. Although, be aware that some information in one section might apply to another section as well. For example, information on teen suicide may also apply to adults who are suicidal.

Assessments you'll find in this chapter:

1) *Test Your Self Adult Depression Assessment* is an original assessment developed from questions from two of the most popular public-domain assessments out there on depression: *The Hamilton Rating Scale for Depression13* and the *Zung Self-Rating Depression Scale.*[14]

2) *Test Your Self Teen Suicide Assessment* is meant to test if an adolescent or young adult is planning to attempt suicide. It is heavily influenced by Stan Kutcher and Sonia Chehil's Tool for Assessment of Suicide Risk for Adolescents (TASR-A)[15] and the Adolescent Suicide Assessment Protocol-20 by William J. Fremouw, Ph.D., Julia M. Strunk, B.A., Elizabeth A. Tyner, B.S., and Robert Musick, MSW/LCSW,[16] as well as the National Institute of Mental Health's Ask Suicide Screening Questions.[17]

3) *The PHQ-9, Adolescent Patient Health Questionnaire[18]* designed to test for signs of clinical depression in teenagers.

4) *Mood and Feelings Questionnaire: Long Version (Child Self-Report)[19]* is for the child in your life that you're concerned about. They can read the assessment and answer the questions themselves or an adult can guide them through each question.

5) *Mood and Feelings Questionnaire: Long Version (Parent Report on Child)*[20] is a questionnaire that's meant to be filled out by an adult who is concerned about the mood of a child.

PART I: DEPRESSION IN ADULTS

There are three types of depression in this section. They happen to be the three types of depression treated most regularly in Nell's office: major depression (sometimes called clinical depression), persistent depression (sometimes referred to as dysthymia) and atypical depression.

Major depression is a mood disorder that causes a persistent feeling of sadness and loss of interest which affects how you feel, think and behave. It can also lead to a variety of physical problems as well. Oftentimes, when you're suffering with major depression completely daily tasks becomes a chore and you can feel that life isn't worth living any longer. Although a person may only have depression once in their life, it's usual they have multiple episodes. During these episodes, symptoms occur daily and for a firm diagnosis of depression need to occur more than two weeks. Symptoms include: feelings of sadness, hopelessness, irritability, loss of interest, sleep disturbances, low energy, changes in appetite, restlessness, a slowing down of motor skills, feelings of worthlessness, trouble concentrating and frequent of recurrent thoughts of death and suicide.

For many people with untreated depression, the symptoms are usually severe enough to interrupt one's daily functioning and / or relationship with others. Over the years many people have complained that they feel generally miserable but don't really know why.

Persistent depression, or dysthymia, is a milder form of major depression but it's chronic. Dysthymia doesn't feel like it comes on in episodes; the symptoms descend like a cloud that won't lift, sometimes lasting for more than two years. Experts aren't sure what causes dysthymia but they believe that genes and family history may play a role. Chronic illness, life stress and certain medications may also increase the likelihood of developing dysthymia especially if one is genetically predisposed to suffer with any type of depression.

Signs of dysthymia mirror those of major depression, although generally speaking, they are less symptomatic as a whole and each individual isn't as intense. In other words, it can feel like a watered-down version of major depression but can be just as disruptive in life and hard to treat.

The last type of depression in this chapter is called atypical depression. Atypical depression is people who feel depressed, a lot, but then have real sustained moments or days of happiness especially when they faced a positive life event. It is atypical because this type of depression doesn't follow the predictable pattern that major depression or dysthymia does. Atypical depression is characterized by a specific set of symptoms related to dietary changes, excessive sleep, feeling exhausted, weighed down, sensitive and extremely moody.

Quick STATS

- It's estimated that between 13 to 25% of elderly Americans suffer from significant symptoms of mental illness, including depression[21]
- In their lifetime, 17.3 (7.1 percent of the population) million adults in the United States will have at least one major depressive episode.[22]
- It can be hereditary[23]

- Women are twice as likely to be diagnosed with depression than men[24]
- The highest rate of suicide in America is adults 65 and older, accounting for 20 percent of all suicides nationwide.[25]

What Causes Depression in Adults?

Depression isn't 'in your head' and it goes beyond simply a chemical imbalance in your brain.[26] It is not simply feeling sad, something that you can just 'get over.' It can be caused by a myriad of factors, anything from genetics, hormones,[27] environmental factors such as a stressful work life, or even traumatic events.[28]

There is concern for adults who feel their depression is unbearable, what may lead to suicide. There's no simple answer as to why people choose to end their life, but common reasons include depression, loss of a loved one, life crisis and stress, trauma, financial troubles, or an illness. Suicide, no matter the age, is often coupled with the belief that life isn't worth living anymore; that whatever situation they're in can't be remedied or improved; that killing themselves in the only way to solve and end a problem.

Test Your Self Adult Depression Assessment

DIRECTIONS: For the following self-assessment, check which box applies to you for the description given. Please answer as honestly as possible.

	Not at all	A little bit	A lot	Significantly
1. I feel downhearted, angry and/or sad more than I used to.				
2. I am bothered by things that did not use to irritate me.				
3. My overall mood has changed.				
4. I have trouble falling asleep or staying asleep and am often tired.				
5. I sleep much more or less than normal.				
6. The mornings are difficult and I have a hard time getting out of bed.				
7. I have little to no desire to do anything outside of my room.				
8. Activities that used to interest me do not interest me anymore.				
9. I feel isolated and disconnected from the people in my life.				
10. There has been a decline in my libido.				
11. My attention span has decreased.				
12. I have a difficult time thinking clearly or making decisions.				

Continue

	Not at all	A little bit	A lot	Significantly
13. I am unmotivated to do anything, especially at work or in school.				
14. I am eating much more or less than I used to.				
15. I have gained or lost weight without changing my exercise regime.				
16. My life feels point-less and I feel helpless.				
17. I am anxious most of the time.				
18. I have had suicidal thoughts recently.				
19. I have contem-plated self-harm.				

SCORING: Note the scores to each of your responses according to the following:

1 = Not at all
2 = A little bit
3 = A lot
4 = Significantly

Write your scores in the table below. Then add up all your scores to get your total score. Write your total in the last row of the table.

Questions #1-10	Your Score	Questions #11-19	Your Score
#1		#11	
#2		#12	
#3		#13	
#4		#14	
#5		#15	
#6		#16	
#7		#17	
#8		#18	
#9		#19	
#10		TOTAL	

INTERPRETATION:

A score between 0-19 is considered a normal range. You most likely are not depressed.
A score between 20-39 indicates that you may be mildly depressed.
A score between 40-59 indicates that you may be moderately depressed.
A score between 60-76 indicates that you may be severely depressed.

What Will Help You

Remember, depression is a complex mental disorder and diagnosing depression is only the first step in recovery. Please bring your self-assessment in to your healthcare provider and discuss the results at length with him or her if you are concerned. Healing from depression isn't, generally speaking, an easy overnight fix unless your depression is specifically caused by an external factor that changes, for example, the seasons changing into winter when it is much colder and darker outside. People who have Seasonal Affective Disorder (SAD) may experience depression at the same time every year when the seasons change. Even then there may be feelings of inadequacy or worthlessness that should be addressed. There are many treatments available and some may include lifestyle changes, therapy, medication or dietary changes.

Here are a few things to consider:

Seek help. The first step in recovery is getting an accurate diagnosis. It's especially important to rule out any physical illnesses that may be contributing to your mood and low energy levels like undiagnosed thyroid disease or IBS.

Treatment. Once you've sought help, and depending on your diagnosis, different treatment methods will be offered to you. From antidepressants, to psychotherapy, to support groups, all treatment options should be discussed with your chosen healthcare provider. They should be able to offer the best advice possible. We encourage people to not rely on medication alone.

If you have Seasonal Affective Disorder (SAD), you may benefit the most from light therapy, spending more time outside, exercising, and making your environments as bright as possible. A trip to a location with your preferred season may also help (e.g., planning a vacation to a tropical, warm area during winter).[29]

Patience. Depression does not go away overnight. Getting better takes a lot of work and patience, but also some potential trial and error. Just because one treatment option doesn't work the way you hoped, doesn't mean everything is a lost cause. Treatment is not a one size fits all solution.

You might have to try a few different methods to figure out what works for you. For example, every therapist is different, with different mannerisms and approaches to treatment. You may not click with the first therapist you schedule an appointment with. That's okay. Find someone you like and feel comfortable talking with.

Avoid negativity. It's crucial that you are aware of how much negativity may be present in your life, especially if you are someone struggling with depression. Be mindful of the people you interact with, the activities you engage in, and the information you consume online.

Looking at social media too much can cause self-judgement by comparing our lives with others'. It may help to take a step back from social media and news on major networks, in the newspaper, or online. As a 2017 APA poll on stress in America found, 56% of adults reported following the news was a source of stress for them.[30] There can often be a lot of negativity on TV and elsewhere online that you may not be aware you're internalizing.

Be mindful of viewing or reading too much negative content online or listening to sad music or videos as well. If you fill your brain with joy, you'll feel more joy.

Reframe your thinking. Negative thoughts we tell ourselves can become true thanks to the self-fulfilling prophecy. When you catch yourself being negative, stop yourself and consider a more balanced, rational, and positive thought. Your thoughts may not change overnight, but in time you can create better thinking habits for yourself. Remember we can be more critical of ourselves than others. Consider practicing positive affirmations, developing a mantra, or talking to yourself like you would a best friend or loved one. This can help build self-confidence and remove self-doubt.

Try to get chores done and have a tidy space. When the area around you is a mess, your mind can feel like a mess too. Making your bed in the morning, cleaning a room in your house, or clearing the dishes from the sink can all contribute to you feeling better about your space, and potentially yourself as well. These activities may help you feel more productive. Also, try your best to take care of yourself and maintain good hygiene. If you are having trouble getting started, start small.

Try not to put things off. Putting off your responsibilities or tasks that you need to get done can make you feel worse about yourself. If you are having trouble starting, try the 10 – or 15-minute rule. Just do something for 10 to 15 minutes, and then you can assess where you are and stop if you want. Sometimes getting started is the hardest part, so once you start, you may feel a lot better about being able to finish.

Support. Never fight your battles alone. Seek refuge in your friends and family's support. Reaching out for emotional support is the right thing to do; letting trusted empathic people in your struggle helps you recover faster and makes them feel useful. Looking to offline and online support groups or your place of worship (if you're religious) might help too.

PART II: DEPRESSION IN TEENAGERS

Teenage Suicide
"The bravest thing I ever did was continuing my life when I wanted to die."
– Juliette Lewis, actress.

Several years ago, the popular Netflix show *13 Reasons Why* dragged teen suicide to the forefront of many people's minds as a stark reminder that yes, teenagers do, in fact, suffer with depression and will attempt suicide as a last effort to end their psychic pain.

If you're reading this section, you must be worried about the potential actions of someone you love – your child, a friend's child, a family member's child. Or, if you're a teenager reading these pages, maybe you're concerned that you might be depressed or do something dangerous to yourself. Teenage suicide is a silent epidemic that needs to be properly addressed in this country.

According to a study done by Ramin Mojtabai at the John Hopkins Bloomberg School of Public Health), from 2005 to 2014, depression in teenagers rose 37 percent impacting 20 percent of adolescents before they reach adulthood.[31] The National Institute of Mental Health calculates that between the ages of 12 and 17, at least 3 million adolescents have experienced one or more major depressive episodes in the last year.[32] In 2017, 13.6 percent of teenagers have made a suicide plan; 7.4 percent have tried to commit suicide; 2.4 percent were only injured.[33] These statistics are worrisome, but it is important to note that the amount of teenagers who have committed suicide is down from previous years (in 2015, 8.6 percent of teenagers committed suicide.)[34]

But what do these statistics mean? What does this trend indicate? In recent years, I feel that there has been a shift in how we discuss teenager suicide, opening up the conversation. Maybe this downward trend has developed because people are willing to talk about the struggles that teenagers go through, allowing them to access resources to prevent suicide.

As we see in adults, there's no simple answer as to why teenagers choose to end their life but common reasons include academic pressure, social pressure, the desire to please parents and guilt if they don't, an erratic and detrimental home life, or a general desire to escape from their life.[35] Frequently, all these reasons can snowball into a depression that may lead to someone taking drastic actions.[36] Social media has also been linked to anxiety and self-esteem issues, and low self-esteem may contribute to depression, anxiety, self-harming behavior, and other problems.[37] Teens (and adults as well) can have a dual diagnosis of both depression and anxiety.

Teens may simply feel that they don't feel right, that they're not happy, and they may not always know why or how it happened. Depression doesn't necessarily need a reason, and even the seemingly smallest problems can potentially set it off. When teenagers feel as if their problems aren't taken seriously, big and small, they may feel disconnected from the adults in their lives. Loneliness and desperation sets in.

Warning Signs of A Potential Suicide Attempt

The list of potential warning signs we've provided is inspired by the American Foundation for Suicide Prevention, The Centers for Disease Control and Prevention, and the National Suicide Prevention Lifeline and Suicide Awareness Voices of Education. You may notice that these signs share many similarities with signs of depression and potentially violent behavior. Adults and friends of a teens at risk should keep an eye out for:

- Changes in sleeping and eating habits
- Withdrawal from friends, family, and social settings
- Isolation – whether self or by peers
- Loss of interest in schoolwork and extracurricular activities
- Alcohol and drug use
- Dangerous risk-taking
- Displayed interest in death and dying
- Increased sense of anxiety, rage, and irritation
- Drastic mood swings not related to puberty
- Threats of physically hurting themselves

Teens or others who are suicidal may feel that they have no reason to live, life is too hard or pointless, they don't deserve to live, or that others in their lives would be better off without them. They may wish that they didn't exist or could simply stop existing. They may be in so much pain that they view suicide as the only way to escape their pain.

Unfortunately, sometimes depression and suicidal behavior in teenagers and young adults goes unnoticed because adults assume teenagers are supposed to be 'moody' and 'act out.' This is why it is even more important that adults and friends remain hyper aware of a teenager's mood, behavior and all of us collectively watch out for any changes in someone's disposition.

Some teens may not even realize they're depressed (as depression manifests in everyone differently) or deny it. Depression doesn't always feel like intense misery that may make someone want to cry all the time. Some people with depression may simply not feel much of anything at all. It may be much harder to recognize this as depression.

"Smiling" or Hidden Depression

It is also incredibly important to understand that many teens (and adults as well) may try to hide their depression altogether. This contrasts with teens who may appear moodier or act out. Instead, many teens put on a "happy face" or a "mask" and try to make everyone believe that they are okay – that they are more than okay, that they are happy even and enjoying life. Some people who are depressed may actually appear like the happiest people you know, and they may never be suspected as someone suffering from depression.

This is a defense mechanism to hide what they are really feeling. One teenager said their classmates saw them as excited and playful, someone who always smiled and laughed.[38] But inside, they were secretly suffering with depression. Another teen isolated themselves. They wanted everyone to see them as happy, even though they were depressed.

Others reported hiding their depression by lying, complimenting and focusing on others, telling others that they're okay, being sarcastic or humorous, socializing, and telling others that they're sick.[39] Teens may have the energy to function well at school or other events because they have the energy to hide their depression from the world. Because of this, they may be more likely to plan and follow through with suicidal thoughts and ideas.[40] This is why "smiling depression" can be so dangerous.

In these situations, it can be much harder to spot signs of depression and potential suicide threats because teens try their best to not let anyone know. Those who do contemplate suicide often keep this information to themselves. They carry it around and withdraw into themselves. The stigma of mental illness can inhibit teens from coming forward, fearing that they may be called weak. They may also feel like no one understands what they're going through, and that they're the only one who feels this way. They're not.

They may not want to worry or disappoint family members. They may believe that family members will consider them a burden, be ashamed of them, misunderstand them, or otherwise not take their thoughts and feelings seriously. They may not want to be treated or perceived differently by their parents, siblings, teachers, friends, classmates, or other relatives, and they may be afraid that if they come forward about how they're feeling, other people will have different behaviors and attitudes towards them.

They may also simply not be at the stage yet where they want to get help and recover from their depression. If they've been depressed for a while, depression may have become all they've known, and teens (and adults as well) can get used to it. They may see depression as part of their identity and be unsure of who they are without it.[41] They may not want to be happy or even be afraid of being happy because the concept is so foreign and removed from their experience. They may also be worried that if they feel happy or joyful feelings, they will eventually feel disappointed, lonely, or letdown.[42] Not wanting to get better yet may reinforce a teenager's feelings that they should be hiding their depression.

According to a 2014 study, about half of teens who briefly experience depression in their teens outgrow it – in other words, their depression doesn't continue into adulthood.[43] This means that the problems that you or your teen may be facing now may not be problems they will face forever. This may be because of the maturation that occurs during these years (as the brain does not fully develop until age 25[44]), learning new skills, and successfully transitioning into adulthood.[45]

In addition to the previous lists of behaviors adults and friends should watch out for in teens, see the following list of hidden warning signs that may be more likely to go unnoticed.

Hidden Warning Signs of Depression

- Appearing overly happy or cheerful all the time – fake smiling and laughing a lot, cracking jokes (pay attention to a person's eyes and face muscles – genuine smiles use more face muscles[46])
- Saying "I'm okay" or "I'm fine" all the time
- Spending a lot of time to themselves behind closed doors or in isolation (e.g., only leaving their bedroom to go to school or work, eat, or go to the bathroom)
- Often looking tired or fatigued
- Frequently saying they're tired or sick
- Frequent lying, making excuses, or telling cover-up stories to explain behavior
- Becoming more defensive, more prone to anger or irritability, or in denial
- Not saying much in conversation; being quiet
- Feeling more intense emotions in general – when feelings are hidden and bottled up, sometimes emotions can leak out[47]
- Sharing less optimistic views[48] – "all or nothing" thinking, being more negative
- Abnormal sleeping, eating, or drinking habits – either too much or too little
- Being disorganized or messy
- Poor hygiene; being unable to care for oneself
- Subtle cries for help – small moments to watch out for where they open up and become vulnerable. Teens concealing their depression may let their guard down for a moment. Someone may also later regret their actions and try to take their call for help back, such as deciding to schedule an appointment with a therapist but then not following through.[49]

Self-Harm

Teens may have thoughts of harming themselves. Like depression, teens and adults may also hide self-destructive behavior. Self-harm can be a coping mechanism to deal with one's emotions, or lack thereof. They may be looking for a physical release or distraction from the emotional pain they're in, or they may be seeking to feel anything at all. They may also harm themselves because it's something in their life that they feel they have control over, or they feel that they must punish themselves. Self-harm may or may not be present in a depressed or suicidal teen. Self-harm also does not automatically indicate that a teen is suicidal.

Some signs of self-harm to watch out for include:[50] [51]

- Feeling like they must injure oneself, or they're addicted to harming themselves
- Feeling disconnected or disassociated from other people or the world
- Hearing voices that tell them to self-harm
- Frequently thinking about self-harm
- Always wearing long sleeves and long pants that cover up arms and legs, even during hot weather
- Avoiding situations where they must undress or show skin in front of others
- Scars or scabs (especially if they're close together or in a pattern, such as small linear lines)
- Fresh cuts, bruises, burns, missing patches of hair, or other wounds that appear regularly (especially if they're close together or in a pattern, such as small linear lines)
- Wounds that are not healing after a while
- Feeling like they can't stop self-harming
- Spending a lot of time by themselves
- Making excuses or telling stories about how they got injured, including saying it was an accident or because they were clumsy
- Acting suspicious, secretive, or jumpy, like they're hiding something
- Impulsive, unpredictable behavior
- Blood on clothing, towels, bedding, or tissues
- Keeping or hiding sharp objects (razors, pencil sharpeners, needles, knives, glass) in unexpected places, such as somewhere in their backpack, locker, or bedroom

Quick STATS on Teenage Suicide:

- Suicide is the second leading cause of death for ages 10 to 24 – more teenagers die from illnesses, diseases and birth defects combined[52]
- Suicide attempts have risen 30 percent between 1999 and 2016, with some states seeing a 58 percent increase[53]
- In 2017, people aged 15 to 24 had a suicide rate of 14.4 percent[54]
- In 2017, 7.4 percent of students attempted suicide and 2.4 percent were injured in a suicide attempt[55]
- Every day, an average of 3,041 suicide attempts are made by someone between the ages of 13 and 18[56]
- Females are more likely to attempt suicide, but males are more likely to die (4 percent more likely, in fact)[57]
- Firearms are used in over half of suicides[58]
- Adolescents are more likely to hang, strangle or suffocate themselves

To test your mental health, take the following *Test Your Self Teen Suicide Assessment*.

Test Your Self Teen Suicide Assessment

DIRECTIONS: Answer the following yes or no questions.

Environment Profile

1. History of suicide in the family	YES	NO
2. Precarious home life	YES	NO
3. Recent loss of loved one	YES	NO
4. Change in living situation or general home life	YES	NO
5. Known psychiatric illness	YES	NO
6. Peer isolation and/or lack of peer support	YES	NO

Behavior and Emotional Profile

7. Anger management issues (irritability)	YES	NO
8. Signs of risky behavior and/or impulse control	YES	NO
9. Substance abuse	YES	NO
10. Shows signs of depression and/or anxiety	YES	NO
11. Feeling hopeless and/or worthless	YES	NO
12. Believing that they would be better off dead	YES	NO
13. Believing that nobody would miss them	YES	NO
14. Speaks of suicidal intentions	YES	NO
15. History of suicidal behavior	YES	NO

SCORING: Based off of 15 questions, if you answered **"Yes" to nine or more,** then the behavior may be leading up to a suicide attempt.

If you answered "Yes" to the questions that specifically address suicide (speaks of suicidal intentions, have a history of suicide in the family or in the past has displayed suicidal behavior), then the chances of another suicide attempt are even higher.

Note, the scoring is not a concrete predictor if a teenager will attempt suicide, but should be more used as a guideline. Concerning results should be shared with a medical provider.

The PHQ-9, Adolescent Patient Health Questionnaire

DIRECTIONS: Answer the following; over the last 2 weeks, how often have you been bothered by the following problems?

	Not at all sure	Several days	More than half the days	Nearly every day
1. Little interest or pleasure in doing things.				
2. Feeling down, depressed or hopeless.				
3. Trouble falling asleep, or sleeping too much.				
4. Feeling tired or having little energy.				
5. Poor appetite or overeating.				
6. Feeling bad about yourself, or that you're a failure or have let yourself or family down.				
7. Trouble concentrating on things, such as reading the newspaper or watching television.				
8. Moving or speaking so slowly that other people could have noticed? Or the opposite – being so fidgety or restless that you have been moving around a lot more than usual.				
9. Thoughts that you would be better off dead or hurting yourself in some way.				

SCORING: Note the scores for each of your responses according to the following:

0 = Not at all
1 = Several days
2 = More than half the days
3 = Nearly every day

If you circled a number greater than zero on any of the problems listed above, please check off how difficult these problems have made it for you to do your work, take care for things at home, or get along with other people?

☐   Not difficult at all
☐   Somewhat difficult
☐   Very difficult
☐   Extremely difficult

Record your scores according to the above key in the table below:

Statements	Your Score
#1	
#2	
#3	
#4	
#5	
#6	
#7	
#8	
#9	
TOTAL	

INTERPRETATION:

If your score is between 1-4 points, this indicates you may have minimal depression.

If your score is between 5-9 points, this indicates you may have mild depression.

If your score is between 10-14 points, this indicates you may have moderate depression.

If your score is between 15-19 points, this indicates you may have moderately severe depression.

If your score is between 20-27 points, this indicates you may have severe depression.

What Will Help You

Now that you have a feeling of what to look for, and perhaps you or a loved one has taken the above assessments, read on and get help.

Talk to someone. Letting someone else know that you are struggling is not a sign of weakness; it's a sign of strength and bravery. If you are a teen and think you might be depressed, I encourage you to talk to a trusted adult in your life. Come forward and say something. Try to be open to getting help and getting better. Your life can significantly improve for the better as long as you are open, even if it may seem like that's not possible for you right now. Depression is highly treatable. Full recovery is possible.

If you are nervous about starting the conversation, consider talking to a parent or guardian you feel closest with first. If that's not an option, consider talking to a school counselor, a teacher, a relative, or another trusted adult. If you feel you can't talk to your parents verbally or in person, consider having someone there with you for moral support, or consider writing your parents a note, a text message, or a letter.

Find a therapist. When looking for a therapist to treat a teenager it's incredibly important to find someone who has experience with treating teenage depression and who can strike up a repour with the teen in question. A teenager must feel at least moderately comfortable opening up to the therapist for any progress to be made. Consider a psychiatric evaluation.

As we mentioned in the earlier section, every therapist is different, and your teen may have to see a few different ones to find the person he or she feels most comfortable with. Talking to a school counselor may also be an option. If you or your teen is a college or university student, they may be able to schedule an appointment with a counselor at their school for free.

Listen and show support. Teenagers want to feel seen and heard. They want to feel that their words, emotions, and actions are understood and validated. You need to show them that you are there for them. Involve them in deciding how their treatment is managed. If you decide everything for them, you may reinstate the notion of being unheard. They may feel helpless and out of control in their own lives but involving them can help them feel more in control. It is important for teens to feel like they have a say. If you suspect your teen may be struggling, talk to them about mental health. Let them know you love them and they can come to you to talk about anything.

Go outside. Disconnect from technology. Sometimes just getting a breath of fresh air can help clear your mind and allow you to focus on being in the present.[59] Try taking a walk or a run. Exercising outside can increase your energy levels.[60] Journaling may also be a healthy outlet for teens to express themselves and their emotions. Or maybe there's a social event your teen can go to. Encourage them to go and try it out, at least once.

Support Groups, like One Recovery. Groups like One Recovery are dedicated to raising awareness in communities for the struggles that teenagers go through and connect teenagers with each other. Finding support in a community can help teenagers, and people of all ages, feel less alone.[61] Teens should also socialize and talk to their friends, reconnect with old friends, or make new friends. Also, think about if you or your teen have any negative social influences in their life. Consider talking to your teen about this.

If you or your teen is self-harming or you suspect that they may self-harm, remove or limit access to sharp objects or anything else that they could use to harm themselves. This may include razors, pencil sharpeners, needles, knives, glass, firearms, or access to many medications, pills, or toxic substances, among other objects.

Strategies to reduce self-harm include:

- Try the Butterfly Project[62] – Using a permanent marker, draw a butterfly wherever you self-harm. Name the butterfly after a loved one. If you harm yourself, the butterfly will die. If you don't, it will live. Draw a new butterfly every time you want to harm yourself. Don't intentionally try to wash or scrub off the butterflies from your skin.
- Snap a rubber band against your wrist whenever you feel the urge to harm yourself.
- Draw lines or pictures on your skin with markers or makeup.
- Hit a pillow or punching bag.
- Scream into a pillow.
- Squeeze ice cubes or a stress ball in your hand.
- Press ice against your skin.
- Take a cold shower.
- Go for a run.

- Identify your emotions and triggers.[63] Get to the root of the problem. Understanding why you harm yourself and what you're feeling when you do may help you better avoid and deal with these situations in the future.
- Learn new coping mechanisms and practice self-care. Distract yourself in healthier ways. Try a creative outlet like writing or drawing. Whenever you feel the urge, try phoning a friend, talking to a family member, counting to yourself in your head, watching a movie or TV show, or taking a walk.[64]

Establish a routine. Start small with encouraging teens to do little things that can lead to a healthier lifestyle. Encourage them to stay active, eat well or socialize with friends. At first there may be resistance, but if you push lovingly enough, positive daily practices go a long way to helping a teen pull out of a depressive state.[65] Remember change is not going to happen overnight, but small steps can go a long way.

Avoid negativity. It's crucial that you are aware of how much negativity may be present in your life (or your teen's life). Be mindful of the people you or your teen interact with, the activities they engage in, and the information they consume online. Social media can be especially harmful to teenagers. The people they follow online, the videos they watch, the music they listen to, the websites they visit, and the content they post can all influence a teenager's mental health.

Reframe your thinking. Negative thoughts we tell ourselves can become true thanks to the self-fulfilling prophecy. When you catch yourself being negative, stop yourself and consider a more balanced, rational, and positive thought. Your thoughts may not change overnight, but in time you can create better thinking habits for yourself. Remember we can be more critical of ourselves than others. Consider practicing positive affirmations, developing a mantra, or talking to yourself like you would a best friend or loved one. This can help you build self-confidence and remove self-doubt.

Try not to put things off. Putting off your responsibilities or tasks that you need to get done can make you feel worse about yourself. If you are having trouble starting, try the 10 – or 15-minute rule. Just do something for 10 to 15 minutes, and then you can assess where you are and stop if you want. Sometimes getting started is the hardest part, so once you start, you may feel a lot better about being able to finish.

If you are a parent or know a teen in your life who is struggling, talk to them about school. If your teen is having problems with a friend, a romantic relationship, a peer, a teacher, or the academic workload itself, it's important that you know what's going on. They may be experiencing a lot of stress concerning their grades, classes, or their social environment. If they are having severe problems with functioning at school, it may be a good idea to talk to their teachers or their school counselor about accommodations.

Consider taking time off from college or university. If you or your teen is a current college or university student, or an upcoming high school graduate thinking about college, it may not be the best idea to continue your studies right now. Taking a semester off (or a year, or longer) to evaluate and treat depression may be the best course of action. You can always return to school when you are feeling better and are able to prioritize your education and earning good grades more heavily. Remember that nothing is more important than your mental health.

Raise awareness. To beat a problem, one must understand the problem.

PART III: DEPRESSION IN CHILDREN

As difficult as it is to write or speak about, children also suffer with mental health issues and disorders. Parents, caregivers and teachers must be open to the fact that children need our help, too. Many children live with undiagnosed depression, like teenagers, because adults attribute their negative, anxious, or lethargic moods and symptoms to "normal" stages of childhood development.

Quick STATS

- Children can get depressed. In fact, there are reports of children as young as preschoolers displaying signs of depression[66]
- When children show signs of depression at an early age, they are often untreated, and those symptoms linger into adolescence and adulthood.[67]
- 7.1% (4.4 million) of American children between 3 and 17 have anxiety
- 3.2 % (1.9 million) of American children aged 3 to 7 have been diagnosed with depression
- Between 2003 and 2007, 5.4% of children aged 6 – 17 had ever been diagnosed with anxiety or depression
- Yet, between 2011 and 2012, the number rose to 8%
- Nearly 80% of children between 3 and 17 years old receive help for depression

MOOD AND FEELINGS QUESTIONNAIRE: Long Version (Child Self-Report)

DIRECTIONS: This form is about how you might have been feeling or acting **recently.** For each question, please check how you have been feeling or acting *in the past two weeks.*
- If a sentence was not true about you, check NOT TRUE.
- If a sentence was only sometimes true, check SOMETIMES.
- If a sentence was true about you most of the time, check TRUE.

	NOT TRUE	SOMETIMES	TRUE
1. I felt miserable or unhappy.			
2. I didn't enjoy anything at all.			
3. I was less hungry than usual.			
4. I ate more than usual.			
5. I felt so tired I just sat around and did nothing.			
6. I was moving and walking more slowly than usual.			
7. I was very restless.			
8. I felt I was no good anymore.			

9. I blamed myself for things that weren't my fault.			
10. It was hard for me to make up my mind.			
11. I felt grumpy and cross with my parents.			
12. I felt like talking less than usual.			
13. I was talking more slowly than usual.			
14. I cried a lot.			
15. I thought there was nothing good for me in the future.			
16. I thought that life wasn't worth living.			
17. I thought about death or dying.			
18. I thought my family would be better off without me.			
19. I thought about killing myself.			
20. I didn't want to see my friends.			
21. I found it hard to think properly or concentrate.			
22. I thought bad things would happen to me.			
23. I hated myself.			
24. I felt I was a bad person.			
25. I thought I looked ugly.			
26. I worried about aches and pains.			
27. I felt lonely.			
28. I thought nobody really loved me.			
29. I didn't have any fun in school.			
30. I thought I could never be as good as other kids.			
31. I did everything wrong.			
32. I didn't sleep as well as I usually sleep.			
33. I slept a lot more than usual.			

SCORING: Note the scores to each of your responses according to the following:

0 = Not true

1 = Sometimes

2 = True

Write your scores in the table below. Then add up all your scores to get your total score. Write your total score in the last row of the table.

Questions #1-17	Your Score	Questions #18-33	Your Score
#1		#18	
#2		#19	
#3		#20	
#4		#21	
#5		#22	
#6		#23	
#7		#24	
#8		#25	
#9		#26	
#10		#27	
#11		#28	
#12		#29	
#13		#30	
#14		#31	
#15		#32	
#16		#33	
#17		TOTAL	

INTERPRETATION: Scores range from 0 to 66. The higher your score, the more likely you have more severe depressive symptoms. If you score higher than 27, this indicates you most likely have depression and you should talk to your healthcare provider about a further clinical assessment.

MOOD AND FEELINGS QUESTIONNAIRE: Long Version (Parent Report on Child)

DIRECTIONS: This form is about how your child might have been feeling or acting **recently.** For each question, please check how s/he has been feeling or acting *in the past two weeks.*
- If a sentence was not true about your child, check NOT TRUE.
- If a sentence was only sometimes true, check SOMETIMES.
- If a sentence was true about your child most of the time, check TRUE.

	NOT TRUE	SOMETIMES	TRUE
1. S/he felt miserable or unhappy.			
2. S/he didn't enjoy anything at all.			
3. S/he was less hungry than usual.			
4. S/he ate more than usual.			
5. S/he felt so tired s/he just sat around and did nothing.			

6. S/he was moving and walking more slowly than usual.			
7. S/he was very restless.			
8. S/he felt she was no good anymore.			
9. S/he blamed himself or herself for things that weren't his/her fault.			
10. It was hard for s/he to make up his/her mind.			
11. S/he felt grumpy and cross with his/her parents.			
12. S/he felt like talking less than usual.			
13. S/he was talking more slowly than usual.			
14. S/he cried a lot.			
15. S/he thought there was nothing good for him/her in the future.			
16. S/he thought that life wasn't worth living.			
17. S/he thought about death or dying.			
18. S/he thought his/her family would be better off without him/her.			
19. S/he thought about killing him/herself.			
20. S/he didn't want to see his/her friends.			
21. S/he found it hard to think properly or concentrate.			
22. S/he thought bad things would happen to him/her.			
23. S/he hated him/herself.			
24. S/he felt s/he was a bad person.			
25. S/he thought s/he looked ugly.			
26. S/he worried about aches and pains.			
27. S/he felt lonely.			

Continue

28. S/he thought nobody really loved him/her.			
29. S/he didn't have any fun in school.			
30. S/he thought s/he could never be as good as other kids.			
31. S/he did every-thing wrong.			
32. S/he didn't sleep as well as s/he usually sleeps.			
33. S/he slept a lot more than usual.			
34. S/he wasn't as happy as usual, even when s/he was praised or rewarded.			

SCORING: Note the scores to each of your responses according to the following:

0 = Not true
1 = Sometimes
2 = True

Write your scores in the table below. Then add up all your scores to get your total score. Write your total score in the last row of the table.

Questions #1-17	Your Score	Questions #18-34	Your Score
#1		#18	
#2		#19	
#3		#20	
#4		#21	
#5		#22	
#6		#23	
#7		#24	
#8		#25	
#9		#26	
#10		#27	
#11		#28	
#12		#29	
#13		#30	
#14		#31	
#15		#32	
#16		#33	
#17		#34	
		TOTAL	

INTERPRETATION: Scores range from 0 to 66. The higher your score, the more likely your child has more severe depressive symptoms. If you score higher than 27, this indicates your child most likely has depression and you should talk to your child's healthcare provider about a further clinical assessment.

What Will Help You

Proper treatment for a child suffering with depression will make a world of difference in a child's life. Early intervention is key. Remember that untreated depression in early childhood can continue into adulthood.[68] Comprehensive treatment also involves parent education; teaching a parent how to deal with their child's depression ensures that all the right steps are being taken to handle the situation effectively. Below are our top suggestions.

1. **Medical Attention and Therapy.** Professional help will teach a child how to manage, cope and control their depression (and moods) so they can live life to the fullest during this stage. Seeing a doctor is necessary. A parent or caregiver must rule out any physical cause of a child's depression, like an undetected illness or vitamin deficiency. As I've said before, depression isn't "all in one's head" so to speak.

2. **Exercise and eat well.** Feeding a child a healthy diet and ensuring the child is developing proper exercise habits does wonders for a child's mental health.

3. **Take up a new activity.** Encourage a child to be curious. Require them to try new things, often, even if they are uncomfortable at first.

4. **Meet with a friend.** Socialize your child with other positive children. Try setting a weekly lunch or dinner date. Get them involved in group activities or team sports.

5. **Disconnect from Tech and Go outside.** Being in nature, experiencing a different environment than constantly being indoors, can increase endorphins, improve self-esteem and self-worth, and create mindfulness.[69]

6. **Read.** Although this is typically done alone, reading to a child is a great way to help with cognitive function and generally is a great way to bond with a child.

7. **Talk to them about school.** If your child is having problems with a friend, a peer, a teacher, or the academic workload itself, it's important that you know what's going on. They may be experiencing a lot of stress concerning their grades, classes, or their social environment. If they are having severe problems with functioning at school, it may be a good idea to talk to their teachers or their school counselor about accommodations.

For all these activities, I suggest you make a daily chart with your child to help him or her chart all their positive progress.

Resources

In this book, I've talked a lot about what resources are available for you. Pacer's Kids Health, Child Mind Institute, Active Minds, Worry Wise Kids, and Families for Depression Awareness all deal directly with depression in children and teenagers and are great resources to help in suicide prevention. Of course, there is also the National Suicide Prevention Lifeline and the National Alliance on Mental Illness to aid in this endeavor. **For the full list of resources, please see the Appendix in the back of this book.**

CHAPTER 8: HOW BAD IS MY ANXIETY?

If your symptoms are negatively interfering with your daily functioning, treatment will help. However, as you read on and take the following assessments, keep in mind that some anxiety is good; it lets you know when you're in a dangerous situation, when you're expanding by trying something new that's a challenge, and when you need to change something about your life that is no longer serving you.

Anxiety is a big problem for Americans. According to the World Health Organization (WHO), 1 in 13 people worldwide have anxiety.[70] In the United States alone, 42 million Americans (18.1% of the population) suffer from a panic or anxiety disorder.[71] Billions are spent treating patients with anxiety[72] and those are just the numbers of people who report their symptoms to their doctors or healthcare providers. It's safe to assume many more Americans live with undiagnosed and untreated anxiety.

In a 2018 poll by the American Psychiatric Association (APA), 39% of Americans reported their anxiety increased compared to the previous year. Another 39% reported equal levels of anxiety. Sixty eight percent of those participants ranked keeping themselves or their families safe as their number one concern, tied with health concerns (68%), and paying bills or expenses (67%).[73] An average of 4.6 work days are missed every month because of anxiety disorders. Reduced work performance due to anxiety affects an additional 5.5 work days monthly.[74]

Adults and children alike suffer with anxiety disorders. Similar to adults, children with untreated anxiety disorders are more likely to have poor work performance at school. They're also more likely to miss out on crucial social experiences and abuse substances. For many children, anxiety usually presents itself alongside other disorders including depression, eating disorders, and ADHD.[75]

Types of Anxiety Disorders

There are several different types of anxiety disorders:

- *Generalized Anxiety Disorder (GAD)* – characterized by excessive, persistent worry about many aspects of one's life, which may include health, finances or relationships.
- *Social Anxiety Disorder (SAD)* – characterized by anxiety about social interactions or social performance situations (ex: going to a work conference)
- *Panic Disorder (PD)* – characterized by severe, immediate anxiety symptoms like profuse sweating, heart palpitations, dizziness (panic attacks)
- *Acute Stress Disorder* – characterized by short-lived anxiety occurring immediately after a trauma
- *Adjustment Disorder* – characterized by anxiety developed in anticipation or response to a major life-changing event (ex: marriage, relocation, divorce, bereavement)
- *Anxiety resulting from a medical condition* – characterized by anxiety developed in conjunction with short – or long-term illnesses

- *Illness Anxiety Disorder (IAD)* (also known as *hypochondriasis* or *health anxiety*) – characterized by a persistent fear of having serious health issues despite evidence to the contrary. People with this disorder may have no symptoms or mild symptoms that they then interpret to indicate a serious medical issue.
- *Substance-Induced Anxiety Disorder* – characterized by anxiety or panic that directly results from misusing or withdrawing from drugs, alcohol, medications, or exposure to toxic substances
- *Phobias* – Specific phobias are characterized by intense, irrational fear of certain objects, events, places, or situations (ex: needles, blood, spiders, flying). A phobia such as Agoraphobia is characterized by a perception of being in an unsafe space with no clear way to escape. This phobia may manifest in a fear of crowded public spaces.
- *Separation Anxiety Disorder* – characterized by persistent anxiety over being away from home, being away from loved ones, or losing loved ones
- *Selective Mutism* – characterized by not speaking in specific situations or to specific people, despite being physically able to speak

Notable Mentions: OCD, BFRB, Hoarding Disorder, and PTSD

In the DSM-5, Obsessive-Compulsive Disorder (OCD) and Post-Traumatic Stress Disorder (PTSD) are not classified as anxiety disorders, although we mention them here because they have been classified as such in previous editions. While OCD and a few related disorders will be discussed below, PTSD is addressed in Chapter 20 of this book.

- *Obsessive Compulsive Disorder* – characterized by intrusive and obsessive thoughts and compulsive behaviors. People with OCD may often realize that their behaviors (rituals) are irrational, but they still feel like they must do them. In the United States, it's estimated that around 1 in 40 adults and 1 in 100 children have OCD.[76]
- *Body-Focused Repetitive Behaviors (BFRB)* – characterized by compulsive body-focused behaviors unintentionally damaging the body, such as hair-pulling (trichotilomania), skin-picking (excoriation), and onychophagia (nail-biting). While there isn't much research out there on these disorders, current research suggests that OCD and BFRB are strongly linked[77]
- *Hoarding Disorder* – characterized by excessive saving and difficulty getting rid of personal possessions, to the extent that working or living in places where items are hoarded can be extremely challenging. In severe cases there can be health and safety concerns for anyone living in a hoarder's home. Hoarding can also cause relationship conflicts. Compulsive hoarding is classified as a compulsive disorder. Hoarding is also most common among older adults[78]

What Does the DSM-5 stand for?

The DSM-5 stands for *Diagnostic and Statistical Manual of Mental Disorders, Fifth Edition*. It's a valuable diagnostic resource that defines and classifies mental health disorders. It is published and periodically revised by the APA.

Signs & Symptoms of Anxiety

- Excessive worrying or nervousness
- Sense of impending danger

- Not being able to control worry
- Lack or difficulty concentrating (on anything other than worry)
- Avoiding situations that may trigger anxiety (or having the urge to avoid those situations)
- Feeling excessively self-conscious or self-doubting
- Perfectionism
- Irrational fears
- Personality changes
- Agitation
- Restlessness
- Irritability or anger
- Fatigue (weakness or tiredness)
- Sweating
- Trembling
- Muscle tension
- Increased heart rate
- Sleep problems (trouble falling or staying asleep)
- Rapid breathing (hyperventilation)
- Having gastrointestinal (GI) problems, such as chronic indigestion (ex: IBS)

Signs & Symptoms of Panic Attacks

Panic attacks are sudden, intense periods of fear experienced over a short time frame (up to 10 minutes), although multiple panic attacks can occur which may seem like they're lasting longer.

- Sudden overwhelming fear
- Palpitations
- Sweating, chills, or hot flashes
- Trembling or shaking
- Breathing difficulties such as shortness of breath, feeling of being choked or smothered
- Chest pain
- Pounding or racing heart rate
- Nausea
- Abdominal pain
- Feeling dizzy, lightheaded or faint
- Headache
- Numbness or tingling in limbs or entire body
- Sense of terror or impending doom
- Sudden fear of death
- Fear of lack of control
- Feeling crazy
- Derealization or depersonalization – feeling detached from oneself or surroundings

Panic Attack vs. Anxiety Attack

Despite very similar signs and symptoms, anxiety attacks and panic attacks are not the same:

Panic Attacks	Anxiety Attacks
• Can occur without a trigger • Sudden, intense, disruptive • Subsides shortly after it starts	• Response to perceived stressor • Gradual, varies in intensity • Can last for long periods of time

Possible Triggers of Panic or Anxiety Attacks

- Work
- Social situations
- Caffeine, drug or alcohol misuse or withdrawal
- Medications or supplements
- Various phobias
- Memories of past trauma
- Worry over experiencing another panic attack

Risk Factors of Anxiety or Panic Attacks

- An anxious personality – According to the Big Five Personality Traits (also known as the Five Factor Model of Personality), people who score high in neuroticism may be more likely to develop anxiety and other mood disorders.[79]
- Existing mental health issues (ex: depression, bipolar)
- Biological family members with anxiety or panic disorders
- Experiencing stress due to a chronic medical condition or serious illness
- Alcohol dependence, drug abuse and withdrawal
- Persistent stress (health, family, finances, work, or school can all be factors)
- Recently experiencing a stressful event (divorce, bereavement)
- Experienced past trauma or witnessed a traumatic event (ex: children who endure abuse or trauma at a young age may develop an anxiety disorder as an adult)
- Being female – women are twice as likely as men to have GAD, PD, and phobias[80]

Because so many people suffer with anxiety worldwide, for this chapter we're providing a variety of self-assessments. Self-assessments included in this chapter are the following:

1) **Generalized Anxiety Disorder 7 Scale (GAD-7).**[81] The Generalized Anxiety Scale screens for the presence of a severe anxiety disorder, which may include Generalized Anxiety Disorder, Panic Disorder, and Social Phobia. This anxiety scale is a brief diagnostic tool that is meant to assess if your current mental health state may need further investigation. It should be noted that this scale in particular only asks about your anxiety within the past two weeks. If you're not sure after taking this test if you have an anxiety problem, consider any major temporary events in your life that may be causing you stress or any medication you are on that may be affecting how you've felt in the last few weeks. Consider if your anxiety has been present beyond just the past two weeks.

2) **Hamilton Rating Scale for Anxiety.**[82] The Hamilton Rating Scale for Anxiety is another scale that rates anxiety. It can be used to assess a person's anxiety level for the first time, or it can

be used to track anxiety symptoms (and see which ones appear or subside) over a period of time.

3) **Social Interaction Anxiety Scale (SIAS).**[83] The SIAS assesses the severity of a person's social interaction anxiety, and from there, if they may have a social anxiety disorder. This scale measures worry when talking about oneself or meeting and getting along with others in various social situations.

4) **Worry Domains Questionnaire (WDQ).**[84] The WDQ was developed to measure what's called non-pathological worry. This instrument is unique in that it includes a variety of sources of worry for people to think about, including personal, social, and financial worries.

Generalized Anxiety Scale (GAD-7)

DIRECTIONS: For each statement check the box that corresponds with the most accurate response. Consider each statement carefully before choosing.

Over the last 2 weeks, how often have you been bothered by the following problems?

	Not at all sure	Several days	Over half the days	Nearly every day
1. Feeling nervous, anxious or on edge				
2. Not being able to stop or control worrying				
3. Worrying too much about different things				
4. Trouble relaxing				
5. Being so restless that it's hard to sit still				
6. Becoming easily annoyed or irritable				
7. Feeling afraid as if something awful might happen				

If you checked off any problems, how difficult have these made it for you to do your work, take care of things at home, or get along with other people?

- ☐ Not difficult at all
- ☐ Somewhat difficult
- ☐ Very difficult
- ☐ Extremely difficult

SCORING: Note the scores for the responses you checked according to the following:

0 = Not at all sure
1 = Several days
2 = Over half the days
3 = Nearly every day

The score ranges from **0 to 21 points.**

Write your scores in the table below. When finished, add up all your scores to produce your total.

Statements	Your Score
#1	
#2	
#3	
#4	
#5	
#6	
#7	
TOTAL	

INTERPRETATION:

- **If your total score is between 0 and 4**, you may not have an anxiety disorder.
- **If your total score is between 5 and 9**, you may have mild anxiety. You should be aware of your anxiety and monitor it, and you may want to have your doctor or mental health professional in the loop to monitor your anxiety over time as well.
- **If your total score is between 10 and 14**, you may have moderate anxiety. This indicates a possibly serious condition.
- **If your total score is 15+**, you may have severe anxiety. Your condition is most likely serious and you should consider treatment as soon as possible.

* If your score is 10 or greater, you should consider talking to your doctor about your anxiety. Ask about getting further assessed for an anxiety disorder, which may include a mental state examination, some diagnostic questioning, or a referral to a mental health professional.

Hamilton Rating Scale for Anxiety

> **DIRECTIONS:** This scale consists of words on the left with a list of symptoms for each that a person with anxiety may experience. Read each work and its symptoms and think about how often you've experienced them recently.

Item			Rating
1.	Anxious	Worries, anticipation of the worst, fearful anticipation, irritability	——
2.	Tension	Feelings of tension, fatigability, startle response, moved to tears easily, trembling, feelings of restlessness, inability to relax	——
3.	Fears	Of dark, of strangers, of being left alone, of animals, of traffic, of crowds	——
4.	Insomnia	Difficulty in falling asleep, broken sleep, unsatisfying sleep and fatigue on waking, dreams, nightmares, night-terrors	——

Continue

5.	Intellectual (cognitive)	Difficulty in concentration, poor memory	——
6.	Depressed Mood	Loss of interest, lack of pleasure in hobbies, depression, early waking, diurnal swing	——
7.	Somatic (muscular)	Pains and aches, twitching, stiffness, myoclonic jerks, grinding of teeth, unsteady voice, increased muscular tone	——
8.	Somatic (sensory)	Tinnitus, blurring of vision, hot and cold flushes, feelings of weakness, pricking sensation	——
9.	Cardiovascular Symptoms	Tachycardia, palpitations, pain in chest, throbbing of vessels, fainting feelings, missing beat	——
10.	Respiratory Symptoms	Pressure or constriction in chest, choking feelings, sighing, dyspnea	——
11.	Gastrointestinal Symptoms	Difficulty in swallowing, wind, abdominal pain, burning sensations, abdominal fullness, nausea, vomiting, borborygmi, looseness of bowels, loss of weight, constipation	——
12.	Genitourinary Symptoms	Frequency of micturition, urgency of micturition, amenorrhea, menorrhagia, development of frigidity, premature ejaculation, loss of libido, impotence	——
13.	Autonomic Symptoms	Dry mouth, flushing, pallor, tendency to sweat, giddiness, tension headache, raising of hair	——
14.	Behavior at Interview	Fidgeting, restlessness or pacing, tremor of hands, furrowed brow, strained face, sighing or rapid respiration, facial pallor, swallowing, belching, brisk tendon jerks, dilated pupils, exophthalmos	——

TOTAL   ——

SCORING: If you don't experience a symptom, write 0 in the rating column.

If you only mildly experience a symptom, write 1 in the rating column.

If you moderately experience a symptom, write 2 in the rating column.

If you severely experience a symptom, write 3 in the rating column.

If you experience a symptom so severe that it's negatively affecting your functioning, write 4 in the rating column.

When you're finished, add up all your scores and note your total score at the bottom.

INTERPRETATION:

- **If your total score is between 0 and 17**, you may have mild anxiety. This level of anxiety may not be indicative of a serious problem, but it may have the potential to develop into one.
- **If your total score is between 18 and 24**, you may have mild to moderate anxiety. You should consider potential treatment options and think about which one(s) may work best for you in managing your anxiety.
- **If your total score is between 25 and 30**, you may have moderate to severe anxiety. Your anxiety may be negatively impacting your day-to-day life. You should seek professional help and get a proper evaluation.

- **If your total score is 30 and above**, you may have very severe anxiety. You should work with a mental health professional to be properly evaluated and develop a treatment plan for your anxiety.

Social Interaction Anxiety Scale (SIAS)

DIRECTIONS: For each item check the appropriate box to indicate the degree to which you feel the statement is characteristic or true for you.

Characteristic	Not at all	Slightly	Moderately	Very	Extremely
1. I get nervous if I have to speak with someone in authority (teacher, boss, etc.).					
2. I have difficulty making eye contact with others.					
3. I become tense if I have to talk about myself or my feelings.					
4. I find it difficult to mix comfortably with the people I work with.					
5. I find it easy to make friends my own age.					
6. I tense up if I meet an acquaintance on the street.					
7. When mixing socially, I am uncomfortable.					
8. I feel tense if I am alone with just one other person.					
9. I am at ease meeting people at parties, etc.					
10. I have difficulty talking with other people.					
11. I find it easy to think of things to talk about.					
12. I worry about expressing myself in case I appear awkward.					
13. I find it difficult to disagree with another's point of view.					
14. I have difficulty talking to attractive persons of the opposite sex.					
15. I find myself worried that I won't know what to say in social situations.					
16. I am nervous mixing with people I don't know well.					
17. I feel I'll say something embarrassing when talking.					

Continue

18. When mixing in a group, I find myself worrying I will be ignored.					
19. I am tense mixing in a group.					
20. I am unsure whether to greet someone I know only slightly.					

SCORING: Once you have completed the assessment, add up all your scores from each statement (excluding statements #5, #9, and #11) as follows:

0 = **Not at all** characteristic or true of me
1 = **Slightly** characteristic or true of me
2 = **Moderately** characteristic or true of me
3 = **Very** characteristic or true of me
4 = **Extremely** characteristic or true of me

Write your scores and your total in the table below. *Note that statements #5, #9, and #11 are excluded from the table.*

Questions #1-12	Your Score	Questions #13-20	Your Score
#1		#13	
#2		#14	
#3		#15	
#4		#16	
#6		#17	
#7		#18	
#8		#19	
#10		#20	
#12		TOTAL	

INTERPRETATION:

- **If your total score is equivalent or greater than 34**, you may have a social phobia, which means you may avoid specific social situations. You may be fine in certain other situations. You may fear being judged, embarrassed, or rejected.
- **If your total score is equivalent or greater than 43**, you may have social anxiety, which means you may avoid social situations in general, regardless of the specific circumstances surrounding an event or the people you're with. You may also have the fear of being judged, embarrassed, or rejected.

Worry Domains Questionnaire (WDQ – Short Form)

DIRECTIONS: For each item check the appropriate box to indicate the degree to which you feel the statement is most accurate to you.

I worry ...	Not at all	A little	Moderately	Quite a bit	Extremely
1. that I'll never achieve my ambitions					
2. that I will not keep my workload up to date.					
3. that I am not able to afford things					
4. that I feel insecure					
5. that I can't afford to pay bills					
6. that I leave work unfinished					
7. that I lack confidence					
8. that I am unattractive					
9. that I will lose close friends					
10. that I haven't achieved much					

SCORING: Note the following scores for each of your responses:

0 = **Not at all** accurate

1 = **A little** accurate

2 = **Moderately** accurate

3 = **Quite a bit** accurate

4 = **Extremely** accurate

Once you have completed the assessment, write down all your scores from each statement, add them up, and indicate your total score in the table below.

Questions #1-5	Your Score	Questions #6-10	Your Score
#1		#6	
#2		#7	
#3		#8	
#4		#9	
#5		#10	
		TOTAL	

INTEPRETATION: There are multiple subscales in the brief WDQ:

To assess your anxiety surrounding relationships, sum the scores for #8 and #9: _____

To assess your confidence level, sum the scores for #4 and #7: _____

To assess your anxiety about the future, sum the scores for #1 and #10: _____

To assess your anxiety surrounding work, sum the scores for #2 and #6: _____

To assess your anxiety surrounding finances, sum the scores #3 and #5: _____

The higher you score, the more frequently you worry about the above topics.

- **If you have a score between 0 and 2**, you do not have a lot of worry. You either have no worry or it's very mild.

- **If your score is between 3 and 4**, you have a moderate amount of worry. Consider monitoring your anxiety over time to see if it improves or worsens. You may want to look into strategies to manage your current levels of anxiety.
- **If your score is between 5 and 6**, you have a severe amount of worry. You should seek evaluation and guidance from your doctor or a mental health professional.
- **If your score is between 7 and 8**, you have a very severe or extreme amount of worry. If you have not already, seek professional help.

What Will Help You

If you feel like your anxiety is severely negatively impacting your day-to-day life, you should consider seeking professional help. Fortunately, there are several treatment options available that can help reduce or control your anxiety.

Counseling or Therapy. It's important to get help early and nip your symptoms in the bud as anxiety can worsen over time and it tends to be harder to treat the longer you wait. There are several psychotherapies that you can try to reduce or manage your anxiety, including Cognitive Behavior Therapy (CBT), Dialectical Behavior Therapy (DBT), exposure therapy, group therapy, and brain stimulation therapy. Some people have also reported success with hypnosis. For more information on the various types of treatments available, see section IV in the book.

Medication. There are several medications on the market now that can ease symptoms of anxiety, but they should not be considered without a) a thorough medical evaluation and b) should only be taken in conjunction with another form of supportive therapy like talk therapy. Consult your doctor about which medication is right for you, and talk to them before starting or stopping any medication. Make sure to obtain proper consent regarding side effects.

Avoid negativity. It's crucial that you are aware of how much negativity may be present in your life, especially if you are someone struggling with depression or anxiety. Be mindful of the people you interact with, the activities you engage in, and the information you consume online.

For example, sometimes looking at social media too much can bring us down, because others' lives can appear so perfect. It's a bad habit to compare yourself to others and their social media feeds. It may help to take a step back from social media and news on major networks, in the newspaper, or online. As a 2017 APA poll on stress in America found, 56% of adults reported following the news was a source of stress for them.[85] There can often be a lot of negativity on TV and elsewhere online that you may not be aware you're internalizing.

Be mindful of viewing or reading too much negative content online or listening to sad music or videos as well. If you fill your brain with joy, you'll feel more joy.

Holistic treatments. You can practice stress management or relaxation techniques, such as guided imagery, breathing exercises, tensing and relaxing your muscles, massage, acupuncture, yoga, and other healing touch therapies. Additionally, you could try expressing your thoughts and feelings through music or art, and / or practice meditation and mindfulness which has proven to be as good if not better than medication.[86] Work to replace any negative thoughts with positive ones. You can try ASMR videos on YouTube that have helped some with depression, anxiety, and falling asleep at night.[87]

Physical exercise. Taking care of your body can be critical to mental wellness. Establish regular physical activity. If you don't usually exercise, start small, and slowly increase your physical activity. Exercise is a great stress reducer, and it may help you in many other areas of your life, not just with anxiety.

Sleep. In addition to exercise, you should get a proper night's sleep. Sleep deprivation will literally make you feel emotionally unstable.

Diet. Eat a healthy, nutritious diet. Some research has found that consuming probiotic-rich and fermented foods can alleviate anxiety,[88] such as yogurt, miso, soy milk, kimchi, pickles, and cheese.

Stay hydrated. Drinking water is incredibly important. Dehydration can be a contributing factor to anxiety. Water helps with increasing energy levels, boosting cognitive function, improving physical importance, curing headaches and illnesses and flushing out your body.[89] While drinking plenty of water also helps with things such as weight loss[90] and maintaining a clear complexion,[91] it goes deeper than staying acne free. Staying hydrated is beneficial to your body on the whole and improves your bodily functions.

While every medical professional seems to have a differing opinion how exactly how much water you should drink a day, the overall idea is that your daily consumption depends on your activity level. A general rule of thumb is 125 fluid ounces for men and women 90 ounces.[92]

If you're having trouble drinking plain water, don't worry; a lot of the foods we consume on a regular basis already have water in them so here are some alternatives: watermelon, grapefruit, grapes, cucumbers, and oatmeal. Also consider smoothies, fruit juices, sports drinks, and fruit-infused waters. Although, if you do choose to drink juices, keep in mind that some juices are high in sodium and sugar which may, in the long run, dehydrate your body.

Other ways to keep hydrated include always keeping water with you (preferably in a reusable water bottle), tracking your water intake (using an app, or setting reminders), and drinking when you feel hungry (sometimes you may think you're hungry when you're actually thirsty). If you are in a hot environment, be sure to drink more water. Aim to sip your water throughout the day and not gulp it down; this makes it easier to reach your daily goal but also ensures you don't overdo it in a short period of time.

Social support. It's crucial to build and maintain social support networks throughout your life: friends, family, clergy, colleagues you can trust and mentors. You may also want to look into local peer support groups to meet others facing similar struggles. In the age of the Internet, even online peer support groups can be helpful and provide a good social outlet.

Whatever treatment you go with, work with your doctor and mental health professionals to develop a treatment plan that works for you, take action, and stick to your plan.

CHAPTER 9: BULLY OR BULLIED? ASSESSMENTS TO SEE IF YOU'RE ONE OR THE OTHER

Have you ever heard that if a child is bullied, by let's say their father, they're more likely to bully others – including their own children one day? This phenomenon is absolutely true. Adult children admit that they struggle with anger and rage (and all the shame and guilt that pours out of them afterwards) as parents only to learn that their own mother or father were also bullies. Are some people more aggressive than others by nature? Yes, but bullying is a learned behavior and its impact can be felt for generations to come.

This chapter will help you figure out if you're being a bully or being bullied in your life. It will also help parents help their children, whether they suspect their child is being bullied or is the bully.

Quick STATS

- 160,000 children skip school each day to avoid being bullied[93]
- Less than half (43 percent) of students notify an adult about being bullied[94]
- 28% of children in grades 6-12 and 20% of high school students are bullied[95]
- In 2016, 34% of students were reported to have been cyber-bullied[96]

But, what exactly is bullying?

Bully, as defined by the American Society for the Positive Care of Children, is "an imbalance of power: kids who use their power, physical strength, access to embarrassing information, or popularity – to control or harm others…Repetition bullying behaviors happen more than once or have the potential to happen more than once."[97]

The severity of bullying can range from something as seemingly harmless as teasing to something much more severe as physical violence. Characteristics of a bully, child and adult, include anger management issues, easily frustrated, inability to take responsibility for their actions, and violent tendencies. Typically, those who bully do so as a way to vent their feelings and cope with their insecurities.

Bullying is no longer just what happens on the playground. Cyber-bullying is a major problem, especially for kids. As a parent it is difficult to know just how many times your child is being bullied (or bullying others) because, more often than not, children tend to keep the act of bullying to themselves.

The Connection between Bullying and Gun Violence

Bullying is a form of aggression and studies clearly demonstrate there's a connection between bullying and gun violence.[98] This is precisely why when we talk about gun violence prevention we talk a lot about spotting and curbing bullying behaviors.

For example, according to a study conducted by the *Journal of Adolescent Health*, those who are bullied are three times more likely to have access to guns than those who aren't.[99] Students who reported only cyberbullying were three times more likely, as well, but those who experienced both cyberbullying and traditional bullying were six times more likely to have access to guns.[100] The cause of these correlations, unfortunately, remains unclear but that doesn't diminish the message – we must worry about children who are aggressive or who are experiencing aggression from other children having access to firearms.[101]

With a greater exposure to guns, there's a higher chance that next time someone is upset, their actions can turn violent. If more than twenty percent of children feel they're bullied,[102] we should all be worried that easy access to guns paves the way to increased gun violence.

It's important for kids, parents, school officials, employers, employees, and citizens to know the signs of a bully. Do you have a gut feeling that your child is not behaving how they should when at school? Is your child afraid to go to school? Or, are you struggling with someone in your own life – personally or professionally – who is aggressive and consistently intimidating? We focused on those three aspects of bullying for this chapter and created three separate assessments that address:

1) Test 1: Is Your Child Being Bullied?
2) Test 2: Is Your Child a Bully?
3) Test 3: Are You Being Bullied?

The following self-assessments are based upon several quizzes: *Am I Being Bullied (Self-Assessment Test)* by PSYCOM, Pacer Center's Teens Against Bullying *Are You Being Bullied? Test* and West Virginia Department of Education's *Am I a Bully?* We have also researched bullying attitudes on resources such as *Stop Bullying, Safe Kids* and *American Academy of Child and Adolescent Psychiatry* to compile these assessments. The questions and languages from those resources have been modified for our needs. Regarding the last assessment, while we tend to focus on bullying in children younger than eighteen, it is important to note that this type of aggressive behavior may carry on into college, adulthood and into the workplace.

TEST 1: IS YOUR CHILD BEING BULLIED?

DIRECTIONS: For each item check the box with the most appropriate answer. In this assessment answer 'How many times a week your child…'

	Never	1-2 times	3-4 times	More than 5 times
1. Is teased, upset, been called names and/or made to cry by another child?				
2. To your knowledge, has your child been physically threatened by others?				
3. Is reluctant to go to school or socialize with other children?				
4. A teacher has expressed concern for their well-being, whether it concerned socially or even their school world.				

Continue

5. Has expressed feelings of isolation amongst children their own age.				
6. You have noticed a change in their general mood – they seem sad, are angrier or are moodier than normal.				

SCORING: Note your scores for each response according to the following:

0 = Never
1 = 1 or 2 times
2 = 3 or 4 times
3 = 5 or more times

This test has a range of **0 to 30 points.**

Write your scores in the table below. When finished, add up all your scores to produce your total.

Statements	Your Score
#1	
#2	
#3	
#4	
#5	
#6	
TOTAL	

INTERPRETATION:
If your score is higher than 15, there is a large chance that your child is being bullied. In this case, see below for resources that can help you move forward and deal with this situation.

TEST 2: IS YOUR CHILD A BULLY?

DIRECTIONS: For each item check the box with the most appropriate answer. In this assessment answer 'How many times a week your child…'

	Never	1-2 times	3-4 times	More than 5 times
1. Teases and upsets other children.				
2. Gets very angry and fights with people.				

3. Says hurtful comments about other children.				
4. Encourages others to fight and be violent.				
5. Was violent to other children.				
6. Threatens to hurt other children or adults, or even expressed violent thoughts.				

SCORING: Note your scores for each response according to the following:

0 = Never
1 = 1 or 2 times
2 = 3 or 4 times
3 = 5 or more times

The test has a range of **0 to 18 points.**

Write your scores in the table below. When finished, add up all your scores to produce your total.

Statements	Your Score
#1	
#2	
#3	
#4	
#5	
#6	
TOTAL	

INTERPRETATION:

- **If your score is between 0-5 points,** this indicates that your child is most likely not a bully.
- **If your score is between 6-10 points,** this means that your child may not be a bully, but you should monitor their actions and be careful about how their actions develop.
- **If your score is between 11-15 points,** this indicates that your child displays some bullying behavior.
- **If your score is higher than 15 points,** this shows your child is most likely a bully.

TEST 3: ARE YOU BEING BULLIED SELF-ASSESSMENT?

DIRECTIONS: In the following assessment, check off how often you have felt these emotions in the past two weeks.

	Never	Rarely	Sometimes	Often
1. Do people make hurtful comments (imitate, verbally harass, mock your appearance, for example) about you?				
2. Do you feel disconnected from people around you, either at work, at home or other places?				
3. Have you heard of rumors being spread about you?				
4. Do you dread going to work, school or social events because you fear being rejected and mocked?				
5. Are you anxious when you have to interact with others?				

SCORING: Note your scores for each response according to the following:

0 = Never

1 = Rarely

2 = Sometimes

3 = Often

The assessment has a range of **0 to 15 points.**

Write your scores in the table below. When finished, add up all your scores to produce your total.

Questions	Your Score
#1	
#2	
#3	
#4	
#5	
TOTAL	

INTERPRETATION:

- **If your score is between 0-3,** this indicates you are probably not being bullied.
- **If your score is between 4-9,** this indicates you may not be a victim of bullying, but you should watch out for any behavior that escalates.
- **If your score is between 10-12,** this indicates you're most likely being bullied.
- **If your score is higher than 12,** this indicates you're being bullied.

What Will Help You

What can you do if your child is a bully? Seek out professional help for you and your child. If your child is the bully, get them into therapy to explore why they are bullying other children at school (or you!) at home. Work with their school, teachers, doctors and other supportive healthcare providers like nutritionists to curb this behavior. Family counseling can also be a very effective treatment option since bullying is also learned or condoned at home. Focusing on teaching healthy conflict resolution techniques is a must.

What to do if you're the bully? Whether it's just seeing a therapist or going to anger management classes, to learn how to curb your aggression, addressing behavior head-on is the only way to change.

What to do if your child is being bullied? Speak up. Is the physical and / or emotional health of your child in danger? If so, you'll need guidance on how to rectify the situation. If the bullying is happening at school, work with the school staff to both alert them to the problem and then come up with a plan of action for your child.

Seek therapy for your child. This may seem obvious but support is necessary and giving your child the space to talk about their feelings, or any trauma that's insured, can be incredibly therapeutic. A well-trained professional will be able to provide your child with the tools to heal and community resources that are available.

Teach your child, with the therapist, to speak up for themselves and set boundaries with aggressive children who make them uncomfortable.

What to do if you're being bullied? Speak up. If you're an adult, having a conversation with the person who's bullying you is highly recommended. If someone at work is the perpetrator, human resources should be there to help, although we recognize that those systems 1) aren't always effective and 2) reporting can have negative impacts on career advancement, even in this day and age. If this is the case, we recommend speaking to an attorney.

Take a look at Chapter 15, *"Are You in an Unhealthy Relationship? A Chapter on Abuse"* for more helpful tips on how to effectively deal with a bully or aggressive person in your life.

CHAPTER 10: SPOTTING POTENTIALLY VIOLENT BEHAVIOR & GUN VIOLENCE

Learn to Identify At-Risk Individuals Before They Hurt Others

Includes: *"Know the Signs"* Checklist

Nell Up Close and Personal:

Mass shootings have become routine events in America. A report conducted by the Federal Bureau of Investigations found that between 2000 and 2013 there has been a 16% increase in active shooting incidents. The same report declared that between 2007 and 2013 there were an average of 16.4 shootings a year, compared to 6.4 annually from 2000 to 2006. In 2018 alone, there were 328 mass shootings resulting in 365 killed and 1,301 were injured.[103]

If you're reading this chapter you're concerned about the state of American or possibly the state of someone you know. The following information and checklist will help you identify someone who may potentially be at risk for hurting others and themselves. We know educating people on how to intervene saves lives.

The morning we began writing this chapter – May 31, 2019 – sitting around my dining room table in Connecticut, somewhere in Virginia a man named DeWayne Craddock emailed his bosses and resigned from his job of nine years as a civil engineer for the city of Virginia Beach. He was an employee, by all accounts, who was in good standing. Later that day, as I was making coffee for my research assistants, the news feeds on our smartphones started to blow up. Mr. Craddock walked into his former office building and indiscriminately shot and killed eleven municipal workers and one contractor. We sat, speechless, looking at each other. I had the same sick feeling in my stomach as I did six years prior.

You see, I live just a dozen miles from Newtown, Connecticut where the shooting at Sandy Hook took place on December 14th, 2012, sending a nation into mourning. I treated several individuals from that community over the next few years. They came into my office grief stricken, confused and suffering with PTSD. It was heartbreaking work for everyone involved. As a therapist, it's the kind of work you wish you didn't have to do.

As a mother, I now worry each time I drop my kids off at school or take them into crowded public spaces like movie theaters, train stations or our local shopping mall. As a therapist I worry about the kids who are bullied, disgruntled, don't feel as if they belong to their community, who have a brewing untreated and unidentified mental illness, an appetite for playing violent video games and access, somehow, to guns.

I also worry about those children's parents; the mother who may not know what to do with her son who has stopped interacting with "real" people because he's online 24/7, the father whose son's grades have plummeted and no longer enjoys the activities he once loved.

I worry about extremists, how they recruit men and young adults, often online, and encourage crimes against humanity. An extremist is someone who subscribes to intense religious or political views and believes in resorting to actions that are often violent. What plans are these groups devising right now, as I type? Where will they unleash their fury next?

A study done by the Anti-Defamation League (ADL) claims that in 2018, over 50 murders were linked to right-wing extremists.[104] While many of the extremist incidents are large cases of violence, it does happen on a smaller scale, homicide; the murders of Matthew Shepard and Emmett Till. Drawing upon links to Islamist extremism and white-supremacy, the ADL's study highlights a sad truth about the American landscape in its current climate – there's an abundance of hate and xenophobia: Pittsburgh Tree of Life shooting in 2018; Christchurch Mosque Shootings of 2019; Sutherland Spring Church Shooting in 2017; Sri Lanka Easter Bombings in 2019; Orlando's Pulse Nightclub Shooting in 2016; 9/11.

I also worry about the adverse side effects of the psychiatric medications we prescribe to children and adults who are depressed or anxious. Some of these medications are known to cause a propensity for violence and suicidal ideation. I do not think, no I know, the public hasn't been properly warned of this. Patients are usually prescribed pills so fast the idea of informed consent remains a foreign concept.

Quick STATS:

- 27 drug regulatory agencies warn users of the following side effects: mania, psychosis, violence and homicidal inclinations
- 65 incidents of mass murders or shootings have been committed by individuals who have used drugs; the US FDA has reported 1,531 cases of psychiatric drug induced homicides[105]
- Reports indicate that "up to 60% of perpetrators of mass shootings in the United States since 1970 displayed symptoms including acute paranoia, delusions, and depression before committing their crimes."[106]

*** From our understanding, there is yet to be a federal investigation into the connection between violence and psychotropic drugs

Will and I agree that to lower incidences of gun violence in America we must have more restrictive gun laws, reexamine the way we clinically treat (or have been under-treating at risk individuals), and we must teach every single person who will listen how to *Know the Signs* of gun violence so we can intervene before another tragedy occurs.

Sandy Hook Promise is an organization – created in the wake of the 2012 shooting – that seeks to educate students, parents, teachers and professionals about how to prevent future gun violence. Heavily influenced by Sandy Hook Promise,[107] and with their permission, we created the following "Know the Signs" assessment; this is what you need to look for in a potential shooter. The following assessment is a baseline of worrisome traits someone with the propensity to commit an act of mass violence might display.

Assessment: *Know the Signs*

DIRECTIONS: Check all that apply to the person you're concerned over.

Aggressive and Violent Demeanor
- ☐ Making violent threats to others – either verbally or online
- ☐ A history of reckless, intimidating and/or vicious behavior
- ☐ Angers easily and fails to resolve conflicts
- ☐ Bringing weapons to school, work, or another public place (or talking about bringing weapons to these places or harming others in any way)
- ☐ Destruction of property
- ☐ Boasting about violent subjects – past/future attacks – and praising those who did them
- ☐ Spending a lot of time reading or posting violent or hateful content online
- ☐ Expressing hatred towards a specific person, group of people, or ideology
- ☐ Warning friends or specific peers to stay away from school, work, or an event

Behavioral Changes
- ☐ Mental illness – diagnosed or undiagnosed
- ☐ Change in sleeping or eating habits that results in a physical change
- ☐ Significant personality shift and overall demeanor
- ☐ Lack of empathy towards people and/or animals
- ☐ Drop in quality of schoolwork, work productivity, and interest in extracurricular activities
- ☐ Researching past attacks, guns, upcoming events or places where there will be crowds, and making plans
- ☐ Purchasing, attempting to purchase, or otherwise gaining access to guns

Social Isolation and Antisocial Behavior
- ☐ Sudden withdrawal from peers and activities at home, at school, and/or at work
- ☐ Victim of social rejection or has become socially ostracized and bullied by peers
- ☐ Decrease in engagement with others and their interests
- ☐ Lack of discipline or respect for authoritative figures
- ☐ Access or use of drugs and/or alcohol

Signs of Suicide
- ☐ Talking about suicide; either harming oneself or citing past examples of someone who has
- ☐ Expressing feelings of despair or hopelessness
- ☐ Displaying concerning behaviors: withdrawal from social interactions, a change in sleep and eating, increased agitation

What Will Help You

Report. Discuss the results of these assessments with a trusted adult, teacher, school social worker, therapist, doctor, employer or law enforcement official. It's imperative to act now and be safe rather than wait and be sorry. You are not alone. Lean on those who are specially trained to handle these types of situations.

If you're a parent worrying about your own child's behavior see a pediatrician or a medical healthcare professional who can give you the best recommendations for your child. Please, don't be ashamed if your child starts to show signs of a mental illness, especially paranoia.

Some signs of paranoia include reluctance to confide in others, distrust in people and institutions, and constant suspicion.[108] Just because a person is suffering with paranoia doesn't mean that they will act out violently, but symptoms of paranoia seriously alter a person's ability to use good judgement and exercise proper impulse control. Some studies suggest there's a strong correlation between paranoia and violence. Paranoia is a symptom of a severe mental illness – immediate medical help is critical.

Get involved. One of the ways to deal with tragedy and trauma is through action and building community. Action heals us, gives us a sense of direction and added purpose. It's how we move forward and cultivate corrective healing experiences. Reach out and join organizations such as *Sandy Hook Promise*, *Everytown for Gun Safety, Moms Demand Action for Gun Sense* and *the Coalition to Stop Gun Violence* to engage in your local community's movement to prevent gun violence. Even if you cannot donate your time, consider donating money and resources to organizations.

Take action. Through the organizations mentioned above, or on your own, you can demand change. Speak to your local or state government about implementing more thorough background checks, instate safer gun-ownership restrictions and demand that all reported threats are properly investigated. Waiting for something to happen before you act only allows for more incidents to happen. Teach and practice inclusivity at all times. Speak up against hate.

Chapter 11: Do I Have an Eating Disorder or Disordered Eating?

Nell's Comments on this Subject as a Therapist and a Mother

Here's what I tell my ten-year-old daughter when she asks me what it's like to work with an eating disorder patient.

"It feels like an enormous responsibility. I've known women and girls who have died from heart attacks because they didn't feed their bodies enough food, and I'm personally terrified of a tragedy happening on my watch. You quickly learn as a therapist that reasoning with someone who has an eating disorder is like trying to reason with a drug addict; they're fixated on food just like an alcoholic is fixated on booze. As they spiral further and further into the disorder it's harder and harder to pull them out. They're dehydrated and malnourished. They don't think clearly. In their weakened state they become so obsessive and compulsive about food and exercise you feel as if something else inside of them is taking over entirely. Your heart breaks for them. Your heart breaks for their mom or their dad or their husband or wife — who look just as scared and lost as the patient."

My intention isn't to scare her, but I am, with all my motherly might, trying to combat the messaging she gets every day – that a girl must be thin in order to be loved – with the truth: eating disorders are life threatening. This is why psycho-education and early detection is so important. With proper medical care, those with eating disorders can resume suitable eating habits and thrive emotionally and psychologically.

For a quick overview on eating disorders and disordered eating, read on. The self assessment picked for this chapter – the *SCOFF* – will help you determine if you or someone you love is struggling with food addiction or compulsion.

Eating disorders are a serious mental illness that affects the relationship people have with food. Individuals who suffer with them are compulsively fixated on body shape, weight, and the amount of food they intake. Eating too little or too much leads to poor nutrition, negatively impacting your body *and* overall health. Negative health impacts can vary depending on the actual eating disorder diagnosis, however, common side effects include heart problems, breakdown of the digestive system, bones, teeth, mouth and one can even develop other diseases.[109] And, we both want to note here, that a person with an eating disorder doesn't necessarily look a certain way; eating disorders affect people of all ages, sizes, cultures, and religion.

Although eating disorders are seen throughout the world, the United States accounts for 30 million of the 70 million people who have been diagnosed with one.[110] This is an alarming statistic, but on some level makes sense; Americans live off of convenience food (fast or frozen food), they're constantly being sold yo-yo diets, and they literally invented the concept of snacking on processed foods.

Quick STATS:

- Anorexia Nervosa has the highest mortality rate of any mental illness.[111]
- Lifetime prevalence of binge eating disorder is 3.5% in women and 2% in men.[112]
- People with anorexia are 56 times more likely to commit suicide than non-sufferers.[113]
- Binge Eating Disorder was found to usually start during late adolescence or in the early twenties.[114]
- In childhood (5-12 years), the ratio of girls to boys diagnosed with AN or BN is 5:1, whereas in adolescents and adults, the ratio is much larger – 10 females to every one male.[115]
- 51% of girls 9 and 10 years old feel better about themselves when they're dieting.[116]
- Body-based bullying can have a severe impact on a girls' attitude and behavior. Girls who suffered teasing by members of their families were 1.5 times more likely to try binge eating and/or other dangerous weight-control methods within five years.[117]

Disordered Eating vs. Eating Disorder?

Disordered eating is used to describe **a range of irregular eating behaviors** that may or may not warrant a diagnosis of a specific eating disorder. *Eating disorders* are **illnesses** in which the person suffering experiences severe disturbances in their eating behaviors and related thoughts and emotions. There are five types of eating disorders listed in the DSM-5 to help therapists and doctors properly diagnose patients.

Symptoms of disordered eating include:[118]

- Frequent dieting
- Anxiety associated with specific foods
- Skipping meals
- Rigid rituals and routines surrounding food and exercise
- Feelings of guilt and shame associated with eating
- Preoccupation with food, weight and body image that negatively impacts quality of life
- A feeling of loss of control around food, including compulsive eating habits
- Using exercise, food restriction, fasting or purging to "make up for bad foods" consumed

Types of Eating Disorders

Anorexia Nervosa is diagnosed when patients weigh at least 15 percent less than the normal healthy weight expected for their height. People with anorexia generally refuse to eat and exercise compulsively. Major symptoms include limited poor intake, fear of being "fat" and problems with body image or denial of low body weight.

Bulimia Nervosa is an eating disorder characterized by binging and purging. Although people who suffer from bulimia may frequently diet or compulsively exercise, their weight can fluctuate because they tend to binge eat frequently and then use laxatives or throw up to feel less full. This makes them feel "out of control" and they often hide the behavior. Warning signs may include: tooth decay, reflux, intestinal problems and chronic sore throat.

Binge Eating Disorder is diagnosed when a person regularly binges on large amounts of food but does not try to get rid of the food afterwards (as one would with bulimia). Serious health complications can arise from this disorder particularly severe obesity, diabetes and cardiovascular disease.

Eating Disorder (not otherwise specified). This category was created for people who are presenting with some eating disorder symptoms but either haven't lost enough weight or haven't experienced symptoms for enough time in order to qualify for a full diagnosis.

Two other conditions co-occur with eating disorders – body dysmorphia and exercise anorexia. Body dysmorphic disorder is a mental illness involving obsessive focus on a perceived flaw in appearance. The flaw may be minor or it may even be imagined. Exercise anorexia is when people manage their calorie intake by obsessively exercising. It's important to remember that people with disordered eating habits (as to full blown eating disorders) may also be experiencing significant physical, emotional and mental stress.

What causes an eating disorder?

New evidence suggests that heredity may play a part in why some people develop eating disorders, but many people who develop one have no prior history. Research has found that people with anorexia and bulimia tend to be perfectionists with low self-esteem which in turn makes them extremely critical of themselves and their bodies. For example, they usually "feel fat" even when they are severely underweight. And many times, eating disorders occur together with other psychiatric disorders like anxiety, panic, obsessive compulsive disorder or alcohol addiction.[119]

Quick STATS on Eating Disorder recovery:

- With treatment, 60% of eating disorder sufferers make a full recovery[120]
- Without treatment, 20% of people suffering from anorexia will prematurely die from eating disorder related health complications, including suicide and heart problems.[121]
- Inpatient treatment of an eating disorder in the US ranges from $500 – $2,000 per day. Long-term outpatient treatment, including therapy and medical monitoring, can cost $100,000 or more. Thankfully insurance companies now usually cover eating disorder treatment.[122]
- Eating disorders statistics tell us that in order for treatment to be successful, it must be multifaceted. It must include medical care, mental health care, and nutritional education and counseling[123]
- Eating disorders research is very under-funded. The National Institute of Health allocates only 93 cents towards research funding for every person diagnosed with an eating disorder. In comparison, they give $88 for every person diagnosed with autism. This is painfully low.[124]

We have collected the following assessment for you to complete if you suspect yourself or a loved one may have an eating disorder:

S.C.O.F.F Assessment[125] was developed by British researchers as a brief screening tool for eating disorders. Only five questions, it will give you or someone you know a snapshot of one's relationship with food. "SCOFF" is an acronym with each letter representing one of the five "yes/no" screening questions.

SCOFF: A Quick Assessment for Eating Concerns

DIRECTIONS: Circle "yes" or "no" in response to each question.

1. Do you make yourself **s**ick because you feel uncomfortably full?	YES	NO
2. Do you worry you've lost **c**ontrol over how much you eat?	YES	NO
3. Have you recently lost more than 15 pounds (**o**ne stone) in a three-month period?	YES	NO
4. Do you believe yourself to be **f**at when others say you are too thin?	YES	NO
5. Would you say **f**ood dominates your life?	YES	NO

SCORING: Give yourself one point for every question you answer with a "yes".

INTERPRETATION: Answering "yes" to two or more of the questions indicates it is "quite likely" the respondent has a complicated relationship with food. They should seek an evaluation by a qualified professional, preferably someone with a background in assessing eating concerns.

What Will Help You

Weight gain. Assisting patients with regaining weight to a healthy level, and for bulimia patients helping them stop the binge purge cycle is key.

Psychotherapy. Addressing the underlying emotional problems that caused, triggered or made the eating disorder worse is necessary in order to maintain long term health.

General Medical Care. Because of the serious physical problems caused by these illnesses nutritional management and nutritional counseling is critical to help a patient rebuild their physical well-being, learn and practice healthy eating habits.

Inpatient Treatment. For recovery of eating disorders, there's inpatient care treatment options at many reputable and well-run centers across the United States. For those who don't know what inpatient treatment is, it's when patients are admitted into hospitals or rehabilitation centers for help. There's usually a 24-hour medical staff on hand that helps patients. Patients also participate in educational classes and group therapy.

Outpatient Treatment. There are intensive and non-intensive outpatient treatment options for people suffering from eating disorders. This is an option for people who don't need constant medical attention and can manage their disorder largely on their own — with assistance and support from family and medical personnel — depending on the severity of the disorder. These programs can include medication, therapy, nutritional counseling, and regular doctor visits to assess physical health. Some centers may even offer virtual outpatient therapy sessions.

Holistic Treatment. There are a variety of holistic treatments you can implement in your daily life in addition to a clinical treatment plan you've established with medical professionals. These holistic treatments include yoga, mindfulness-based therapy, meditation, remedial massage, kinesiology, acupuncture, and creative therapies such as art and dance.

CHAPTER 12: DO I DRINK TOO MUCH ALCOHOL?

If you're reading this chapter, you're clearly concerned about your own drinking habits or the habits of someone you care about. Below is some useful information and an original assessment that helps people figure out where they fall on the problem drinking spectrum.

Drinking is a major problem in the country. Studies estimate that 15 million Americans struggle with some level of alcohol disorder every single day. It takes a toll on our economy; heavy drinkers are 4 to 8 times more likely to be absent from work than non-drinkers and they cost employers somewhere between $33 billion $68 billion in losses each year, according to research done by the United States Office of Personal Management. Alcoholism also takes a toll on families on our families. More than 10 percent of U.S. children live with a parent who has an alcohol problem.[126] Alcoholism doesn't discriminate. People from all walks of life are at risk. In fact, as anyone who has ever attended a 12-step meeting knows, it's actually one of the greatest common denominators amongst us. And sadly, out of those who do struggle, only 8% ever receive treatment.[127] In my opinion, alcohol is and always has been the gateway drug.

Is alcoholism a disease?

Alcoholism, like other drug addictions, is medically defined as a chronic, progressive and potentially fatal disease. Those suffering from alcoholism experience an incessant craving to drink, an increased tolerance to drinking, and eventually they become physically dependent on alcohol. Problem drinkers continue to abuse alcohol despite the many negative consequences their destructive habits have on their lives and the lives of their loved ones.

Clinical experience indicates that people are either born with an allergy to alcohol or they're not.

Some of us can tolerate alcohol well, we never want too much, we know when to slow down and we never let it seriously impair our judgement. Others, well, others have such a taste for alcohol that the idea of having just one drink doesn't compute. This doesn't mean the problem drinkers suffer from a lack of self-disciplined. We all know high functioning alcoholics who can be very disciplined at everything else but their drinking. But for some of us, we can't say *no thank you* in the face of alcohol.

Alcoholism is technically caused by a combination of biological, genetic, psychological, environmental and social factors including:
- Frequency of use
- Age at which alcohol was first consumed
- Certain demographics such as age, gender and genetic background
- Family history of alcoholism
- Having a parent who is an alcoholic increases one's risk by 4x
- Prenatal exposure to alcohol
- Overall health

Am I an Alcoholic?

It's hard to always tell if someone is drinking too much. If you think it's a problem, it probably is a problem. Oftentimes, when you question someone about their drinking you have to wade through their answers to find the truth. You may be surprised to learn that most healthcare providers are trained to add two drinks to every instance of drinking someone discusses. When people drink, they lose track of how many cocktails they're consuming and they're ashamed to tell that truth.

Denial

The refusal to admit the truth or reality of the condition.

With denial, a person with alcohol use disorder has impaired insight into their condition. Denial is a common symptom of alcohol use disorder and it can keep the person from seeking treatment. Oftentimes, friends and family members will also deny how bad the situation has become.

People in denial try to rationalize their behavior, dismiss it, blame others or outside circumstances, conceal their drinking, make comparisons to others as a way of suggesting their drinking problem isn't that bad, make false promises to stop, and generally exhibit defensive behavior when their drinking habits come into question.

Signs of Alcohol Abuse and Alcoholism:

- Frequent intoxication
- Binge drinking
- Mood changes
- Work performance issues
- Bloodshot eyes
- The smell of alcohol
- Tremors
- Excessive use of mints or mouthwash
- Slurred speech
- A decline in hygiene and self-care
- Drinking alone
- Frequent disputes with others
- High tolerance to alcohol or a sudden change of physical affect
- Memory loss
- A preoccupation with drinking and alcohol
- Hiding use
- Interference with professional functioning (e.g., job loss)
- Drinking prior to occasions where alcohol will be served
- Alcohol related arrests: public intoxication, DUI, lewd behavior, altercations
- Changes in behavior while intoxicated: impulsivity, anger, sexual promiscuity
- Feeling remorseful or humiliated by drinking-related behavior
- Loss of relationships because of one's drinking
- Neglect of other activities

While the above indicators are signs of alcohol abuse, in order to diagnose someone with alcoholism that person must show signs of physical dependence on alcohol such as: they need increased amounts of alcohol to feel intoxicated, they can't seem to quit drinking even when they want to, they seemingly can't control how much alcohol they consume and they must drink (or use other drugs) to avoid withdrawal symptoms.

What's a clinical definition of binge drinking?

Binge drinking is defined by periodic, extreme overindulgence. If a man consumes five or more standard drinking during one social occasion or a woman consumes four or more standard drinks in one occasion it's considered binge drinking.

To assess whether you have a drinking problem, or if a person you care about may be at risk for an alcohol disorder, take our *Alcoholic Screening* below.

The following test is an original assessment we created using inspiration from the *Michigan Alcohol Screening Test (MAST)* and the *Alcohol Use Disorders Identification Test (AUDIT)*.

Alcoholic Screening

DIRECTIONS: Circle "yes" or "no" to the following questions.

1. Do you have more than eight drinks per week?   YES   NO

2. Do you black out from drinking on a regular basis?   YES   NO

3. Do you ever drink first thing in the morning after a night of drinking to get you going or cure your hangover symptoms?   YES   NO

4. Does any near relative or close friend ever worry or complain about your drinking?   YES   NO

5. Is it difficult for you to stop drinking after one or two drinks?   YES   NO

6. Do you feel guilty about your drinking?   YES   NO

7. Have you ever attended an Alcoholics Anonymous (AA) meeting?   YES   NO

8. Have you fought with people when you drink?   YES   NO

9. Has drinking ever created problems between you and a near relative or close friend?   YES   NO

10. Has a family member or close friend gone to anyone for help about your drinking?   YES   NO

11. Have you lost friends because of your drinking?   YES   NO

12. Has your employer ever brought up your drinking, for example, absenteeism?   YES   NO

13. Have you ever lost a job because of your drinking?   YES   NO

14. Do you neglect your obligations – e.g., family or work – for two   YES   NO
or more days in a row because you were drinking?

15. Do you drink before noon fairly often?   YES   NO

16. Have you ever been told you have liver trouble, such as cirrhosis?   YES   NO

17. After heavy drinking, do you experience delirium tremens (DTs),   YES   NO
severe shaking, visual or auditory (hearing) hallucinations?

18. Have you ever gone to anyone for help about your drinking?   YES   NO

19. Have you ever been hospitalized because of drinking?   YES   NO

20. Has your drinking ever resulted in your being hospitalized in a   YES   NO
psychiatric ward?

21. Have you ever gone to any doctor, social worker, clergyman, or   YES   NO
mental health clinic for help with any emotional problem in which
drinking was part of the problem?

22. Have you been arrested more than once for driving under the   YES   NO
influence of alcohol?

23. Have you ever been arrested, or detained by an official for a few   YES   NO
hours, because of other behavior while drinking?

SCORING: Give yourself one point for every answered "Yes."

TOTAL: _____

INTERPRETATION: A total score of eight or more indicates hazardous drinking or alcohol dependence and further evaluation by a healthcare professional is recommended.

What Will Help You

Changing your drinking habits or making the decision to live is a sober life is no small task for those who are addicted to alcohol. As they say in recovery, the first step is recognizing your drinking is a major problem: your life has become unmanageable and your behavior is affecting the people around you. The good news, there is so much support out there for people with alcohol problems it's incredible, including many free support groups. If you want help it's yours for the taking.

There are two schools of thought when it comes to alcohol disorder treatment; behavior modification vs. complete abstinence from drinking. People ask me all the time if I think it's possible for someone who struggles with alcohol addiction to consciously cut back on how much they drink so they don't have to give up drinking all together. The short answer…yes, it is possible. Find out what are your triggers are, what types of alcohol your body cannot handle and then teach yourself to drink responsibly. But, hear me out – this person is the exception to the rule. Most people who struggle with drinking will eventually need to make the tough decision to quit drinking all together.

What path a person takes towards recovery is a deeply personal choice, one that's based on a variety of factors unique to that individual's life and the magnitude of their problem. Anyone suffering with addiction, on any level, should seek counseling. They should also be treated for any underlying mental health issues that may have been ignored for far too long.

Someone who is trained to help people with alcohol disorders can also recommend rehab facilities. It's important to note that detoxing from chronic alcohol abuse is dangerous on your own. Alcohol withdrawal symptoms include seizures, strokes or even heart attacks in high-risk patients. Medically supervised detoxes are performed at inpatient treatment centers or local hospitals. Many people have successful recoveries because of checking into a good rehab facility or local outpatient program.

There are some medications on the market designed to stop or reduce drinking and prevent relapse which your doctor should be able to prescribe. These medications should only be taken under the close supervision of a medical professional.

Support groups and 12 step programs like AA are incredible. You make the decision to quit drinking, fellowship keeps you sober. Support groups teach you coping skills, provide built-in accountability partners and free talk therapy. When you talk to someone about how you're feeling, the load lightens.

CHAPTER 13: DO I HAVE A DRUG PROBLEM?

The authors' intention with this chapter is to bring people hope. We assume that anyone reading the following is worried about someone in their life or they're worried about their own drug use. The following information and assessment provided is a starting point; the first step to recovery is admitting you have a problem.

Drug addiction affects so many lives; anyone from a suburban mother, to a corporate banker, to a midwestern farmer can fall prey to addiction. In 2017, 19.7 million Americans aged 12 and older abused substances.[128] Not only are drug users and addicts affected, but so are their family, friends and loved ones. We all know that there are numerous physical, psychological, social, and financial problems that can occur when a person becomes addicted to drugs. Drug addiction now costs our nation more than $740 billion every year in crime prevention, lack of work productivity dollars and healthcare expenses.[129] And, the problem is only getting worse. Opioid addiction is at an all-time high as you'll see from some of the statistics we mention below.

What's the difference between drug abuse and drug addiction?

Drug addiction is the compulsive seeking and use of drugs despite the negative effects drugs have on the mind and body. It is regarded as a substance use disorder. It's important to note that drug *addiction* differs from drug *abuse*. Drug abuse is when a person uses drugs beyond their appropriate amount. Addiction is much more serious. A person who is addicted to drugs experiences a range of physical, social, psychological, and other symptoms as a result. Drug addiction is a chronic, complex disease. A drug addict will engage in compulsive use that is difficult for them to control, despite the harmful effects. They may not have the capability to stop. Continued drug use alters the brain to the point where simply having the intention or willpower to quit isn't enough. Long-term, some areas of the brain that can be affected by drug use include judgment, decision-making, and behavioral decisions.[130] Relapse is common, which means an addicted person should be monitored closely and continuously working with a supportive network of professionals and loved ones to recover.

STATS:

- Drug use is highest among 18 to 25-year-olds[131]
- The same year, 9.4 percent of men were addicted, while only 5.2 percent of women[132]
- 443,000 minors between the ages of 12 and 17 have abuse problems[133]
- 6.8 million Americans with an addiction problem also have a mental illness[134]
- There were 70,237 overdose deaths in 2017[135]
- From 1999 to 2017, the sale of painkillers to doctors, hospitals and other medical clinics has increased 4 times[136]
- Between July 2016 and September 2017, opioid overdoses increased 54 percent in 16 states[137]
- In 2015, 2 million Americans had a substance use disorder involving prescription pain relievers[138]

- Of the 64,000 drug overdose deaths in 2016, 40% involved a prescription opioid[139] [140]
- Every day in the United States, there are over 130 overdose deaths related to opioids[141]

Is drug addiction a disease?

There's not one single cause of substance abuse and addiction. Someone can have several risk factors and never become addicted while another can only have one and still become addicted. While several risk factors can be present in early childhood and adulthood, anyone at any life stage can also become addicted to drugs.

Drug addiction can be caused by a myriad of factors including:

- *Genetics* – Genes account for half of a person's addiction risk.[142] For example, people whose parents are drug abusers may be 45% to 79% more likely to abuse them too.[143] Predisposition to alcoholism may also be connected to a predisposition for drug abuse.
- *Environment* – This can include factors such as family/home life and stability, friends, stress, abuse or trauma, economic status, and ease of access to drugs.[144] Growing up in poverty, living with a drug user, aggressive childhood behavior, poor social skills, and a lack of parental guidance or supervision may all increase the chances of a person developing a drug addiction.[145] [146]
- *Mental Illness* – Some people may turn to drugs to cope with existing mental health problems,[147] such as depression and anxiety.
- *Age* – Drug addiction is more likely to occur when drug use starts at a young age. A 2001-2002 National Institute on Alcohol Abuse and Alcoholism (NIAAA) survey found young adults between 18 and 24 were more likely than other age ranges (25-44, 45-64, and 65+) to have both an alcohol and drug use disorder.[148] With their brains still developing, teenagers may be more likely than adults to make poor decisions, such as trying drugs for the first time. Over half of new illicit drug users in 2013 were under 18.[149] Some minors start using drugs even younger, around ages 12 and 13.[150]
- *Drug Choice* – Cocaine, heroin, and methamphetamines may be more physically addictive than other drugs like alcohol or marijuana. Withdrawing from cocaine or heroin can also be painful, which may lead a person to want more of it, and also use it more regularly.[151]
- *Use* – Drugs that are smoked or injected are more addictive,[152] with more powerful but short-lived effects, compared to those that are swallowed. Drug users who smoke or inject may be more likely to use their drug of choice, and their use tends to increase as their tolerance builds.
- *Metabolism* – People process and absorb drugs differently. A drug may last for a longer or shorter period of time depending on a person's metabolic rate.[153]

SIGNS OF DRUG ADDICTION

If you think you or someone you know is addicted to substances, here is a list of signs to watch out for. Be aware that symptoms can vary depending on the drug of choice, and how recently the drug was taken.

Physical Symptoms

- Change in eating and sleeping patterns, such as developing insomnia or having food cravings at odd hours
- Deterioration of the body's appearance – losing weight or muscle, gaining weight, abandoning personal hygiene, odor and appearance

- Heightened or altered perception of visual, auditory, taste, and/or reality
- Bloodshot eyes and larger or smaller pupils
- Involuntary eye movements
- Slurred or rambling speech
- Drowsiness
- Dry mouth
- Changes in heart rate, blood pressure, and/or body temperature
- Slowed breathing
- Slowed reaction time
- Reduced pain sensation
- Lack of muscle control, including muscle cramping or relaxation
- Dizziness, nausea or vomiting
- Decreased or lack of coordination
- Tremors, chills and sweating
- Abdominal pain
- Constipation
- Mouth sores or rashes (if smoking or inhaling drugs)
- Nose sores or rashes (if snorting drugs)
- Needle marks (if injecting drugs)
- Some withdrawal symptoms include headaches, chest tightness, heart palpitations, diarrhea, stomachaches, muscle twitches, muscle aches, and tingling

Behavioral Symptoms

- An intense need for drugs or to get high, such as needing more of the drug on a more regular basis over time – daily, or several times a day (this may indicate a drug tolerance)
- Behaving out of the ordinary for this particular person
- Aggressive or impulsive behavior
- Engaging in dangerous or illegal activities (driving while under the influence, using dirty needles, having unprotected sex, stealing money or prescriptions)
- Involvement with law enforcement and other legal issues
- Neglect of work, school, home life, and other responsibilities
- Abandoning personal interests and hobbies, including ones they really enjoyed
- Becoming more secretive or suspicious, isolating themselves
- Desperate, sudden and unexplained financial difficulties
- Suddenly requesting money from family or friends without explanation
- Hiding stashes of drugs in various places where others are unlikely to find them
- Continual use of substances, even if the drug is causing physical or psychological harm to their body, or life has taken a turn for the worse

Psychological Symptoms

- Always thinking about drugs – whether it's how to get them, how they can use them, or how to recover from them

- Personality or attitude changes
- Anger and irritability
- Hyperactivity or agitation
- Lethargic or unmotivated
- Anxious or paranoid
- Denial that they may have a substance problem
- Mood or energy changes (may be rapid shifts; mood swings), such as an elevated, euphoric mood and energy or depressed mood
- Struggling with concentration or memory
- Decreased mental ability
- Confusion
- Inattentive to surroundings
- Experiencing hallucinations, delusions, flashbacks, blackouts, or panic attacks

Potential Consequences of Drug Addiction

There are several potential complications and consequences of drug addiction, and the health risks can be very serious, especially if drug use is combined with other drugs.

- Overdose
- Injury or accidents
- Incarceration
- Neurological damage (which may be permanent)
- Cardiovascular problems (collapsed veins, blood vessel and heart valve infections, artery issues)
- Increased risk of infectious diseases such as hepatitis and HIV from shared needles and a weakened immune system, as well as STDs from unprotected sexual activity
- Unwanted and/or high-risk pregnancies from unprotected sex
- Respiratory diseases such as chronic bronchitis and various cancers (lung, mouth, neck, and stomach cancers) from smoking
- Infertility
- Seizures, strokes, or heart attacks
- Limb damage
- Poor nutrition
- Poor dental health (lost teeth, gum disease)
- Fetal damage if a woman is pregnant (can lead to miscarriage, premature birth, low birth weight, neonatal abstinence syndrome, cognitive or behavioral problems)
- Coma
- Death

If you think you or someone you know may suffer from a drug addiction, we encourage you or them to take the *Drug Abuse Screening Test* below.

The **Drug Abuse Screening Test (DAST-10)**[154] was developed to determine possible involvement with drugs in the past 12 months. This test does not include the use of alcohol. "Drug abuse" refers to (1) the use of prescribed or over-the-counter drugs in excess of the directions and (2) any nonmedical use of drugs.

The various classes of drugs may include cannabis (marijuana, hashish), solvents (e.g., paint thinner), tranquilizers (e.g., Valium), barbiturates, cocaine, stimulants (e.g., speed), hallucinogens (e.g., LSD) or narcotics (e.g., heroin, oxycodone). Remember that the questions do not include alcoholic beverages.

Drug Abuse Screening Test

DIRECTIONS: Please answer every question. If you have difficulty with a statement then choose the response that is mostly right.

In the past 12 months…

1. Have you used drugs other than those required for medical reasons? YES NO

2. Do you abuse more than one drug at a time? YES NO

3. Are you unable to stop abusing drugs when you want to? YES NO

4. Have you ever had blackouts or flashbacks as a result of drug use? YES NO

5. Do you ever feel bad or guilty about your drug use? YES NO

6. Does your spouse (or parents) ever complain about your involvement with drugs? YES NO

7. Have you neglected your family because of your drug use? YES NO

8. Have you engaged in illegal activities in order to obtain drugs? YES NO

9. Have you ever experienced withdrawal symptoms (felt sick) when you stopped taking drugs? YES NO

10. Have you had medical problems as a result of your drug use (e.g. memory loss, hepatitis, convulsions, bleeding)? YES NO

SCORING: Score 1 point for each question answered: "Yes," except for question 3 for which a "No" receives 1 point.

TOTAL: _____

INTERPRETATION:

Score	Degree of Problems Related to Drug Abuse	Suggested Action
0	No problems reported	None at this time
1-2	Low level	Monitor, reassess at a later date
3-5	Moderate level	Further investigation
6-8	Substantial level	Intensive assessment
9-10	Severe level	Intensive assessment

If your score is 0, you may not have a drug addiction.

If your score is 1 to 2, you may not have a serious problem with drugs at this time, but a drug addiction can always develop over time. You should be conscious of your drug use and re-assessed in the future to determine that your drug use does not develop into anything more severe. Be aware that drug use can rapidly get out of your control.

If your score is 3 to 5, you may have a moderate problem with drug addiction. Consider talking to family, friends, or a medical professional about your drug use.

If your score is 6 to 8, you may have a substantial problem with drug addiction. At this point, you should seek help from a medical professional if you haven't already.

If your score is 9 to 10, you may have a severe problem with drug addiction. Definitely seek help before your condition can worsen even further.

What Will Help You

Working in the recovery space, with patients who are struggling with addiction, is most rewarding. Witnessing personal transformation is inspiring. Watching someone go from being a heroin addict living on the streets to a fully functioning, upstanding member of their community – thriving parent, daughter, sister, friend, employee, employer and mentor – is exciting.

Recovering from drug addiction is no easy or simple feat. It takes dedication, the right resources (there is no single treatment that will work for everyone), and support. If you know someone in your life who you suspect may have a drug addiction, avoid preaching to them or using threats or emotional appeals. You want to encourage them to talk to you about what's going on, not put them down or shame them. It is important to reserve judgment.

However, do not enable their behavior by making excuses for them or protecting them. Don't try to take complete control. You can't force them to stop taking drugs. Remember, addiction is more than just willpower. Ultimately, if they want to change their lives, they have to be willing to change themselves. They need to have autonomy of their own decisions, as do you. If you're struggling to support an addict on their journey, attend an Al-Anon meeting. Al-Anon family groups are fellowships of relatives and friends of alcoholics who share their experience, strength and hope in order to solve their common problems.

Rehab. Is highly recommended. Getting assistance from medical professionals and a treatment facility provides support.

Detoxification. In order to move forward with recovery, the first step is detoxification, where the drug gets out of the person's system while trying to limit withdrawal symptoms. Acute withdrawal is the first stage of withdrawal, with many dangerous physical symptoms. Depending on what substances were used, withdrawal symptoms and the duration vary. Typically, acute withdrawal symptoms begin a few days into detox and last anywhere from five to ten days, or even several weeks. If withdrawal is severe, medications may be able to help under professional guidance.

The second stage of withdrawal, post-acute withdrawal, has more psychological symptoms. When a person has reached post-acute withdrawal, their brain chemistry is working on returning to normal. Post-acute withdrawal symptoms can last up to two years after drug use has stopped. Symptoms can be managed with professional help, counseling, and intervention.

Pharmacological Treatments. It may seem counterproductive to suggest drugs as a way of easing out of abusing substances, but there are many drugs that do just that. Methadone, Buprenorphine, and Naltrexone are just a few examples that specifically help with opioid addiction, which is prevalent in the American drug culture right now. When these substances are taken, it makes the user not want to take other drugs, limiting drug cravings and minimizing withdrawal for an eventual and gradual drug-free lifestyle.

Out Patient Care. Patients who choose out-patient care can live at home while recovering. During this time, it is common to continue therapy and attend support group meetings, self-help groups, or 12-step programs to feel a sense of community. There are also many online forums and support groups which drug addicts in recovery might find beneficial.

Outpatient behavioral treatment can consist of CBT, multidimensional family therapy (to improve family functioning), motivational interviewing (to encourage change and behavioral adjustments), and contingency management (also known as motivational incentives, to encourage drug abstinence through positive reinforcement). Treatment can be time-consuming with multiple weekly sessions at first. Over time, less frequent treatment sessions may be needed.

Support networks. Friends and family who will support you in recovery is key.

12 Step Programs. It's important to seek help outside of your close friends and family to maintain recovery. Narcotics Anonymous holds daily meetings worldwide.

Therapy. Therapies can offer strategies for users to cope with abstinence, prevent relapse, work through relapse if it occurs, and resolve any underlying issues with their relationships, jobs, or other aspects of their lives. They can also work through any other mental health issues.

Did you know this?

An additional out-patient resource is the reSET® mobile application. This app is a digital therapeutic tool for people with drug addiction. It's available via prescription-only, and it's meant to supplement other treatments.

Chapter 14: How's Your Love Life? Take Our Relationship & Marriage Assessment

Our intention for this chapter, first and foremost, is to help you have a little fun with your partner. We've provided a few assessments that help you test the temperature of your relationship and, at the end, we give you a few tips to improve things between you and your romantic partners — whether you're married or not.

Navigating love is not for the faint of heart. Nell has treated hundreds of couples over the years in her office. Some come in having just found out their partner is having an affair, some are lonely, married to workaholics — some are workaholics themselves and have ignored their husband or wife for years. Many couples come in during times of high stress: the birth of a baby, a move, financial hardship, death of a loved one or a new medical diagnosis. Others walk into my office not speaking to one another; communication has broken down, resentments have built up, someone doesn't feel adored and "is over it," another feels totally unappreciated and already has one foot out the door.

Without fail, however, the best couples she sees are the ones who come in *before* things get bad. Sometimes they come in when nothing is really wrong at all. They simply want to "check in" with a professional to make sure they're evolving together into the best versions of themselves. It's much easier to tweak a relationship before things get way off course. Feeling stuck in a rut (or an unfulfilling relationship) doesn't have to be a way of life.

Quick STATS

In 2017, 87% of Americans said they believed in true love.[155] In the same year, 2,236,496 nuptials took place in the United States. Those are some hopeful statistics given that in 2017, 787,251 marriages also ended in either divorce or annulment.

What's the State of Your Relationship?

If you and your partner are experiencing any of the problems below, you should consider that there may be areas of your relationship that can be improved. The fewer signs you identify with, the better, as this indicates only a few areas needing improvement

Signs of Low Relationship Satisfaction

- Poor communication (or a lack of it)
- Frequent arguments (the opposite can also occur, when you don't argue at all because you avoid talking about problems)
- Becoming easily frustrated by what your partner says or does
- Unable to visualize a future together (or visualizing a happy future **without** your partner)

- Decrease or lack of physical intimacy
- Feeling disconnected or distant from one another
- Not spending quality time together (or no longer enjoying time together)
- Not feeling loved, respected, trusted, or prioritized by your partner
- Investing in other relationships rather than the one with your partner (children, family members, friends, affair partners)
- Disagreeing on important long-term goals and aspects of life (this may include marriage, finances, religion, where you want to live, household chores, and children, among others)
- Having difficulty remembering when you and your partner were last happy
- Feeling like you're only staying together out of convenience, because you've been together so long (*sunk-cost fallacy*), or for the sake of any children you both have
- Not willing to work on your relationship

Signs of High Relationship Satisfaction

- Being supportive of one another in day-to-day life and all their goals
- Having similar senses of humor, interests, habits, or mannerisms
- Taking an interest in what your partner enjoys
- Being willing to compromise on what you do together or talk about
- Doing fun things together (and having a good time)
- Wanting to spend more time together
- Frequent and open communication
- Listening to your partner and feeling like you're being heard back
- Engaging in both non-sexual and sexual physical touch
- Being inattentive to other attractive people
- Accepting your partner as they are, including all their flaws
- Being able to spend time apart and be your own person without any dependency
- Agreeing on important long-term goals and aspects of life (this may include marriage, finances, religion, where you want to live, household chores, and children, among others)
- Being able to work on issues together, and having those resolutions make you stronger
- Not having too much conflict or drama – there are more good moments than bad
- Forgiving and moving past issues that come up in your relationship
- Feeling fulfilled and committed to the relationship
- Feeling loved, respected, trusted, and appreciated by your partner
- Feeling like you belong with your partner (not wanting to be with anyone else)
- Visualizing a happy future together

The Locke & Wallace Marital Adjustment Test (MAT)[156] is a 15-question assessment that measures relationship satisfaction. It was originally used to showcase the differences between well-adjusted and mal-adjusted couples. While it's classified as a marital test, you can use it to assess any romantic relationship.

We have also provided the **Positive-Negative Relationship Quality Scale (PN-RQ)**,[157] which assesses both positive and negative relationship qualities (or lack thereof) in a relationship. In this assessment you will determine how much of each positive and negative quality is present in your relationship.

Encourage your partner to take the assessments themselves to assess their own satisfaction and their view on the qualities of your relationship. It's possible that you might have very different answers to the same question. Afterwards, compare your answers and see how your overall relationship satisfaction and qualities match up.

Locke & Wallace Marital Adjustment Test (MAT)

DIRECTIONS: Circle or shade in the dot on the scale line which best describes the degree of happiness everything considered of your romantic relationship.

1. Circle One: *Male Female*

O   O   O   O   O   O   O
Very   Happy   Perfectly
Unhappy   Happy

DIRECTIONS: State the approximate extent of agreement or disagreement between you and your partner on the following items. Place a checkmark in the corresponding box for each row.

	Always Agree	Almost Always Agree	Occasionally Disagree	Frequently Disagree	Almost Always Disagree	Always Disagree
2. Handling Family Finances						
3. Matters of Recreation						
4. Demonstration of Affection						
5. Friends						
6. Sex Relations						
7. Conventionally (right, good, or proper conduct)						
8. Philosophy of Life						
9. Ways of dealing with in-laws						

DIRECTIONS: Circle one letter in each statement:

10) When disagreements arise, they usually result in:
    (a) Partner A giving in
    (b) Partner B giving in
    (c) Agreement by mutual give and take

11) Do you and your partner engage in outside interests together?
    (a) All of them
    (b) Some of them
    (c) Very few of them
    (d) None of them

12a) In leisure time do you generally prefer:
    (a) to be "on the go"
    (b) to stay at home

12b) Does your partner generally prefer:
    (a) to be "on the go"
    (b) to stay at home

13) Do you ever wish you had not married? (If not married, do you ever wish you had not gotten together with your partner?)
    (a) Frequently
    (b) Occasionally
    (c) Rarely
    (d) Never

14) If you had your life to live over again, do you think you would:
    (a) Be with the same person
    (b) Be with a different person
    (c) Not be with anyone at all

15) Do you ever confide in your partner:
    (a) Almost never
    (b) Rarely
    (c) In most things
    (d) In everything

SCORING: Look at the response tables below. Each response has a score associated with it. Note your answer to each question and record the scores you received in the Scoring Table.

Very Unhappy			Happy			Perfectly Happy
O	O	O	O	O	O	O
0	2	7	15	20	25	35

	Always Agree	Almost Always Agree	Occasionally Disagree	Frequently Disagree	Almost Always Disagree	Always Disagree
2. Handling Family Finances	5	4	3	2	1	0

3. Matters of Recreation	5	4	3	2	1	0
4. Demonstration of Affection	8	6	4	2	1	0
5. Friends	5	4	3	2	1	0
6. Sex Relations	15	12	9	4	1	0
7. Conventionally (right, good, or proper conduct)	5	4	3	2	1	0
8. Philosophy of Life	5	4	3	2	1	0
9. Ways of dealing with in-laws	5	4	3	2	1	0

10) When disagreements arise, they usually result in:
    (a) Partner A giving in – 1 point
    (b) Partner B giving in – 1 point
    (c) Agreement by mutual give and take – 10 point

11) Do you and your partner engage in outside interests together?
    (a) All of them – 10 points
    (b) Some of them – 8 points
    (c) Very few of them – 3 points
    (d) None of them – 0 points

12a) In leisure time do you generally prefer:
    (a) to be "on the go"
    (b) to stay at home

12b) Does your partner generally prefer:
    (a) to be "on the go"
    (b) to stay at home

(If you and your partner both answered "stay at home", give yourself 10 points. If you both answered "on the go", give yourself 3 points. If you disagreed with your partner, give yourself 2 points.)

13) Do you ever wish you had not married? (If not married, do you ever wish you had not gotten together with your partner?)
    (a) Frequently – 0 points
    (b) Occasionally – 3 points
    (c) Rarely – 8 points
    (d) Never – 15 points

14) If you had your life to live over again, do you think you would:
    (a) Be with the same person – 15 points
    (b) Be with a different person – 0 points
    (c) Not be with anyone at all – 1 point

15) Do you ever confide in your partner:
    (a) Almost never – 0 points
    (b) Rarely – 2 points
    (c) In most things – 10 points
    (d) In everything – 10 points

Record your scores for each question in the table below.

Questions	Your Score	Partner's Score
#1: Degree of Happiness in Relationship		
#2: Handling Family Finances		
#3: Matters of Recreation		
#4: Demonstration of Affection		
#5: Friends		
#6: Sex Relations		
#7: Conventionality		
#8: Philosophy of Life		
#9: Ways of Dealing With In-Laws		
#10: Who Gives In During Disagreements		
#11: Engaging in Outside Interests		
#12a. Leisure Time Preference		
#12b: Partner's Leisure Time Preference		
#13: On Having Gotten Together		
#14: Would you do it again?		
#15: Confiding in Partner		
TOTAL		

Add up all your scores for each of the 15 questions and write your total number down in the table above.

INTERPRETATION: The higher your score, the higher your relationship satisfaction.

If you have a high score, this means you have a strong relationship with your partner and it's going in a positive direction. You are satisfied in your relationship.

If you have a low score, you may be unhappy, and there may be several areas of your relationship that you and your partner could work on.

Positive-Negative Relationship Quality Scale (PN-RQ)

DIRECTIONS: Considering only the **positive** qualities of your relationship and ignoring the negative ones, rate your relationship based on the following statements. Fill in the appropriate bubble to indicate the extent that a statement is true:

My relationship is….	Not At All True	A Little True	SomewhatTrue	Mostly True	Very True	Completely True
Enjoyable	O	O	O	O	O	O
Pleasant	O	O	O	O	O	O
Strong	O	O	O	O	O	O
Alive	O	O	O	O	O	O
Fun	O	O	O	O	O	O
Full	O	O	O	O	O	O
Energizing	O	O	O	O	O	O
Exciting	O	O	O	O	O	O

DIRECTIONS: Considering only the **negative** qualities of your relationship and ignoring the positive ones rate your relationship based on the following statements. Fill in the appropriate bubble to indicate the extent that a statement is true:

My relationship is….	Not At All True	A Little True	SomewhatTrue	Mostly True	Very True	Completely True
Miserable	O	O	O	O	O	O
Bad	O	O	O	O	O	O
Empty	O	O	O	O	O	O
Lifeless	O	O	O	O	O	O
Unpleasant	O	O	O	O	O	O
Dull	O	O	O	O	O	O
Weak	O	O	O	O	O	O
Discouraging	O	O	O	O	O	O

SCORING: Assign each of your responses a value according to the following key. Write your scores in the Scoring Table below.

5 = Completely True
4 = Very True
3 = Mostly True
2 = Somewhat True
1 = A Little True
0 = Not At All True

Now add up all your scores for both positive and negative qualities and write your total numbers down at the bottom of the table.

Positive Statements	Your Score	Partner's Score	Negative Statements	Your Score	Partner's Score
#1: Enjoyable			#1: Miserable		
#2: Pleasant			#2: Bad		
#3: Strong			#3: Empty		
#4: Alive			#4: Lifeless		
#5: Fun			#5: Unpleasant		
#6: Full			#6: Dull		
#7: Energizing			#7: Weak		
#8: Exciting			#8: Discouraging		
TOTAL			TOTAL		

INTERPRETATION:

The higher your positive score, the more positive relationship qualities you have. The more positive relationship qualities you have, the stronger your relationship is.

The higher your negative score, the more negative relationship qualities you have. The more negative relationship qualities you have, the weaker your relationship is.

To gain a better understanding of both yourself and your romantic partner, it may be helpful to look into different approaches to romantic relationships, communication, and love. Chapman's *Five Love Languages* is one approach we will explain below.

Chapman's Five Love Languages

Have you ever heard of the five love languages? The five love languages are distinct ways we express love for one another. Dr. Gary Chapman developed the five love languages after counseling married couples for years. He ended up writing a book, *The Five Love Languages: The Secret To Love That Lasts*, explaining the concepts fully. In the decades that have followed, his book has been read by millions worldwide and many couples have reported success with implementing the practices in their relationships and daily lives.

Chapman's five love languages are:

1. *Words of Affirmation* – These consist of compliments, words of appreciation, and encouragement. They are meant to build up a partner. Examples include saying "I love you", "I appreciate you" and "I'm here for you."
2. *Acts of Service* – These consist of any action or behavior one performs on behalf of their partner, because they want to show their love or care for them. Examples include doing housework, fixing one's car, or cooking your partner a meal after a hard day.
3. *Giving and Receiving Gifts* – This love language consists of giving or receiving physical objects as gifts.

4. *Quality Time* – Quality time is not just about spending time with one another. It's about spending meaningful time, really engaging with your partner and doing fun activities you can both enjoy together.

5. *Physical Touch* – This love language is all about physical contact and affection, whether sexual or not.

In his book, Dr. Chapman argues that everyone has a different primary love language. After knowing each other's love language, both partners, according to Dr. Chapman, should be able to focus on giving each other what they need, according to their primary love language. In this scenario, knowing your love language (as well as your partner's), may vastly improve your relationship.

What Will Help You

Make an effort. It is important that both parties are invested in putting forth an honest effort to improve their relationship. Both partners must also accept responsibility for their individual shortcomings in the relationship in order to move forward. No one is perfect, but we can all try to do better. You should strive for greater communication and awareness of your own needs and actions as well as your partner's, and commit to taking the steps necessary to work on your relationship.

It can be easy to stop trying and fall back onto familiar habits. If you think you've been trying less, try to put more effort into yourself and your relationship, and your partner may notice the positive change.

Keep it fresh. To keep the conversation fresh, and to continue learning about one another, consider asking each other new questions that you might not have thought of before. When you start asking new questions, you may realize you don't know them as well as you may have thought. Frequent communication is key here.

Don't dwell on the past. Additionally, it's important to focus on the present, avoid dwelling on the past (unless there are serious unresolved issues in your past that needs to be discussed). Try to move forward with more kindness and appreciation for your partner and all you do for one another. Be positive in your interactions. Speak honestly. Remember no one can read your mind, and that includes your partner. Take the time to truly listen to one another, especially before you speak.

Dedicate time to each other. Establishing a regular date night can also help keep the spark alive. You should both set aside at least one night for one another. Go out and have fun! Do something exciting. Don't just sit at home all the time. And when you're with each other, really be present. Put away your phones and other distractions. Focus on one another. Remember the good times. Remember that you're partners, and you're in this together. Alternatively, try to find more time in your day-to-day lives to reconnect.

Seek therapy. It may also be helpful to sit down with a relationship or marriage counselor if you think you and your partner have deeper underlying issues that you'd like to resolve with the help of a professional. Even if you don't, seeing a counselor can improve your communication overall. Individual therapy may help improve your relationships as well. Working on oneself inevitably improves the quality of the partnership.

CHAPTER 15: ARE YOU IN AN UNHEALTHY RELATIONSHIP? A CHAPTER ON ABUSE

Assess if You're in an Abusive Relationship or You're the Abuser

Nell Daly Counsels Patients on Relationships

Do you feel manipulated and controlled by your significant other? Do they criticize your actions and try to control who you socialize with? Do they call you names? Put you down? Bully you? Give you the silent treatment for days on end? Have you ever been physically assaulted by them? Pressured or forced you into having sex when you didn't want to? If the answer is yes to any of these questions, we ask you to keep reading.

"Don't drink the Kool-Aid," I said to Anna, a patient I began treating in the summer of 2015. Anna was an accomplished marketing director, fabulous dresser and adoring mother of one little four-year-old girl. She was married to Joe for seven years.

"What do you mean by that?" she asked, head cocked to the side, her purse sitting neatly on her lap.

"I mean each week you come in here and tell me stories of how your husband grabbed your phone while you were in the shower and read all your text messages, called your terrible names in front of Ruby, and makes you sleep on the couch if you look at him 'the wrong way.' The list goes on and on. Don't drink his Kool-Aid, Anna. You are not the problem. You are not crazy, a bitch, a loser or a terrible mother. He's abusive, very very abusive."

"I don't know what I did to deserve this kind of treatment," she replied, eyes cast downward.

"Anna, even if you had 'done something wrong' make no mistake, no one, absolutely no one has the right to treat another human being this way."

Here's the thing about abusive relationships, sometimes you're in so deep it's easier than you think to lose sight of what's "normal" behavior and what's not. To make things more complicated, in my experience abusers don't consciously begin relationships abusing the person they're now hurting. Abusers, whether consciously or unconsciously, use the old "bait and switch" method; they court someone hard and then slowly, over time, wear them down with their abusive behavior. This also means the one being abused often clings to ideas of what the person they love *once was* or *has the potential* to be. Do the words *but he wasn't always this way* sound familiar to you? I'm sure anyone reading this has had a friend say this to you at some point in your life.

In Anna's case, her husband controlled the finances, owned the home she moved into when they got married, and he was constantly threatening her that if she left him she wouldn't "have a pot to piss in." He said he would tell a judge she cheated on him, even though she hadn't, and she would lose custody of her daughter. Anna was now petrified to leave her husband because it would mean, at some point during any given week, she would have to leave her sweet vulnerable daughter alone with him too.

Walking out on Joe was no light matter. Anna was sitting in my office very vulnerable; if she left him she was at an even greater physical risk than if she stayed. Many times this can feel like a lose-lose situation.

Quick STATS:[158]

- Every minute, 20 people are abused. This equals ten million cases per year
- Daily, domestic abuse hotlines receive over 20,000 calls
- Women between the ages of 18-24 are more likely to be abused
- 1 in 4 women experience abuse in their lifetime, while for men it's only 1 in 9
- 1 in 7 women have been physically injured by their partners
- 1 in 5 women have been sexually assaulted in the USA
- Between 14 and 25 % of women are sexually assaulted in their relationship
- 66.2 percent of women have reported being stalked by current or past partners
- 1 in 3 female murder victims are killed by their partners
- Yearly an estimated 4,000 women are killed due to domestic violence[159]
- Between 2003-2014, 10,018 deaths were caused because of domestic abuse
- If they leave the relationship, women are 70 times more likely to be killed in the following two weeks than if they stayed
- Only slightly more than half of abuse cases are ever reported to the police

Emotional vs. Physical Abuse

There are two main types of abuse: physical and emotional. Physical abuse includes, but is not limited to, hitting, kicking, pushing, leaving bruises and/or cuts, sexual abuse, burns and broken bones. Emotional abuse consists of manipulation, the need to control someone and the environment around you, gas lighting (the psychological manipulation of an individual with the intention of making them question their sanity) and calling someone hurtful names, just to name a few transgressions. It's important to note that while physical abuse is easier to spot than emotional abuse, emotional abuse is just as damaging and traumatizing to the victim.

Below are two different risk-assessment tests we've developed just for you. One is for the person who is potentially being abused, the other is for the potential abuser. The following self-assessments are a conglomeration from several assessments, including *Psych Central's Domestic Violence Screening Quiz*, *Break The Cycle's Quiz*, *Love Is Respect Is my Relationship Healthy Quiz* and knowledge taken from The National Domestic Violence Hotline's fact sheet characterizing abuse.

Test 1: Are You Being Abused?

Are you feeling manipulated, controlled or afraid for your physical well-being? Is there something in your gut that's telling your current relationship is unhealthy? If so, take Test 1.

Test 2: Are You Being Abusive?

Are you constantly paranoid your partner is lying to you? Do you have the need to control them – whether it be their thoughts, actions, clothing choices or friend groups? Have past relationships, or family members or friends ever told you that your behavior is manipulative, domineering and overly aggressive? If the answer is yes, take Test 2.

***Please note that even though these tests are worded to imply the abuser is a romantic partner, you can insert anyone – family members, friends, mentors – into many of the questions to assess if anyone in your life is being abusive towards you or someone you love.

Test 1: Are You in An Abusive Relationship?

DIRECTIONS: For each item, check the most appropriate box. In the past four weeks, has your partner done any of the following:

	Never	Sometimes	Most of the time	All the time
1. Checked in on you when you weren't together? Got angry if you didn't respond?				
2. Have they tried to control what you wear?				
3. Have they controlled who you socialize with?				
4. Have they isolated you from friends and family?				
5. Have they made you nervous to be around them?				
6. Have they made you feel obligated to have the same opinion as them in fear they will be upset if you don't?				
7. Have they accused you of having affairs?				
8. Have they belittled what you've said or done? Especially while in public?				
9. Are you ever embarrassed by how your partner treats you?				
10. Have they coerced you into doing anything you didn't want to do?				
11. Have they pressured you into having sex with them?				
12. Does your partner threaten to harm you physically?				
13. Have they threatened to harm you or themselves if you were to break up with them?				
14. Have they actually harmed you?				
15. Have they increased their violence?				
16. Have they justified their behavior with an excuse?				

SCORING: Assign your responses scores according to the following:

1 = Never
2 = Sometimes
3 = Most of the time
4 = All the time

The assessment ranges from **16 points to 64 points.** Based off of your answers and the scoring key above, give yourself a score from 16-64. Write your scores in the table below and then add them up to get your total. Write your total in the last row of the table.

Questions #1-8	Your Score	Questions #9-16	Your Score
#1		#9	
#2		#10	
#3		#11	
#4		#12	
#5		#13	
#6		#14	
#7		#15	
#8		#16	
		TOTAL	

INTERPRETATION:

If you scored between **0 and 16 points,** then this relationship is likely not abusive. That does not mean traits of abusive behavior are not present, but it does not display common characteristics of abuse.

If you scored from **16 to 32 points,** then your relationship may be abusive. Watch out for characteristics that may develop that could indicate abuse.

If you scored between **32 and 48 points**, then you're most likely in an abusive relationship.

Finally, if your score is **48 to 64 points**, then your relationship shares many characteristics with an abusive relationship.

* This assessment is designed to indicate signs of abuse. It's a starting point to get you thinking more deeply about your relationships. Even if your scores DO NOT indicate signs of abuse, if you feel physically or emotionally threatened, seek further help.

Test 2: Are You Being Abusive?

DIRECTIONS: For each item, check the most appropriate box. Answer if you, in the past four weeks, have done any of the following:

	Never	Sometimes	Most of the time	All the time
1. Have you checked in on your partner when you weren't together? Did you get angry if they didn't respond?				
2. Have you tried to control what they wear?				
3. Have you tried to control who they socialize with?				
4. Have they expressed feelings of being isolated from friends and/or family?				
5. Have you noticed they seemed nervous to be around you?				
6. Do they always have the same opinion as you? Would you get mad if they didn't?				
7. Have you accused your partner of having affairs or lying about their whereabouts?				
8. Have you belittled them or their words when you're in public?				
9. Are you ever embarrassed by your partner's behavior?				
10. Have you ever coerced them into doing anything they didn't want to do?				
11. Have you pressured them into having sex with you?				
12. Did you threaten to harm your partner? (Or have you harmed your partner?)				
13. Have you ever threatened to harm yourself if they leave you?				
14. Has your violent actions increased?				
15. Do you always have an excuse that justified your behavior?				

SCORING: Assign your responses scores according to the following:

1 = Never
2 = Sometimes
3 = Most of the time
4 = All the time

The assessment ranges from **16 points to 60 points.** Based off your answers and the scoring key above, give yourself a score 16-60. Write your scores in the table below and then add them up to get your total. Write your total in the last row of the table.

Questions #1-8	Your Score	Questions #9-15	Your Score
#1		#9	
#2		#10	
#3		#11	
#4		#12	
#5		#13	
#6		#14	
#7		#15	
#8		TOTAL	

INTERPRETATION:

If you scored between **0 and 16 points,** then you're probably not acting in an abusive. That does not mean you don't, sometimes, show signs of abusive behavior, but your responses do not display common characteristics of abuse.

If you scored from **16 to 32 points,** then you do show some signs of being an abuser. It is hard to say one way or another based on this scoring system, but watch out for characteristics that may develop that could indicate abuse.

If you scored between **32 and 48 points,** then you're most likely the abuser in your relationship.

Finally, if your score is **48 to 60 points**, then your relationship shares many characteristics with an abusive relationship.

What Will Help You

Take a moment and consider taking one or more of the following steps:

If you're the one being abused:

1. **Report.** Is your physical wellbeing in danger? If so, you'll need guidance and protection to remove yourself from the situation. Helpful advice is to document everything and work with the authorities, although these systems are far from perfect, you need to protect yourself. Examples include reporting incidents to the police, seeing a doctor, filing a restraining order, carefully removing yourself from the situation, ect.
2. **Seek therapy.** This may seem obvious, but support is necessary! Talking about the relationship will provide clarity and relief. Trauma left untreated has many negative ramifications. A well-trained professional will be able to provide you with tools to heal, community resources or facilitate couple's counseling – depending on your relationship status.
3. **Set boundaries.** Whether you decide to remove yourself from a situation or not it's important to state to your abuser what will and will not be tolerated moving forward. This might include cutting off all contact. Keep yourself safe above all else.

** For friends and family members of the abused, provide a safe haven, education, and resources.

If you're the one who is being abusive:

1. **Seek therapy.** People can transform their behavior with intense professional help. There are therapists who specialize in working with abusers.

2. **Attend anger management classes.** More often than not, abusive behavior stems from a person's need to vent frustrations, they exhibit a lack of impulse control and depending on the case, may have deeply held misogynistic or racist beliefs that influence the way they treat a partner or loved one. These classes seek to help a person reframe and redirect their anger, once triggered, so they are able to deal with anger in a healthier way. These types of classes also teach a person how to become more aware of your actions and usually some relaxation strategies.

3. **Properly treat untreated mental illness or drug addiction**, (which correlates to rates of violence). Violence can come from a place of mental illness or substance abuse. There is no denying that being in an altered state allows for humans to behave in a way that they might not normally. By getting clean or treating an underlying mental illness, you can practice healthy behavior.

If you feel you need to remove yourself from your current situation or need help doing so, please reach out to the National Domestic Violence Hotline or the Emotional Abuse hotline for confidential support. All numbers are listed in our resource section at the back of the book.

CHAPTER 16: DO I HAVE THE BABY BLUES? TESTING YOUR MOOD DURING PREGNANCY AND POSTPARTUM

It is natural for women to experience mood changes during pregnancy, including feeling more tired, irritable or worried. However, while mild mood changes during pregnancy are common, mood symptoms can become severe enough to require treatment by a healthcare provider.

If your symptoms interfere with your daily functioning and they persist for at least two weeks – ASK FOR HELP. Depression and anxiety during pregnancy can worsen and continue into the postpartum period. Untreated perinatal mood disorders can have an adverse effect on both the mother's and baby's health. If you're worried about a pregnant or postpartum partner, daughter, sister or friend, keep reading and help the at-risk mom fill out these carefully curated assessments.

Looking for some guidance and a whole lot of answers? Here's the deal on all baby-related moods that deserve the attention of a well-trained therapist or family doctor.

When Nell first went into private practice, she specialized in what's called *perinatal mood and anxiety disorders*. Why? Because as she was finishing her clinical training, she gave birth to her first child and eventually developed a horrible case of postpartum depression.

At the time there wasn't much information out there on perinatal mood disorders. Google searches brought up obscure websites with scant information. Mom blogs weren't popular yet. And doctors weren't required to ask you how YOU felt during your follow up visits – every question seemed to center around the health of the baby. Many women, including Nell, were afraid to speak up.

Times were different back then.

Quick STATS:

- Up to 1 in 7 women experience PPD[160]
- For half of women diagnosed with PPD, this is their first episode of depression.[161]
- About half of women who are later diagnosed with PPD may have begun experiencing symptoms during pregnancy[162]
- According to The American Congress of Obstetrics and Gynecologists between 14-23% of women will struggle with some symptoms of depression during pregnancy.[163]
- More than 1 and 10 women experience antenatal (prenatal) anxiety during their pregnancy.[164]

- Many new moms experience what's commonly called "the baby blues" – a mild, brief bout of depression – for a few days or weeks after giving birth.[165]
- It's estimated that 10 to 20 percent of new moms will experience a more severe form of depression or an increase in anxiety that doesn't easily resolve on its own. This can happen at any time during the first 12 months after birth.[166]
- Postpartum psychosis is a rare, serious mental illness that affects one in 500 to 1000 new mothers. The onset is usually within the first six weeks after delivery and may cause the mother to completely lose touch with reality.[167]

Women suffering with a perinatal mood disorder tend to worry, a lot, about what other people think. In fact, excessive worrying is a telltale sign something is wrong. Mothers worry that if they tell someone how they are feeling, they would most certainly take the baby and be admitted to the closest emergency room.

Brooke Shields's groundbreaking memoir *Down Came the Rain* is a moving account on her deeply painful struggle with postpartum depression.

Finally, someone was willing to tell the truth.

Nearly fifteen years later, research and the social stigma surrounding perinatal mood disorders have come a long way. This is due, in large part, to the brave women with large platforms who've spoken up about their own struggles with mood disorders during or after pregnancy: Gwyneth Paltrow, Serena Williams and Rachel Hollis come to mind. And the amount of public information available to women now as opposed to then is a testament to the elected officials who have fought long and hard to pass bills demanding better healthcare for women and children.

When Nell opened her private practice on 5th Avenue a year after reading Brooke's book, she made it a point to help new mothers and their concerned family members. She organized support groups, completed advanced clinical training at major teaching hospitals and applied for research grants. She eventually became the New York State Co-coordinator for *Postpartum Support International*, a worldwide non-profit organization that helps women suffering with perinatal mood disorders find resources and get the help they deserve.

From all of that invaluable on-the-ground experience, here are the golden truths gleaned after more than a decade in the field that mothers, fathers, and family members need to know when supporting a pregnant or postpartum mother.

Quick DEFINITION:

Perinatal Mood and Anxiety Disorders are mood and anxiety symptoms that occur during pregnancy or up to one year postpartum. "Perinatal mood and anxiety disorders" is also an "umbrella term." Underneath it there are several specific diagnoses.

Disorders Related to Pregnancy

- Depression During Pregnancy
- Anxiety During Pregnancy

Disorders Related to Postpartum

- Postpartum Depression
- Postpartum Anxiety Disorders (intrusive thinking, panic attack, obsessive compulsive behaviors / thought patterns)
- Postpartum Psychosis

As far as we've come in this particular field of study, many lay people – those who aren't healthcare workers – still don't realize the varied faces that "postpartum depression" can take. In fact, the term postpartum "depression" is a bit of a misnomer. Oftentimes we commonly say *postpartum depression* when the experience is usually coupled with symptoms of severe anxiety. Over the last several years there has been a real push by health care advocates to educate Americans that postpartum depression oftentimes manifests as uncontrollable painful anxiety, as noted in the disorders listed above.

Risk Factors

Risk factors do not cause perinatal mood disorders. I list them here only to make you aware of the factors that can potentially make you vulnerable to perinatal depression and anxiety. A good exercise is to check all that apply and discuss the results with your healthcare provider.

- ☐ Type A personality type (perfectionist, overachiever, overly self-reliant)
- ☐ A history of severe PMS
- ☐ A history of attempted suicide or suicidal ideation
- ☐ A history of drug or alcohol abuse
- ☐ History of a mental disorder, specifically bipolar, depression or anxiety
- ☐ Family history
- ☐ If a mother experiences depression or anxiety during pregnancy she is at greater risk of developing a mood disorder postpartum
- ☐ Inadequate support: lack of childcare, financial stress
- ☐ Medical problems with a previous pregnancy or birth including loss
- ☐ A history of domestic violence
- ☐ A history of sexual assault
- ☐ Relationship issues with partner or husband, father of the child

Symptoms often associated with a mood disorder during pregnancy and then during the postpartum phase.

Common Mood Complaints During Pregnancy

One of the hard things about being a pregnant woman who is experiencing symptoms of anxiety or depression is that it's difficult for the pregnant woman to realize if she is in emotional trouble or she's simply experiencing a "normal" pregnancy. Each and every pregnancy is unique and "normal" is personal to every individual.

Countless women came into Nell's office over the years, with swollen bellies and swollen feet, apologizing for their feelings and unsure if they actually need help. They would begin their first session with me by saying things like: "I'm so sorry I'm crying. I hate complaining. Shouldn't I be happier? I hate feeling like a burden to everyone."

If you think you're not feeling well, you're not feeling well. It's not for anyone else to judge. And if you have a thoughtful partner or friend who asks, "Hey, you don't seem like yourself, are you ok?" and you burst into tears, or your heart sinks, listen to your gut and seek treatment and support. Untreated anxiety and depression during pregnancy affects maternal fetal outcomes and puts you at risk for a post baby mood disorder.

Symptoms of Depression / Anxiety During Pregnancy:

- Feeling sad, hopeless, excessive crying
- Lack of interest in becoming a mother
- Feeling as if you're going to be a worthless mother
- Excessive anxiety over the future: health of your child, life plans
- Sleep issues: insomnia or never feeling fully rested
- Suicidal thoughts or fantasies
- Remarkably low energy
- Loss of appetite, little to no weight gain
- Experiencing symptoms that feel similar to panic attacks
- Extreme irritability

Common Mood Complaints During the Postpartum Phase

Women who are suffering with postpartum depression or anxiety are what I call slippery fish. Sometimes they appear as they are – frazzled, unkempt, disorganized, crying or nervous. Other times they appear very "put together" – hair blown out, clothes freshly pressed with an impeccably cared for baby is a bigger concern. Masks take a lot of energy to hold up. Common symptoms are:

Symptoms of Depression / Anxiety During Postpartum:

- Constant crying
- Feeling disconnected from the baby
- Experiencing intrusive thinking often centered around some act of violence, like harming the baby or being harmed themselves
- Stuck in a loop and exhausted from worrying about the same thing over and over all day long

- Experiencing an increase in obsessive compulsive thinking or behaviors, for example, charting every waking minute of their newborn's day, obsessing over baby products, food contamination, breastfeeding and sleep schedules, daycare options
- Experiencing panic attacks

The best way to describe what it feels like to have a postpartum mood disorder is: *the worst* case of PMS you've ever been through, then times that by ten.

A Note on Postpartum Psychosis:

Postpartum psychosis is a serious illness that can be life threatening. Often mothers who develop postpartum psychosis are having a severe episode of a mood disorder, usually bipolar (manic-depression) disorder with psychotic features.

To be clear, if a woman is hallucinating, mentions suicide at all, and doesn't feel "guilty" about any intrusive thoughts she's having about harming herself or her baby, she is having a medical emergency and needs to be brought to a hospital emergency room immediately. Don't be afraid to call 911. Let those who are trained to deal with a mental health crisis do their job.

Postpartum Psychosis Symptoms include:

- Delusional thinking (thoughts not based in reality)
- Hallucinations (hearing or seeing things that aren't there)
- Disorganized thinking

We have picked out three wonderful self assessments to help you figure out if you, or someone you love, is suffering with a perinatal mood disorder. In 2006, New Jersey became the first state in the US to pass a law mandating universal screening, education and referral for postpartum depression. Since then 13 other states have followed their lead.

Test 1:

The Edinburgh Scale,[168] found below, is the most common assessment used on new mothers during postpartum OBGYN or pediatrician follow-ups. **A careful clinical assessment should be carried out to confirm the diagnosis.** The EPDS will not detect mothers with anxiety disorders, phobias, or personality disorders. If you're worried that you or someone you know may be suffering with a pregnancy related mood disorder The Edinburgh Scale is a great way to obtain a baseline.

Test 2:

If you or any woman you love answers question #10 on the Edinburgh Scale with a 1, 2 or 3 ("the thought of harming myself has occurred to me) the following test should be given and treatment should be sought out immediately. **The Suicide Assessment for a Positive EPDS Screen (#10)**[169] was developed by The Postpartum Stress Center of PA, founded by Karen Kleinman who has dedicated her life's work to helping expectant and new mothers. We have republished it here with her permission.

Test 3:

Since so often mothers who are suffering with a perinatal mood disorder show symptoms of anxiety, instead of or in addition to depression, we wanted to include the **Perinatal Anxiety Screen Scale**[170] owned by the Government of Western Australia's Department of Health.

EPDS (The Edinburgh Scale)

> **DIRECTIONS:** As you have recently had a baby we would like to know how you are feeling. Please mark the answer that comes closest to how you have felt IN THE PAST 7 DAYS not just how you feel today.

What is your baby's age? _____

1) I have been able to laugh and see the funny side of things:
   (a) As much as I always could (0)
   (b) Not quite as much now (1)
   (c) Definitely not so much now (2)
   (d) Not at all (3)

2) I have looked forward with enjoyment to things:
   (a) As much as I ever did (0)
   (b) Rather less than I used to (1)
   (c) Definitely less than I used to (2)
   (d) Hardly at all (3)

3) I have blamed myself unnecessarily when things went wrong:
   (a) Yes, most of the time (3)
   (b) Yes, some of the time (2)
   (c) Not very often (1)
   (d) No, never (0)

4) I have been anxious or worried for no good reason:
   (a) No, not at all (0)
   (b) Hardly ever (1)
   (c) Yes, sometimes (2)
   (d) Yes, very often (3)

5) I have felt scared or panicky for not very good reason:
   (a) Yes, quite a lot (3)
   (b) Yes, sometimes (2)
   (c) No, not as much (1)
   (d) No, not at all (0)

6) Things have been getting on top of me:
   (a) Yes, most of the time I haven't been able to cope at all (3)
   (b) Yes, sometimes I haven't been coping as well as usual (2)
   (c) No, most of the time I have coped quite well (1)
   (d) No, I have been coping as well as ever (0)

7) I have been so unhappy that I have had difficulty sleeping:
   (a) Yes, most of the time (3)
   (b) Yes, sometimes (2)
   (c) Not very often (1)
   (d) No, not at all (0)

8) I have felt sad or miserable:
   (a) Yes, most of the time (3)
   (b) Yes, quite often (2)
   (c) Not very often (1)
   (d) No, not at all (0)

9) I have been so unhappy that I have been crying:
   (a) Yes, most of the time (3)
   (b) Yes, quite often (2)
   (c) Only occasionally (1)
   (d) No, never (0)

10) The thought of harming myself has occurred to me:
   (a) Yes, most of the time (3)
   (b) Yes, quite often (2)
   (c) Not very often (1)
   (d) No, not at all (0)

SCORING: The score that corresponds with each response is in parenthesis next to it. Add up all your scores as indicated. Write your total below.

TOTAL: _____

INTERPRETATION:
A score of 10 may require a repeat assessment, as depression symptoms may be present.
A score of 12 indicates that depression is likely and further assessment by a trained healthcare provider is recommended.
If any answer other than "No, not at all" is circled for item number 10, further assessment is required right away. Please contact your healthcare provider immediately.

Suicide Assessment For A Positive EPDS Screen (#10)

> **DIRECTIONS:** Check all that apply and discuss the results with your healthcare provider.

- ☐ How often are you having thoughts of hurting yourself?
- ☐ Are you able to describe them?
- ☐ Have you ever had thoughts like this before?
- ☐ What happened the last time you had these thoughts?
- ☐ Does your partner know how bad you are feeling? If not, why not?
- ☐ Who do you consider your most primary connection for emotional support?
- ☐ Does this person know how you are feeling? If not, why not?
- ☐ Does anyone in your family know how you are feeling?
- ☐ Have you ever acted on suicide thoughts before?
- ☐ How do you feel about these thoughts you are having?
- ☐ Do you have specific thoughts about what you would do to harm yourself?
- ☐ If you do have a plan, do you know what is keeping you from acting on it?
- ☐ Are there weapons in your home?
- ☐ Do you have access to medications that could be harmful to you?
- ☐ Is there anything else you can think of that [can be done] right now to help you protect yourself from these thoughts?
- ☐ Have you thought about what the implication would be for your baby?
- ☐ Do you feel able to contact [your healthcare provider] if you feel you cannot stop yourself from acting on these thoughts?

Perinatal Anxiety Screening Scale (PASS)

> **DIRECTIONS: Over the past month, how often** have you experienced the following? Please check the box that **most closely** describes your experience for **every** question.

	Not at all	Sometimes	Often	Almost Always
1. Worry about the baby/pregnancy				
2. Fear that harm will come to the baby				
3. A sense of dread that something bad is going to happen				
4. Worry about many things				
5. Worry about the future				
6. Feeling overwhelmed				
7. Really strong fears about things, e.g. Needles, blood, birth, pain, etc.				
8. Sudden rushes of extreme fear or discomfort				

9. Repetitive thoughts that are difficult to stop or control				
10. Difficulty sleeping even when I have the chance to sleep				
11. Having to do things in a certain way or order				
12. Wanting things to be perfect				
13. Needing to be in control of things				
14. Difficulty stopping, checking				
15. Feeling jumpy or easily startled				
16. Concerns about repeated thoughts				
17. Being 'on guard' or needing to watch out for things				
18. Upset about repeated memories, dreams or nightmares				
19. Worry that I will embarrass myself in front of others				
20. Fear that others will judge me negatively				
21. Feeling really uneasy in crowds				
22. Avoiding social activities because I might be nervous				
23. Avoiding things which concern me				
24. Feeling detached like you're watching yourself in a movie				
25. Losing track of time and can't remember what happened				
26. Difficulty adjusting to recent changes				
27. Anxiety getting in the way of being able to do things				
28. Racing thoughts making it hard to concentrate				
29. Fear of losing control				
30. Feeling panicky				
31. Feeling agitated				
Global Score				
TOTAL				

SCORING: A total PASS score is obtained by adding all of the items on the PASS. Write your scores for each item in the Scoring Table below according to the following:

0 = Not at all
1 = Sometimes
2 = Often
3 = Almost Always

The score ranges from **0 to 93 points.**

When finished writing down your scores, add them up to produce your total. Either write your totals in the table above or the table below.

Questions #1-16	Your Score	Questions #17-31	Your Score
#1		#17	
#2		#18	
#3		#19	
#4		#20	
#5		#21	
#6		#22	
#7		#23	
#8		#24	
#9		#25	
#10		#26	
#11		#27	
#12		#28	
#13		#29	
#14		#30	
#15		#31	
#16		TOTAL	

INTERPRETATION: A **cut-off score of 26** is recommended to differentiate between high and low risk for presenting with an anxiety disorder.

Recommended Severity Ranges:

Anxiety Severity	Range of Scores
Asymptomatic	0-20
Mild-moderate symptoms	21-41
Severe symptoms	42-93

The PASS is **not** a diagnostic scale. However, for clinical purposes, it can be useful to have some indication of the nature of the anxiety symptoms being experienced. In addition, the answers to **item 7** should be considered individually, as this item is a **clinical indicator of phobia.**

Some Points to be Aware Of:

1) Dads get depressed too; have them take the tests below if you're worried about an expectant or new father.

2) Sometimes symptoms of a perinatal mood disorder show up immediately. Other times a woman can be fine for the first three month and then quickly – or slowly – start to feel "not herself." The

six-week mark is where all the euphoria of having a new baby wears off and the chronic loss of sleep starts to take its toll on a family's psychological health. However, women can be nine months postpartum with symptoms when few were present before.

3) "Does quitting nursing make you feel better?" Nursing and the emotional ramifications of stopping vary mother to mother.

I nursed all three of my children because it came easy for me and I was too lazy to wash bottles and make formula in the middle of the night. Many women feel a lift in mood once they stop nursing and the last of the postpartum hormones wash out of the system a few weeks later.

4) **Just because you had a perinatal mood disorder with one child doesn't mean you'll have it again.** I wanted to highlight that sentence because a) it's true and b) gives women hope. Yes, you're at a greater risk but you'll also know how to nip it in the bud earlier and you'll have better support systems in place. The reverse can also be the case; you can be on cloud nine with your first baby and then really struggle with the second.

Nell happened to have a horrible case of postpartum anxiety with her first child. "With my second—a little girl born in the summertime, who nursed for five minutes a few times a day and slept twelve hours a night—it was the single happiest time of my life. I was blissed out, literally, the first year of her life."

5) Treating the struggles and heartbreaks women face when it comes to fertility, pregnancy loss and stillborn grief has also been a large focus of Nell's work. Do to the content restrictions we have for this particular book, please see our Extended Resource Guide for more information on those topics. In no way should any of those experiences be minimized. They are incredibly painful life events that don't often get the attention they deserve. Women must be given emotional, physical and spiritual support during those tender times as well.

What Will Help You

Getting help for depression or anxiety related to pregnancy or postpartum is essential. Symptoms do not typically resolve without some combination of therapies and support. You'll never get these months back with your baby. You deserve to feel sustained moments of joy as a new mother. The sooner you treat your symptoms the better. No one gives you a medal for needless suffering.

- Seeing a therapist trained in perinatal mood disorders is the first line of treatment. Not only will they educate you and help you put words to your experience, they will become a resource for you to draw upon. Talk therapy is essential, effective and will make you feel hopeful again.

- Some women supplement talk therapy with psychiatric medication. There are pros and cons when taking this road so make sure you clearly understand the risks and the benefits. Medications should be used only in conjunction with talk therapy.

- Many women crave support groups and 12 step programs. Support groups for new moms all suffering with a perinatal mood disorder, however, can sometimes make a new mother *more* anxious than less. Hearing about how one mother has thoughts of harming her child isn't always in the best interest of a fragile parent who is already struggling to cope with the day to day demands of new motherhood. Anxiety is catchy. You'll know if you need to tread lightly and seek out Mommy and me classes instead of therapeutic support groups. Spending quality time doing light activities with new moms and dads is healing in itself.

- Electroconvulsive therapy, more commonly referred to as ECT, is a gentle noninvasive holistic approach that has also proven to help many women.

- Lastly, there are plenty of self-care measures that can make a big difference: meditation, dietary changes, healthy sleep habits, acupuncture, exercising, breaks using childcare, just to name a few.

CHAPTER 17: ON POST TRAUMATIC STRESS DISORDER WITH A SPECIAL SECTION FOR ARMED FORCES MEMBERS AND FIRST RESPONDERS

Do your palms sweat when you think about a certain event that happened five years ago? Do you constantly change the subject to avoid thinking or talking about a certain moment? Does thinking about a specific memory make you nervous, angry and generally feel not like yourself? Do you have trouble sleeping at night? Jump at loud unexpected noises? Then, you might have PTSD.

Our bodies and minds don't learn to effectively cope with trauma if we simply pretend like it didn't happen. In America, especially, there's this "pull yourself up by your bootstraps" ethos constantly in the air, or a "suck it up and move on" mantra that we pick up on consciously and unconsciously – all the time – reinforcing our individual and collective silence around trauma. Danielle Bernock, author of *Emerging with Wings: A True Story of Lies, Pain, and the Love That Heals* said, "Trauma is personal. It does not disappear if it is not validated. When it is ignored or invalidated the silent screams continue internally heard only by the one held captive. When someone enters the pain and hears the screams healing can begin."[171] On trauma and PTSD, here are some good assessments and how to heal.

PTSD, the shortened form of Post-Traumatic Stress Disorder, is a psychiatric condition 'triggered' by a stressful and traumatizing event. A traumatic event may include abuse, neglect, military combat, sexual assault or rape, assault, an accident, a medical emergency, a natural disaster, witnessing a death or grave injury, or experiencing any other kind of physical attack or threat to one's safety or that of loved ones.[172] Whether the individual witnesses or experiences the event first hand, a group of symptoms develop as a way for someone to cope with their past. Typically those experiencing PTSD, when triggered, relive their trauma again and again. This makes them feel like their life or safety is currently in danger. These triggers can include certain sounds, people, situations, events, or even smells.

Many people who have undiagnosed and untreated PTSD choose to block out the memories, and the unpleasant sensations that follow, because they're too painful. Yet, in doing so, oftentimes they unintentionally make daily life harder on themselves. If PTSD isn't treated properly, the side effects of a PTSD diagnosis can impact someone's life for years.

Symptoms of PTSD include:
- Flashbacks
- Nightmares or other dreams, or recurring thoughts related to the event
- Avoidance and unwillingness to address trauma (e.g., avoiding places that may trigger bad memories, not wanting to talk, not being able to remember the traumatic situation)
- Experiencing emotional and/or physical reactions to triggers

- Experiencing overwhelming fear or panic attacks
- Blaming self for the trauma
- Feeling anxious, worried, depressed, or hopeless
- Outbursts of anger or aggression
- Unexplained sweating or rapid breathing
- Racing heart, headaches, diarrhea, chronic pain (in the stomach, chest, or lower back)
- Trouble sleeping or concentrating
- Feeling on edge, on guard, mistrustful or easily startled
- Feeling emotionally numb or detached
- No longer enjoying interests or hobbies
- No longer cultivating relationships
- Having eating, drug, or alcohol problems, or engaging in other self-destructive behaviors

Symptoms can vary over time. For example, you or a loved one may not experience many or any of these symptoms unless there is a trigger, although many normal everyday occurrences can be triggers. Additionally, symptoms may not appear right away after an event; sometimes it can take months to develop the disorder. If symptoms persist for over a month following a recent traumatic event, you may have PTSD.[173]

Quick STATS:
- 70% of American adults experienced a traumatic event in their life, of that 70 percent, 20 percent develop PTSD (that's over 31 million adults)[174]
- 10% of women develop PTSD while only 4 percent of men do[175]
- 67% of people exposed to mass violence have PTSD[176]
- Veterans have a higher chance of having PTSD than civilians
- 11-20 % of veterans who served in Operations Iraqi Freedom and Enduring Freedom have been diagnosed with PTSD
- 12% of Gulf War (Desert Storm) veterans experience PTSD annually
- 15% of Vietnam War veterans experience PTSD, as of the late '80s, and the current number is estimated to be much higher[177]
- 7% of veterans suffer from both PTSD and a physical brain injury[178]
- Combat makes up only a small part of the PTSD inducing events in the military
- 55% of women and 38% of men enlisted in the military experience sexual assault
- Yet, only 23% of women in the military report sexual assault while enlisted
- There are roughly 200 special programs run by the VA for PTSD treatment[179]
- Nearly 50% of veterans who have PTSD do not receive the help they need[180]
- An estimated 30% of first responders develop health issues, which may include depression and PTSD[181]

Are Some People More at Risk than Others? Causal Factors
One major causal factor for developing PTSD has to do with what kind of initial support a person receives after the traumatic event occurs. If there's little family or community support, the traumatized person is at a higher risk of developing PTSD related symptoms. If the traumatized person doesn't talk about the event, they're also placing themselves into a higher risk category. In other words, studies show shutting down and remaining silent causes greater long term psychological and emotional damage.[182]

People are also more likely to develop PTSD if they have experienced trauma during their childhood, if their family has a history of mental health problems, or if they have sleep or substance abuse issues.[183] The brain's response to stress and a person's personality type may also be causal factors.[184] Experiencing symptoms of depression and Acute Stress Disorder after a trauma may further increase a person's risk of developing PTSD,[185] as well as experiencing a major negative life event after a disaster occurs.[186] Additionally, women are more likely to develop PTSD than men.[187]

If a person experiences constant exposure to traumatic or stressful circumstances, such as being in a combat situation, or working as a first responder who, because of the nature of their job, must face regular exposure to traumatic situations is also, understandably, at higher risk. These traumatic situations may include witnessing horrifying incidents, failing to help someone, seeing a peer, partner, or child die, or being in a situation that gravely endangers their own life.[188] They also may deal with fires, natural disasters, serious injuries, or dead bodies. Those who arrive first at the scene and those who stay the longest may experience the greatest negative impact on their mental health.[189] We should not leave out here 911 dispatchers who also experience a lot of trauma by fielding disturbing calls and generally at a fast pace.

PTSD is a widespread problem. To help you dig deeper, we've provided several assessments below. One test focuses on general PTSD and how to measure it. The second assessment is directly meant for Veterans and military personnel.

1) **The PTSD Checklist for DSM-5**[190] is meant to assess PTSD for the general population. It is a general guide for PTSD indicators.
2) **The PCL-M**[191] is an assessment for veterans and military personnel.

The PTSD Checklist for DSM-5

DIRECTIONS: Below is a list of problems that people sometimes have in response to a very stressful experience. Please read each problem carefully and then check one of the boxes to the right to indicate how much you have been bothered by that problem in the past month.

	Not at all	A little bit	Moderately	Quite a bit	Extremely
1. Repeated, disturbing, and unwanted memories of the stressful experience?					
2. Suddenly feeling or acting as if the stressful experience were actually happening again (as if you were actually back there reliving it)?					
3. Feeling very upset when something reminded you of the stressful experience?					
4. Having strong physical reactions when something reminded you of the stressful experience (for example, heart pounding, trouble breathing, sweating)?					
5. Avoiding memories, thoughts, or feelings related to the stressful experience?					

6. Avoiding external reminders of the stressful experience (for example, people, places, conversations, activities or situations?)					
7. Trouble remembering important parts of the stressful experience?					
8. Having strong negative beliefs about yourself, other people, or the world (having thoughts such as: I am bad, there is something seriously wrong with me, no one can be trusted, the world is completely dangerous?)					
9. Blaming yourself or something else for the stressful experience or what happened after it?					
10. Having strong negative feelings such as fear, horror, anger, guilt or shame?					
11. Loss of interest in activities that you used to enjoy?					
12. Feeling distant or cut off from other people?					
13. Trouble experiencing positive feelings (for example, being unable to feel happiness or have loving feelings for people close to you)?					
14. Irritable behavior, angry outbursts, or acting aggressively?					
15. Taking too many risks or doing things that could cause you harm?					
16. Being super alert or watchful or on guard?					
17. Feeling jumpy or easily startled?					
18. Having difficulty concentrating?					
19. Trouble falling or staying asleep?					

SCORING: For every answer, note how many points it is worth according to the following:

0 = **Not at all** bothered
1 = **A little bit** bothered
2 = **Moderately** bothered
3 = **Quite a bit** bothered
4 = **Extremely** bothered

Scoring ranges from **0 to 76 points.**

Write your scores in the table below. Then add them up to get your total and write it in the last row of the table.

Questions #1-10	Your Score	Questions #11-19	Your Score
#1		#11	
#2		#12	
#3		#13	
#4		#14	
#5		#15	
#6		#16	
#7		#17	
#8		#18	
#9		#19	
#10		TOTAL	

INTERPRETATION: The higher you score, the higher the chance of PTSD.

THE PCL-M: ASSESSMENT FOR VETERANS AND MILITARY PERSONNEL

DIRECTIONS: Below is a list of problems and complaints that veterans sometimes have in response to stressful military experiences. Please read each one carefully then check one of the boxes to the right to indicate how much you have been bothered by that problem in the past month.

	Not at all	A little bit	Moderately	Quite a bit	Extremely
1. Repeated, disturbing memories, thoughts or images of a stressful military experience?					
2. Repeated, disturbing dreams of a stressful military experience?					
3. Suddenly acting or feeling as if a stressful military experience were happening again (as if you were reliving it)?					
4. Feeling very upset when something reminds you of a stressful military experience?					
5. Having physical reactions (e.g., heart pounding, trouble breathing, sweating) when something reminds you of a stressful military experience?					
6. Avoiding thinking about or talking about a stressful military experience or avoiding having feelings related to it?					
7. Avoiding activities or situations because they remind you of a stressful military experience?					
8. Trouble remembering important parts of a stressful military experience?					

9. Loss of interest in activities you used to enjoy?					
10. Feeling distant or cut off from other people?					
11. Feeling emotionally numb or unable to have loving feelings for those close to you?					
12. Feeling as if your future will somehow be cut short?					
13. Trouble falling or staying asleep?					
14. Feeling irritable or having angry outbursts?					
15. Having difficulty concentrating?					
16. Being super alert or watchful or on guard					
17. Feeling jumpy or easily startled?					

SCORING: For every answer, note how many points it is worth according to the following:

1 = **Not at all** bothered
2 = **A little bit** bothered
3 = **Moderately** bothered
4 = **Quite a bit** bothered
5 = **Extremely** bothered

Scoring ranges from **17 to 85 points.**

Write your scores in the table below. Then add them up to get your total and write it in the last row of the table.

Questions #1-9	Your Score	Questions #10-17	Your Score
#1		#10	
#2		#11	
#3		#12	
#4		#13	
#5		#14	
#6		#15	
#7		#16	
#8		#17	
#9		TOTAL	

INTERPRETATION: The higher you score, the higher the chance of PTSD.

What Will Help You

PTSD can seem like an impossible condition to conquer because it is triggered by everyday events. *It is not impossible to manage.*

If you're suffering from PTSD:

- **Seek therapy.** Therapy has several goals when dealing with PTSD and they include learning how to address and manage symptoms, improving self-esteem, and coping with your past. Remember, treating PTSD soon after the traumatic event is the best way to prevent lingering symptoms.
  - o **Exposure therapy.** One method of healing is actually slowly being exposed to triggers. This helps people face their trauma head on but in a safe environment surrounded by a professional. This method of therapy can be very effective.
- **Learn your triggers.** Triggers are certain smells, sounds, people, situations, ect, that can bring on a memory related to the event. A part of managing PTSD can be learning what triggers you, and learning how to either avoid those triggers and how to effectively cope with them.
- **Have a plan in place.** Because avoiding triggers all the time isn't realistic, it's best to have a plan in place in case you do start to have a PTSD attack. Take deep breaths, find a calm place to sit down, drink water, tell someone. Have a list of emergency numbers of people you can call to help you through the attack.
- **Join a support group.** If therapy isn't for you, there are support groups that you can become involved with that will allow you to get help. Creating this sense of community is a great way to connect with others who know what you're going through and can provide emotional support.

If someone you know is suffering from PTSD, here's a list of things that you can do to help them through this trying time and make their future better:

- **Show them you are there for them.** Listening to them and telling them that you support them is crucial in allowing someone to heal. This builds a sense of emotional backing and understanding.
- **Physically be there for them.** During an attack, if they need someone around them, be a physical grounding presence. Encourage them to spend time with loved ones who can help them stay positive and uplifted.
- **Educate yourself.** Each person suffers with PTSD for different reasons and the symptoms may manifest themselves differently. Providing psychoeducation to a friend or loved one or patient goes a long way towards healing.

Please note: It is difficult for veterans and first responders to acknowledge they may have a problem to either loved ones or a professional who can help them. The culture around both the military and first responder professions is personal sacrifice in the name of community safety. The price tag – one's health.

Many tell me they fear there's still a stigma around receiving mental health services. They're afraid of being deemed weak and do not want to be stereotyped or treated differently in their workplace (or by family and friends), if people find out they're receiving treatment. You need to know 1) you're not alone and 2) your life can improve for the better if you get help. The more we talk about mental health and increase awareness, the more we reduce the stigma.

For a full list of resources, please see our list in the back of the book.

CHAPTER 18: ON AGING, TEST FOR VITALITY & YOUR RISK FOR ALZHEIMER'S

Many people are concerned that their elderly parent, spouse, sibling or friend is starting to show signs of depression, dementia, or what they fear the most – Alzheimer's disease. This can be a highly stressful time for caregivers, loved ones *and* the person showing signs of aging.

For this chapter we wanted to provide you two assessments and one checklist that will help you or a loved one determine how an elderly person is functioning emotionally and cognitively. The assessments we picked give people a baseline from which to work from. We suggest you discuss the results with your healthcare provider.

1) **The Zest for Life Test**[192] (originally called the Life Satisfaction Index), is specifically designed for senior citizens and highly regarded as a measure of overall psychological well-being. This assessment essentially looks at whether the senior in your life is suffering from clinical depression. If you are the person taking the test, taking it along with a trusted friend or partner may be very helpful.

2) **Checklist of Alzheimer's Disease: 7 Warning Signs.** Please note that even the presence of any or all these symptoms is not a sure indicator of Alzheimer's disease.

3) A short **Questionnaire on Cognitive Decline in the Elderly**[193] (Short 1QCODE) which will help you determine if someone you know has declined mentally over the last ten years. It's important, when trying to determine if someone is starting to decline mentally, to remember what that person was like ten years ago compared to now.

Mental Health and the Elderly: A National Concern

In 2015, senior citizens accounted for 14.9 percent (47.8 million) of the American population.[194] By 2035, there will be 78 million Americans over the age 65,[195] and studies show that seniors are at a greater risk of mental health problems than younger people. Roughly twenty percent of senior citizens over the age of 55 have a mental illness and could benefit from treatment.[196] In fact, suicide rates are highest among men over the age of 65[197] and, overall, the elderly account for eighteen percent of suicide deaths.[198]

Many elderly people feel ashamed and do not speak up about their mental health symptoms. Often, the patients, their loved ones and friends, and even their own doctors fail to recognize the signs of mental illness in older people. We, as a society, tend to blame the symptoms of "old age" when we watch an elderly loved one mentally slipping and we tend to think nothing can be done to alleviate the problem. This is simply not true.

Mental Health & the Elderly: A National Concern

In 2015, senior citizens accounted for 14.9 percent (47.8 million) of the American population. By 2035, there will be 78 million Americans over the age 65, and studies show that seniors are at a greater risk of mental health problems than younger people. Roughly twenty percent of senior citizens over the age of 55 have a mental illness and could benefit from treatment. In fact, suicide rates are highest among men over the age of 65 and, overall, the elderly account for eighteen percent of suicide deaths.

Many elderly people feel ashamed and do not speak up about their mental health symptoms. Often, the patients, their loved ones and friends, and even their own doctors fail to recognize the signs of mental illness in older people. We, as a society, tend to blame the symptoms of "old age" when we watch an elderly loved one mentally slipping and we tend to think nothing can be done to alleviate the problem. This is simply not true. There are various treatments and medications on the market that can help lift depression, quell anxiety and slow down the progression of disease.

It's worth reminding our readers that a full battery of diagnostic tests should always be done on anyone complaining of mental health symptoms or if they're showing signs of dementia. Conditions like thyroid disease, Parkinson's and certain types of cancers – for example – should always be ruled out first.

THE "ZEST FOR LIFE" TEST

DIRECTIONS: Please read each statement on the list.
- If you agree with it, circle "AGREE."
- If you do not agree with a statement, circle "DISAGREE."
- If you are not sure one way or another, circle "UNSURE".

1. As I grow older, things seem better than I thought they would be.	AGREE	DISAGREE	UNSURE
2. I have gotten more breaks in life than most of the people I know.	AGREE	DISAGREE	UNSURE
3. This is the dreariest time of my life.	AGREE	DISAGREE	UNSURE
4. I am just as happy as when I was younger.	AGREE	DISAGREE	UNSURE
5. My life could be happier than it is now.	AGREE	DISAGREE	UNSURE
6. These are the best years of my life so far.	AGREE	DISAGREE	UNSURE
7. Most of the things I do are boring and monotonous.	AGREE	DISAGREE	UNSURE
8. I expect some interesting and pleasant things to happen to me in the future.	AGREE	DISAGREE	UNSURE
9. I feel old and somewhat tired.	AGREE	DISAGREE	UNSURE
10. The things I do are as interesting to me as they ever were.	AGREE	DISAGREE	UNSURE

11. As I look back on my life so far,
    I am fairly well satisfied.   AGREE   DISAGREE   UNSURE

12. I would not change my past life even if I could.   AGREE   DISAGREE   UNSURE

13. Compared to other people my age,
    I make a good appearance.   AGREE   DISAGREE   UNSURE

14. I have made plans for things I'll be
    doing a month or a year from now.   AGREE   DISAGREE   UNSURE

15. When I think back over my life, I didn't
    get most of the important things I wanted.   AGREE   DISAGREE   UNSURE

16. Compared to other people, I get down
    in the dumps too often.   AGREE   DISAGREE   UNSURE

17. I've gotten pretty much what I expected
    out of life.   AGREE   DISAGREE   UNSURE

18. In spite of what people say, the lot of the average
    person is getting worse, not better.   AGREE   DISAGREE   UNSURE

SCORING: The questions were presented at random. We scrambled them so that you wouldn't know which categories you were marking, and to make you less self-conscious of your choices. The 18 test items that you have just checked off represent four categories of life satisfaction: *mood, zest for life, agreement between desired and achieved goals,* and *resolve and fortitude.* Each of these categories measures a different quality, and when taken together as a whole they are a measure of the fifth category, self-concept.

The following is a key to the test categories and how to score your answers. Note that the questions are now arranged to fit into the appropriate categories.

CATEGORY	QUESTION	HOW TO SCORE	SCORE
I. Mood	3	A. If you answer *Disagree,* Score 1 point.	
	4	B. If you answer *Agree,* Score 1 point.	
	5	C. If you answer *Disagree,* Score 1 point.	
	6	D. If you answer *Agree,* Score 1 point.	
	7	E. If you answer *Disagree,* Score 1 point.	
	16	F. If you answer *Disagree,* Score 1 point.	

II. Zest for Life	1	G. If you answer *Agree*, Score 1 point.	
	8	H. If you answer *Agree*, Score 1 point.	
	9	I. If you answer *Disagree*, Score 1 point.	
	10	J. If you answer *Agree*, Score 1 point.	
	13	K. If you answer *Agree*, Score 1 point.	
	14	L. If you answer *Agree*, Score 1 point.	
III. Desires Vs. Achievements	11	M. If you answer *Agree*, Score 1 point.	
	12	N. If you answer *Agree*, Score 1 point.	
	17	O. If you answer *Agree*, Score 1 point.	
IV. Resolve & Fortitude	2	P. If you answer *Agree*, Score 1 point.	
	15	Q. If you answer *Disagree*, Score 1 point.	
	18	R. If you answer *Disagree*, Score 1 point.	
V. Self-Concept = Total Score (Questions 1-18 combined)			
		TOTAL	

INTERPRETATION: To understand your total score, refer to the table below.

Point Scores	Explanation
15-18	You're in great shape. Keep doing what you're doing.
10-14	You're in pretty good shape overall. Continue to concentrate on your strengths.
5-9	You may be having difficulties in "aging gracefully," and you may need additional help and support from others.
0-4	You may be at risk both physically and emotionally. You may need to seek informal and professional help for medical support and emotional assistance.

How To Interpret Each Category

There are no exact scores for these categories. Please rate yourself along with a spectrum from high to low.

Category I measures mood tone. This refers to your basic mood. Are you generally happy and optimistic? Do you use positive terms when referring to people and things? Do you take pleasure in life or are you generally depressed, lonely, or blue? Are you often bitter, irritable, or angry?

Category II measures your zest for life versus apathy. This refers to your enthusiasm of response to life and your degree of involvement with activities, persons, or ideas. It doesn't matter whether you're involved alone or with others, whether these are socially approved activities, or whether they give you status. A person who loves to sit at home and knit rates just as high as a person who loves to get out and meet people; what counts is simply your passion. Lower ratings are given for apathy and boredom and involvement in meaningless activities.

Category III measures agreement between your desired and achieved goals. This refers to the degree to which you feel you have achieved your goals in life, whatever they may be. What counts is feeling you've accomplished whatever you think is important. High ratings go not only to someone who says, "I've managed to keep out of jail," but also to someone who says, "I've managed to send all of my kids to college." Lower ratings go to individuals who feel they have missed most of their opportunities or who say, "I've never been suited to my work." Also low on the spectrum are those who want to be "loved" but merely feel "approved of." (Note: Regret for your lack of education is not considered significant, because it is unfortunately a universal response of all people except those who have attained high social status.)

Category IV measures personal resolve and fortitude. This refers to the extent to which you accept personal responsibility for your life. The opposite would be to feel resigned, to merely condone, or to passively accept what life has brought you. Do you accept your life as meaningful and inevitable? Are you relatively unafraid of death? Whether or not you have been a person of high initiative, do you accept resolutely and positively what life has brought you, or not? A person who felt life was a series of hard knocks but stood up to them would get a high rating. Lower ratings would include people who blame themselves too much and those who place blame on others or the world for their own failures and disappointments.

Category V is the measure of self-concept. Your total score is overall measure of your life satisfaction and includes all of the previous four categories. This refers to your concept of yourself– your physical as well as your psychological and social attributes. You might say this is a combination of your self-acceptance, your self-identity, and your self-confidence. High ratings usually go to those who are concerned with grooming and appearance, who think of themselves as wise or mellow, who are comfortable in giving advice to others, who are proud of their accomplishments, who feel important to someone else. Lower rating are scored by those who feel "old", weak, sick, or incompetent; those who feel themselves to be a burden to others; and those who speak disparagingly of themselves or of older people in general.

ARE YOU AT RISK FOR ALZHEIMER'S?

Alzheimer's disease, a form of dementia, is a progressive neurodegenerative disorder of the brain that can lead to a decline in mental function severe enough to disrupt daily life. Persons with this illness may experience confusion, memory loss, personality and behavioral changes, impaired judgment, difficulty finding words, finishing thoughts, or following directions. Early signs may often go unnoticed and the progression and its severity can vary. Eventually, this disease leaves its victims unable to care for themselves.

Quick STATS

- Alzheimer's disease impacts people mostly over the age of 65, but can strike as early as in the forties and fifties[199]
- It is the 6th leading cause of death in the US[200]
- 1 in 3 senior citizens over the age of 85 die with Alzheimer's[201]

- 5.8 million Americans develop it a year[202]
- Women are more likely to develop this disease[203]
- Only 1 in 4 people are ever properly diagnosed[204]
- By 2050, it is believed that there will be roughly 16 million Americans living with Alzheimer's[205]

Forgetfulness, When It's a Symptom vs. When It's a Problem

Having one or more of these symptoms is not a sure sign of Alzheimer's disease. One of the reasons that so few people are properly diagnosed with Alzheimer's is because many people assume these symptoms are just natural signs of aging. The opposite is also true; forgetfulness isn't always the first sign of Alzheimer's disease. Most often a person with Alzheimer's disease first develops abrupt and uncharacteristic mood swings. We hope the following charts will help you to distinguish the normal signs of aging from the more troubling symptoms.

The information presented in this chapter is not intended to scare you but to keep you up to date; knowledge can go a long way in dispelling fears. Anyone who suspects that a loved one may be developing Alzheimer's disease should not jump to conclusions too quickly. Many other illnesses or conditions mimic it such as depression, alcoholism, thyroid disease, anemia, Huntington's and Creutfeld-Jakob disease, diabetes and boredom. Physicians must rule out treatable conditions, before making a correct diagnosis, which typically involves physical and neurological exams.[206]

*** As of the publication of this book new A.D. studies are currently underway at research hospitals around the world, like Bringham and Women's Hospital in Boston, MA. They are hoping to diagnose certain types of A.D. with a simple blood test somewhere in the near future.[207]

An Alzheimer's Disease Comparison Table

Young Adult to Retirement	Elderly Person	Person with Alzheimer's
Is seldom forgetful	Forgets part of an experience (e.g., can remember eating but doesn't remember what fruit was served at lunch)	Often forgets entire experiences (e.g., may not remember eating and demands a meal)
Remembers later	Often remembers later	Rarely remembers later
Acknowledges memory lapses lightly	Acknowledges lapses readily, often with a request for help in recalling information	Acknowledges lapses grudgingly after initial denial and attempts to compensate for lapse
Maintains skills, such as reading words or music	Skills usually remain intact	Skills deteriorate
Follows written or spoken directions easily	Usually able to follow directions	Increasingly unable to follow directions
Can use notes or reminders	Usually able to use notes or reminders	Increasingly unable to use notes or reminders
Can care for self	Usually able to care for self	Increasingly unable to care for self

CHECKLIST OF ALZHEIMER'S DISEASE SYMPTOMS: 7 WARNING SIGNS

*Please note that even the presence of any or all these symptoms is not a sure indicator of Alzheimer's disease.[208]

- ☐ Loss of short-term memory occurs; a person can't learn new information.
- ☐ Loss of long-term memory occurs; a person can't remember personal information, such as birthplace or occupation.
- ☐ Judgement is impaired.
- ☐ Aphasia develops; a person can't recall words or understand the meaning of common words.
- ☐ Apraxia develops; a person loses control over his or her muscles and can't, for example, button shirts or operate zippers.
- ☐ Loss of spatial abilities; a person can't assemble blocks, arrange sticks in a certain order, or copy a three-dimensional figure.
- ☐ Personality changes; a person may become unusually angry, irritable, quiet, or confused.

The Informant Questionnaire on Cognitive Decline in the Elderly

DIRECTIONS: Below are situations where this person has to use his / her memory or intelligence and we want you to indicate whether this has improved stayed the same or it's gotten worse over the past ten years. So for example is this person always forgot where he / she had left things and he/she still does then this would be considered "Hasn't changed much." Please indicate the changed you have observed by circling the appropriate answer.

Compared with 10 years ago how is this person at:

1. Remembering things about family and friends e.g. occupations, birthdays, addresses	Much improved	A bit improved	Not much change	A bit worse	Much worse
2. Remembering things that have happened recently	Much improved	A bit improved	Not much change	A bit worse	Much worse
3. Recalling conversations a few days later	Much improved	A bit improved	Not much change	A bit worse	Much worse
4. Remembering his/her address and telephone number	Much improved	A bit improved	Not much change	A bit worse	Much worse
5. Remembering what day and month it is	Much improved	A bit improved	Not much change	A bit worse	Much worse
6. Remembering where things are usually kept	Much improved	A bit improved	Not much change	A bit worse	Much worse
7. Remembering where to find things which have been put in a different place from usual	Much improved	A bit improved	Not much change	A bit worse	Much worse
8. Knowing how to work familiar machines around the house	Much improved	A bit improved	Not much change	A bit worse	Much worse
9. Learning to use a new gadget or machine around the house	Much improved	A bit improved	Not much change	A bit worse	Much worse
10. Learning new things in general	Much improved	A bit improved	Not much change	A bit worse	Much worse
11. Following a story in a book or on TV	Much improved	A bit improved	Not much change	A bit worse	Much worse

12. Making decisions on everyday matters	Much improved	A bit improved	Not much change	A bit worse	Much worse
13. Handling money for shopping	Much improved	A bit improved	Not much change	A bit worse	Much worse
14. Handling financial matters e.g. the pension, dealing with the bank	Much improved	A bit improved	Not much change	A bit worse	Much worse
15. Handling other everyday arithmetic problems e.g. knowing how much food to buy, knowing how long between visits from family or friends	Much improved	A bit improved	Not much change	A bit worse	Much worse
16. Using his/her intelligence to understand what's going on and to reason things through	Much improved	A bit improved	Not much change	A bit worse	Much worse

SCORING: Assign scores to each of the items as follows:

1 = Much improved
2 = A bit improved
3 = Not much change
4 = A bit worse
5 = Much worse

Write your scores in the table below. Then, add them up according to how many of each category you circled.

Questions #1-8	Your Score	Questions #9-16	Your Score
#1		#9	
#2		#10	
#3		#11	
#4		#12	
#5		#13	
#6		#14	
#7		#15	
#8		#16	
		Much Improved TOTAL	
		A Bit Improved TOTAL	
		Not Much Change TOTAL	
		A Bit Worse TOTAL	
		Much Worse TOTAL	

INTERPRETATION: Look to see where the person you tested fell on the scale. Were your scores much improved or much worse? These reflections are meant to help you facilitate a conversation between extended family members and medical providers who should hear your concerns about your or your loved one's mental health.

What Will Help You

Seek medical attention. If you're concerned about yourself or a loved one, your first step is to find a physician who knows and understands the elderly population. This doctor could be a primary care physician, a neurologist, or a psychiatrist. While Alzheimer's disease is irreversible, there are medications and treatments that can help.

Socializing. Join community classes and find people in your area with common interests. Attend readings at bookstores or go to the theater/movies with friends. Avoiding social isolation has serious health benefits.

Sleep. It may seem obvious, but whether you're fourteen or eighty-four, sleep is crucial to a healthy brain.

Diet and health. This should go without saying but taking care of your health, in general, and eating right is the best way to stay healthy. If you smoke, try quitting or even cut back on the number of alcoholic drinks you have a week.

Reading. Read any kind of material that engages you and enlivens your mind. From the news to a novel, there are a plethora of sources that engage your mind and help keep you involved with the world.

Travel. Interesting companions and new sights, sounds, and sensations keep your mind alive. It's also a great way to connect with new people.

Puzzles and games. From crosswords, jigsaws, chess, bridge (or other card games) and board games, puzzles keep your mind engaged and open to learning more. They can even strengthen your vocabulary and have shown to improve the memory muscle. Even very simple games that involve cognitive function can help. If you or your loved one has vision problems, consider getting puzzles with large pieces.

New activities. It could be sewing, photography or gardening, anything that encourages you to focus on something outside of your normal routine sharpens your intellect.

*** For caregivers: don't take what a patient who is suffering with memory loss personally; remain calm, don't argue with them (it is not something within their control, and they may sometimes be as frustrated or as lost as you may be), try accepting their behavior as part of the disease, and seek help so you can avoid caregiver burnout.

Chapter 19: The Importance of a Spiritual Intake

Being "religious" or choosing a religious affiliation isn't as important as it once was to many people. In 2016, 39% of those polled between the ages of 18 and 29 have no religious affiliation in America.[209] However, from my extensive experience, I've realized there's an extremely positive connection between spirituality and mental health. This is not news, per se.

According to researchers at Duke University and the Department of Medicine at King Abdulaziz University in 2012 who complied data from various sources, thirteen studies conducted since the 1960s have found an advantageous correlation between religion/spirituality and mental health. And, thirty-nine studies show faster healing time from depression as well as a lower chance of becoming depressed when someone has religion to rely on.[210] These studies are just a small sampling of many that reinforce the idea that being religious or spiritual is an effective coping mechanism for people.

In short, it helps to have some sort of belief system to provide guidance, comfort and ballast against the chaos that exists outside of us, and the chaos that inherently exists inside our own hearts and minds. But, *by no means* do you need a spiritual beliefs system in order to function at a high level. Spiritual practices and beliefs resonate with some and not with others. So many of the symptoms I've helped people deal with stem from ambiguous loss, spiritual pain and grief. It's hard to tackle these things in the absence of spiritual work.

Here are the assessments you'll find in this chapter:

For this chapter, we thought it would be helpful provide you with asessments that help you determine the state of your spiritual health. These assessments will get you thinking more deeply about your spiritual health. They are:

1) **Spiritual Wellness Assessment.**[211] This assessment is meant to test how balanced you are spiritually. The spiritual dimension of wellness that you determine in this assessment is about the meaning and purpose that you have in your life.
1) **Functional Assessment of Chronic Illness Therapy – Spiritual Well-Being (FACIT-SP).**[212] Originally developed for people with chronic illnesses, this assessment is a modified version for people who are not ill. You will be provided a series of statements that many people have deemed to be important, and asked to rate how important each one is to you.

The importance of soul work?

When a person is dealing with an immediately painful situation, they have a limited capacity to talk about larger life questions. Painful problems take up time. Persistent symptoms take up energy – more than we think. It isn't until those issues are partially or fully resolved that patients naturally start moving into psycho-spiritual therapy.

Nell always knows when a patient is entering into this last phase of treatment—and they're almost ready to end their sessions with her—because they start asking existential questions like, "*How do you think*

I can connect more deeply with God" or *"how do I create a more meaningful life?"* They speak of spiritual matters instead of small practical to-do lists. They're no longer consumed on a daily basis by the debilitating symptoms that once plagued them when they first came into her office. They feel calm, seen, unburdened and heard. They feel we've done a good job of "unpacking their wounds." They're now coping and functioning at a higher level which ultimately leaves us room to discuss topics like – happiness, fulfillment and peace.

Spirituality vs. Religion

Spirituality and religion may sometimes be used interchangeably, but they are not one and the same. Spirituality is personal and private. It is unique to the individual, directly based on personal experience and can incorporate any number of beliefs, values, attitudes, and practices concerning oneself and the universe. Beliefs and practices can vary widely based on the person.

Organized religion, on the other hand, is dogmatic, with set beliefs, values, leaders, and rituals that dictate how the religion should be followed. There may be some variations in schools of thought, beliefs, leaders, and practices (which may be regarded as sects if they have a large enough following), but there will be major core tenants of the religion that will be believed and followed by all in order to be considered a believer of that religion.

You can be both religious and spiritual. If you're not religious, know you can be spiritual but not religious. You don't need to ascribe to a particular religion or any religion at all to assess your spiritual health (or have good spiritual health). This chapter is for everyone, regardless of religious differences.

Quick Stats:

- In the wake of 9/11, 90% of Americans turned to religion to help them manage the stress.[213]
- 10% of people reported that their respective religion was less important to them after 9/11, especially those who suffered a loss after the tragedy.[214]
- 67% of people say that during their struggle with mental help, their church has shown support.[215]
- In 2017, 27% of Americans consider themselves to be spiritual but not religious.[216]
- 70% of people older than 65 believe in God, while only 51% of people 18-29 years old do.[217]
- 12% of the American population attends church regularly.[218]
- 38% of adults attend a religious service of any denomination and religion weekly.[219]

A Grasp on Death

Through the 20,000+ hour of life stories I've listened to, I've come to realize people are largely driven by their fear of death. We fear death in the three following ways (although some only fear one or two of these ways):

1) We fear how we will die. *What will it feel like? Will I be in pain? Will it be quick or a long drawn out illness?*
2) We fear what's on the other side of death. *Is there a heaven? A purgatory? A hell? Will it be beautiful or will I fall into a black endless hole for eternity?*
3) We fear we won't accomplish all we were meant to before we die. *What will happen to me if I don't make all my dreams come true? How sad will I be if I run out of time?*

Those who have grappled with and then come to terms with some or all of these questions, in my humble opinion, seem to have a calmer sense about them. They're filled with less spiritual angst and, as mentioned above, cope well with every day stress and the grief that surfaces throughout our days.

<u>What is a spiritual crisis?</u>

A spiritual crisis, which also may be called a spiritual emergency or transpersonal crisis, occurs when a person undergoes a change or shift (or multiple changes) of their values, attitudes, beliefs, purpose, or goals as a result of a recent spiritual experience.[220] It is regarded as an identity crisis, and it can occur spontaneously or intentionally.[221]

Experiences that may prompt a spiritual crisis include a near-death experience, an out-of-body experience, a paranormal encounter, an existential crisis, questioning or weakening faith, passionate spiritual or religious practice or devotion, loss of a loved one, thoughts of one's own or a loved one's morality, usage of psychoactive substances, trauma, distress, illness, or some other spiritual, religious, or overwhelming life event.[222]

During this time, the person in crisis may experience different thoughts or perceptions of reality, states of consciousness, intense emotions, visions, somatization (physical reactions of the body in response to the crisis), or other psychological effects that are out of the ordinary. They may be afraid, anxious, or confused (especially if their experiences have occurred suddenly), and they may have difficulty coping with their day-to-day life and responsibilities.[223]

Emerging from a spiritual crisis (which also may be called a spiritual emergence, awakening, or transformation), makes a person likely to have stronger clarity, purpose, meaning, beliefs, attitudes, and values than before. They may be more interested in social, economic, ecological, and health issues,[224] and have a greater worldview.[225] They may feel stronger, more confident, more connected to others or the universe, and liberated after their experience, regarding the crisis as a time for personal development.[226]

Now that you understand more about spirituality and what a spiritual crisis is, take the *Spiritual Wellness Assessment* assessment below.

Spiritual Wellness Assessment

DIRECTIONS: Read each statement carefully and respond honestly by checking the most appropriate box for each statement.

	Almost Always	Sometimes	Very Seldom
1. I feel comfortable and at ease with my spiritual life.			
2. There is a direct relationship between my personal values and daily actions.			
3. When I get depressed or frustrated, my spiritual beliefs and values give me direction.			
4. Prayer, meditation, and/or quiet personal reflection is/are important in my life.			
5. Life is meaningful to me, and I feel a purpose in my life.			
6. I am able to speak comfortably about my personal values and beliefs.			

Continue

7. I am consistently striving to grow spiritually and I see it as a lifelong process.			
8. I am tolerant of and try to learn about others' beliefs and values.			
9. I have a strong sense of life optimism and use my thoughts and attitudes in life-affirming ways.			
10. I appreciate the natural forces that exist in the universe.			

SCORING: Note your scores for each of your responses according to the following:

2 = Almost always

1 = Sometimes

0 = Very seldom

Write down your scores in the table below. Then add up all your scores and write your total in the last row.

Statement	Your Score
#1	
#2	
#3	
#4	
#5	
#6	
#7	
#8	
#9	
#10	
TOTAL	

INTERPRETATION: Your total score indicates how you're doing with your Spiritual Wellness Dimension.

If you have a score between 15 and 20 points, you have excellent strength in this dimension.

If you have a score between 9 and 14 points, there is room for improvement. Look again at the items in which you scored 1 or 0. What changes can you make to improve your score?

If you have a score between 0 and 8 points, this dimension needs a lot of work. Look again at this dimension and challenge yourself to begin making small steps towards growth here. Remember: The goal is balanced wellness.

What Will Help You

Here are some tips we've compiled to help you strengthen your spiritual health or overcome a spiritual crisis.

Know your society and support system, and educate those around you. Understand that you may feel especially confused and misunderstood if you live in a culture, society, or family where spiritual crises and awakenings are not well received, or information regarding them is lacking. Some cultures have a greater spiritual disconnection than others. Western medicine and medical professionals have not traditionally recognized spiritual crises.[227] Family and friends may think you are going crazy, and you may question your sanity as well. Know what you're going through is natural and happens to many. You are not alone. It may help to educate them on what you are going through so that they can be there for you and support you.

Reach out for professional help. Organizations such as the Spiritual Emergence Network have professionals who have dealt with spiritual emergencies before and know what you are going through. They are available to talk to you and help you work through your crisis. Talking to someone early on about your spiritual experiences is important.[228] Any professional you see or talk to should help you normalize and process what you've gone through.[229]

Reflect on your spiritual experience. You can learn a lot from it, perhaps more than you initially might think. Reflect on your journey and think about what you have learned so far, and what you can continue to learn.

Psychospiritual Healing and Holistic Treatments. This healing addresses the inner being, working with our energies and life force.[230] Consider working with a psychospiritual healer. Other holistic treatments can include practicing mindfulness and awareness, engaging in simple physical activity, being outside, eating well, focusing on your breathing, simplifying your life and reducing overstimulation, learning about energy management, receiving reiki, meditating, journaling, and practicing yoga.[231] You may also want to consider ecclesial or spiritually euphoric experiences. All of these should help you overcome and emerge from your spiritual crisis.

PART IV:

GETTING THE HELP YOU NEED AND DESERVE

Part IV: Getting The Help You Need and Deserve

Now that you've tested yourself and read up on some of the most common mental health problems we face, it's time to dig in and do the work to heal yourself, or help someone you care about heal themselves. At the end of each chapter we provided you with a snapshot of things you can do immediately that will alleviate some of your symptoms, but here is a more in depth discussion of the treatment process and options.

Where Do I Go for Help and What Should I Expect?

If you decide to seek help, it's important to know where to go and what to expect.

Hotlines. There are hotlines like the National Suicide Prevention Hotline at your disposal where you will most likely speak to a trained crisis worker or volunteer. While on the phone, the worker is there to listen, provide support, and direct you to local resources. If you are uncomfortable or unable to speak on the phone, there are online chat or text hotlines you can turn to as well. **See the Appendix at the back of this book for a full list of hotlines.**

Therapy. When considering therapy, it's crucial to consider the following: do you need someone with specific expertise? Would a general therapist suffice? What are their qualifications? How much are you willing to pay per session? Does your insurance cover the cost? Luckily, most of this information can be found through a few simple Google searches for therapists in your area, or you may have a friend of a family member that can recommend someone good for you to see.

Keep in mind that the first person you talk to may not be the best person for you. Sometimes, you simply don't mesh with a therapist on a personal level or you feel their area of expertise doesn't align with the type of help you need. *Having a good repour with your therapist is a must.* It's perfectly acceptable to go to someone else if you're not getting "a good vibe." You should feel comfortable talking with your therapist and that you're receiving the right approach to treatment depending on your treatment goals. I always suggest, if you're considering therapy, to look into all your options and don't wait too long – your symptoms will only get worse.

Initial therapy phone interview. Introduce yourself and explain that you are considering therapy. Ask them if they have time to answer a few questions. If they don't, find a time convenient for both of you for a phone meeting. During the conversation, you might want to ask the following: What are your qualifications and experience or training? What is the fee and is insurance accepted? (If you cannot afford the fee, ask them if they offer a 'sliding scale fee.') Is there a charge for initial consultation? What types of therapy are used at the facility? What hours are available for an appointment?

A phone interview will help you select a therapist you think you could work with. After speaking with several therapists, reflect on how you feel about each of them. Did they answer your questions clearly? Do you feel comfortable with them? Are they supportive? Trust your gut instinct – you're picking someone whom you will be speaking to about confidential matters so you want to feel as comfortable with them as possible.

Medication. As a holistic psychotherapist, Nell softly encourages her patients to try alternative treatments before they take medication to control their unwanted mental health symptoms. If a patient feels like medication might be a useful part of their treatment plan, they should speak with their primary care provider or a prescribing psychiatrist.

Before deciding on medication, consider the following: how will this medication help me? What's the right dosage for me? What are the side effects? What's the cost? Will this medication interfere with any other medication I am taking, or vice versa? How soon should I feel a difference? Be aware that you might have to try a few different medications or adjust your dosage several times before you figure out what works best for you. It can take a few weeks to see improvements. You may also experience side effects before you feel like the medication is working. Patience is key.

If you do use medication as a treatment option, it's best taken in conjunction with talk therapy. You should also be aware that taking medication can increase suicidal ideation. For example, medication can activate someone who is severely depressed. Before medication they may be too lethargic to hurt themselves, post-medication they may have more energy to carry out their plan.[232]

Rehab. The intake process begins with a phone call. You or your healthcare advocate and the prospective facility need to discuss, before admission, if that particular center is a good fit for you. On the first day of rehab, a counselor at the clinic will ask you everything they can about your addiction or disease to help them better understand what they need to do to help you. You will talk about what goals you wish to accomplish and how to reach them, as well as best treatment methods. From there, the center will help you get comfortable in the new environment and begin a detox, if necessary. Since building a routine is instrumental in recovery, many rehab centers fill their patients day with activities such as group therapy, individual sessions and social time.

Self-Help Material. Like this book, there are many other self-help resources available to you. There are many national and international organizations, websites, online and offline support groups, and books dedicated to helping people overcome their illnesses and stressors that improve a person's well-being. **See the Appendix at the back of this book for a full list of organizations, websites, and self-help books.**

Whether you choose to seek help through therapy, medication, rehab, or any combination of these, remember to be patient. There may be a lot of trial and error involved before you figure out what works for you. Just because one treatment option doesn't work the way you hope doesn't mean everything is a lost cause. There may also be some days that are worse than others, and moments where you feel like giving up or falling back into old habits. Remember treatment is not a one size fits all solution; healing takes time.

A Brief Explanation of The Most Popular Types of Clinical Treatments

- Psychotherapy, more commonly referred to as 'talk therapy', is the practice of helping people and changing their behavior through dialogue. Psychotherapists help their patients learn how to manage emotions and sort through their problems.

- Cognitive Behavioral Therapy (CBT), a form of psychotherapy, focuses on awareness of one's actions changing the behavior of a patient. Changes in exercise or diet can change cognitive thought. Dialectical Behavioral Therapy (DBT) is a form of CBT.

- Eye Movement Desensitization and Reprocessing (EMDR) is a treatment that allows a patient to mentally decrease the importance of a trauma. Fully process emotions and sort through experiences.

- Nutrition Therapy targets medical conditions and illnesses through a specific diet. Each diet is catered by a medical professional to a specific patient to ensure their conditions are addressed properly with the right type of food.

- Art Therapy consists of journaling, dancing, painting, etc., and is meant to provide a creative outlet to express emotions and foster emotional healing. It is particularly useful in allowing someone to communicate their emotions nonverbally.

- Alternative Therapy is acupuncture, massage therapy, aromatherapy, reflexology, meditation, and yoga.

- Immersive Retreats removes someone from distractions of daily life and gives them time to reflect. Some retreats are catered to yoga or meditation or other specific practices. While there are many institutes around the world in countries like Thailand and India, here are just a few in the United States:
  - Esalen Institute, Big Sur, CA
  - The Omega Institute, Rhinebeck, NY
  - Shambhala Mountain Center – Red Feather Lakes, CO
  - Rolling Meadows Yoga and Meditation Retreats – Brooks, ME
  - Miraval Resort and Spa – Tucson, AZ

How Do I Afford Therapy?

Many people say that they can't go to therapy because they can't afford it. This is unfortunate, and it shouldn't be a deterrent to you getting the help you need. If affordability is an issue, you have options. Talk with your doctor or another professional about low-cost therapy. Here are a few options you may want to consider:

- Check with your insurance provider and employer about what they may cover. Some companies may cover some of the cost of therapy through their Employee Assistance Program (EAP).

- Negotiate. Ask about any available discounts or sliding-scale therapy (which adjusts therapy costs based on income). If one therapist doesn't work for you, ask for a referral to another therapist.

- Look into organizations such as Open Path, which helps provide affordable therapy. Other websites like Open Counseling may be able to provide you with a list of low-cost therapists in your area. Do your research.

- Check out any training clinics or community health centers near you. Supervised graduate students at local universities may be able to see you for a low cost.

- If you are a current college or university student, stop by your school's counseling office. You may be able to meet with a counselor for free. You may also want to speak to your school's accommodation or disability office about any academic accommodations you may need.

- Consider online or group therapy, which may be cheaper than in-person, individual therapy. Online therapy may also fit well around your schedule.

- Take a look at your budget and see if you can cut out or reduce expenses to prioritize treating your mental health.

How Do I Make Time for Therapy?

"I don't have time for therapy." We all make one thousand excuses as to why we can't find the time to take care of our mental health: work demands, parenting demands, life demands all seem to take precedent but in order to get better (and stop wasting time feeling stuck or sad), consider shifting things so you can fit it in. Your biggest regret will be that you didn't enter therapy sooner. Believe me.

If you're struggling with finding the time because you don't seem to get a moment during the work week, consider talking to your employer. You may be able to take leave or shift your hours one day a week for a regular appointment (e.g., coming in earlier or later, leaving during an afternoon and returning). You don't have to disclose the details or your reasons for going to therapy to your employer. In the United States, you have the right to accessible medical treatment. If you feel you cannot talk to your boss directly, consider talking to your HR department first.

You may also consider scheduling your appointment during your lunch break (if you can see a therapist close to the office), in the early morning hours before work, in the evenings after work, or even on weekends.

Talk to a therapist about what will work for *you and your schedule*. You may want to specifically look for a therapist with flexible hours or weekend availability, or someone who is an online therapist so you don't have to spend the travel time making it to an office for face-to-face sessions.

Can You Recommend Self-Care Tips?

Treating yourself right and caring for your mind and body is just as important as seeking medical help. The following are some gentle suggestions for things that I have found help me clear my mind and create a positive mentality. Try doing these to help you feel good about you, your time and your recovery. You probably have already read about many of these tips in previous chapters, so this section may serve as a recap and summary for you.

Socialize with friends and family. It's simple, but being social with people whose company you enjoy is, for me, one of the easiest ways to better my mood and outlook. If you are not physically close to your family or friends, consider giving them a call more regularly or using video chat, texts, or emails to keep in touch.

You may also consider going out and making new friends, becoming a member of a support group, volunteering your time, going to events in your area, or getting involved in a religious community. All of these social outlets may help you easily connect with others. Even online friends and groups of people who can relate to what you're going through may contribute to improving your well-being.

Talk with someone you trust. Even if you don't go to a therapist, speaking with another person is a great way to vent, create a perspective on situations and move forward. Have an open mind. Be open to what your loved ones say; allow them to help you implement changes in your life.

Let yourself feel your emotions. Bottling up feelings may do a lot more harm than good.

Make your "me time" have a purpose. To make sure that downtime is spent being productive, take steps to ensure that you have relaxing activities to fill your time. You can meditate, go for a walk, read a book, listen to a podcast and exercise to create purposeful downtime. Disconnecting from tech and reconnecting with nature may help you. Consider cutting back on time spent browsing your phone, watching TV, or scrolling through social media feeds. Ask yourself how you can make more productive use of your time.

Avoid negativity. It's crucial that you are aware of how much negativity may be present in your life, especially if you are someone struggling with depression or anxiety. Be mindful of the people you interact with, the activities you engage in, and the information you consume online.

For example, sometimes looking at social media too much can bring us down, because others' lives can appear so perfect. It's a bad habit to compare yourself to others and their social media feeds. It may help to take a step back from social media and news on major networks, in the newspaper, or online. As a 2017 APA poll on stress in America found, 56% of adults reported following the news was a source of stress for them.[233] There can often be a lot of negativity on TV and elsewhere online that you may not be aware you're internalizing.

Be mindful of viewing or reading too much negative content online or listening to sad music or videos as well. If you fill your brain with joy, you'll feel more joy.

Work towards a goal. Each day, write down what your intentions are for that day. Create goals you wish to accomplish over time so that each day, week and month serves a purpose and spurs motivation. Think about something you're passionate about or interested in, such as a new hobby you love, a different career, or learning something new, and work towards it.

Reframe your thinking. If you catch yourself being negative, stop yourself and consider a more balanced, rational, and positive thought. Your thoughts may not change overnight, but in time you can create better thinking habits for yourself. Remember we can be more critical of ourselves than others. Consider practicing positive affirmations, developing a mantra, or talking to yourself like you would to a best friend or loved one. This can help build self-confidence and remove self-doubt.

Eat nutritious foods. While there's no shame in having a sugary treat every once in a while, a large part of self-care is making sure what you consume benefits your body, too. The food you eat directly impacts your energy, mood, and overall mentality.

Stay hydrated. Drinking water is incredibly important. Dehydration is a huge factor when it comes to anxiety. Water helps with increasing energy levels, boosting cognitive function, improving physical importance, curing headaches and illnesses and flushing out your body.[234] While drinking plenty of water also helps with things such as weight loss[235] and maintaining a clear complexion,[236] it goes deeper than staying acne free. Staying hydrated is beneficial to your body on the whole and improves your bodily functions.

While every medical professional seems to have a differing opinion how exactly how much water you should drink a day, the overall idea is that your daily consumption depends on your activity level. A general rule of thumb is 125 fluid ounces for men and women 90 ounces.[237]

If you're having trouble drinking plain water, don't worry; a lot of the foods we consume on a regular basis already have water in them so here are some alternatives: watermelon, grapefruit, grapes, cucumbers, and oatmeal. Also consider smoothies, fruit juices, sports drinks, and fruit-infused waters. Although, if you do choose to drink juices, keep in mind that some juices are high in sodium and sugar which may, in the long run, dehydrate your body.

Other ways to keep hydrated include always keeping water with you (preferably in a reusable water bottle), tracking your water intake (using an app, or setting reminders), and drinking when you feel hungry (sometimes you may think you're hungry when you're actually thirsty). If you are in a hot environment, be sure to drink more water. Aim to sip your water throughout the day and not gulp it down; this makes it easier to reach your daily goal but also ensures you don't overdo it in a short period of time.

Get enough sleep. Sleep impacts our mental health. It's important to give your body the rest it deserves. Make sure you're getting enough hours of rest every night. Establishing a regular, reasonable sleep routine is critical to self care. Try to fall asleep and wake up at the same time every day, even on the weekends. If you're struggling with your sleep habits, consider talking to your doctor, investing in a better mattress or alarm clock, avoiding electronic devices before bed, or addressing any stressors in your life that may be affecting you mentally. There may also be certain foods you're eating which contribute to getting a better or worse quality of sleep on any given night.

Exercise. Exercise is so important for staying physically and mentally healthy. Exercise can help you treat depression, anxiety, ADHD, and PTSD, in addition to helping you think more clearly, attain better sleep, achieve higher self-esteem, reduce stress, feel more energy, and practice healthier coping mechanisms.[238] You don't have to limit exercise to just gym time either – go for a run or a bike ride, or play a sport in your spare time.

Practice mindfulness. Practicing mindfulness can help you focus on the moment, and help improve your awareness and acceptance of your current situation. Spiritual practices such as meditation have been proven to have significant health benefits as well, and may be just as effective as medication.[239] Reflect on your life, habits, and your current state and how you are or are not contributing to your growth and well-being. Think about what you're grateful for. Evaluate where you are and where you want to be. Consider your thoughts and emotions, where they come from, and how your thoughts make you feel.

Try holistic treatments. Try practicing stress management or relaxation techniques for when you feel stressed or overwhelmed, such as guided imagery, breathing exercises, and tensing and relaxing your muscles. Additionally, you could try expressing your thoughts and feelings through music, art, or journaling.

Avoid alcohol, drugs, cigarettes and other bad habits, even if you aren't addicted. By avoiding bad habits, you clear distractions and allow yourself to focus on what's important in recovery. It may seem obvious, but the last thing you want to do is trade one addiction for another, so it's smartest just to avoid bad habits altogether.

Take it easy. Everyone needs time to rest and recharge. You may find that you need a mental health day. Or you may need to schedule more time in your day to just breathe. Our lives can be so busy and stressful. Every once and a while you may find that you need to plan some time to sleep in, enjoy some alone time or a hobby you haven't indulged in for a while. Doing nothing in a world that never stops can be curative. Taking a long bath, getting a massage, scheduling a spa day, or buying yourself something nice (such as new clothes that you feel good in) may also help.

How Should I Intervene When I Think Someone Needs Help?

When staging an intervention, or even having a casual conversation with your loved one, it's never an easy task. Interventions are meant to allow you to express your concern and other emotions in a constructive way that doesn't antagonize the person you're addressing. Hopefully, it leads to assistance. It's best to begin the intervention with a plan, knowing exactly what you intend to say. Hiring a professional to help you is always a good idea when feasible. Here are a few things to keep in mind while intervening:

- **Never criticize, berate, or show frustration while talking with your loved one.** Don't blame them for their problems or their mental illness – it's not their fault. Don't trivialize or invalidate their feelings or problems. Don't tell them that their problems don't seem that bad, life isn't fair, or other people have it worse. Even if all of those points may be objectively true, it's not helpful or relevant. Phases such as, "It will be okay," and other generic words of support may not be all that helpful either.
    - o   As an example, take someone with depression. A depressed person can be trapped in a fog that makes it hard to see or understand anything else other than the depression that they're going through in the moment. A loved one with depression cannot just "get over it," "be happier," or "look on the bright side." Even if it may seem that their life is going well and that they have so many things to be happy about, someone can still be very depressed. Depression is unrelated to personal circumstances, although it can be worsened by them.[240]
    - o   Don't make your loved one feel that they're selfish, uncaring about others, or lazy. Understand even small day-to-day tasks and taking care of oneself can be a major challenge for someone struggling with severe mental health issues. It's not that they're lazy or don't care – they're simply dealing with a lot that others can't see, and they may not be able to keep their own head above water.
    - o   Try to stay calm while expressing your concerns, and show them that you care about them and what they're going through in a soothing tone.
- **Remind them that they're not alone, and they can speak to you about anything.** The stigma of mental illness can inhibit people from coming forward, fearing that they may be called weak. They may also feel like no one understands what they're going through, and that they're the only one who feels this way. They're not. They may also be afraid of reactions from loved ones. They may not want to worry or disappoint family members, inconvenience others, or feel like a burden. They may also be nervous about not being taken seriously, or being perceived differently. It's important to reassure them that they are supported no matter what.
- **Provide specific examples of how their destructive behavior makes you feel** and impacts people. Use "I" statements that are focused on you and what you're feeling, and not your loved one.

- **Show them support** and encourage them to maintain a routine. Encourage them to get help by reminding them to take care of themselves on a daily basis by sleeping and eating properly, or even by accomplishing smaller tasks like dressing in the morning.
- **When encouraging them to get help, remind them that you are there for them.** Don't undermine their struggle. Take it seriously. Say expressions such as "How else can I help," "I'm worried about you and want to help, if you'll let me," or "I'm concerned about you." Make sure you follow through and are actually there for them if they need it. Someone may get the impression that others *say* that they're there for them, but they don't truly mean it. Show them you're there through genuine actions in addition to words, and consider checking up on them if you haven't heard from them recently.
- **Be patient.** Recovery is a lengthy process. Your loved one will not be "fixed" or feel better overnight. Be patient, understanding, and willing to listen if your loved one wants to talk (you may also find that your loved one doesn't want to talk, and that's okay too). Consider checking in with your loved one regularly. Ask how they are and reserve judgment.
- **Educate yourself and those around you.** Mental illness can be incredibly difficult to understand. Properly educating yourself about mental health and a loved one's mental illness may be especially necessary if you have had no personal experience with their illness, or if you come from a family or society where mental health isn't properly addressed. Try to educate yourself and dispel any misconceptions you may have that could potentially be harmful to your loved one. Consider educating other family members and friends as well.
- **Recognize you are not a substitute for a therapist** or another trained mental health professional. While it's important to support a loved one who needs you, they should not be overly-reliant on you. Dependency can develop which may make it difficult for a person to cope with and recover from their illness on their own. If someone is *too* supportive, they may also be enabling poor behavior that is not conducive to recovery.
  - Remember, you must help yourself first before helping someone else. It can be so difficult to support someone with mental illness, and a family member or friend may not always be able to provide the support one needs.
  - Be mindful of and take care of your own mental health if you feel supporting your loved one may be too much for you. Being around someone who is suffering can take a negative toll on the health of those around them, and it's important for both family members and the person who's struggling to recognize this.
  - Family members and friends may need to step back and distance themselves a bit, lean on their own support system, or encourage their loved one to speak to their doctor or a mental health professional if they need to talk to a therapist (if they don't have one), schedule more regular therapy sessions, or talk to their doctor about other options.
- **Recognize your loved one's mental illness or actions are not your fault.** It may seem easy for someone to think they should have seen signs and noticed sooner, especially if a loved one hid the signs of their mental illness or addiction, but someone's else's mental illness is not your fault unless you're the abuser.
- **Get help for yourself if you need it.** As we mentioned above, family members and friends may sometimes need to take a step back from loved ones to address their own mental health. If you have recently learned of a loved one's mental illness or that they have done something (such as if they have harmed themselves, harmed others, or committed suicide), you may be in shock or have

difficulty processing the triggering event, especially if their behavior is completely unexpected or out of character for them. You may be wrecked with guilt, shame, or regret thinking that you didn't do enough. You may believe that something you did or said may have driven someone to feel or think a certain way, harm themselves, harm others, or kill themselves. You may ruminate on the notion that if you didn't do those things, or acted differently, your loved one might be fine today.

o   If you are in this situation, again, please know it's not your fault. You are not to blame for someone else's thoughts or actions. Don't beat yourself up. There's nothing more you could have done, seen, or said in the moment. Remember we all make our own choices. You are not responsible for what someone else does.

o   If you're struggling after learning that your loved one has harmed themselves, harmed others, or committed suicide, please talk to someone, let yourself feel all your emotions (do not push your grief aside), and get the help and support for yourself that you need. Give yourself time away from work or other obligations if you can and stay away from drugs and alcohol. Look into grief counseling and support groups in your local area. Reach out to family and friends for support.

o   If you know someone who is struggling after someone in their life has committed suicide, please try to be supportive and think of them and check in every once and a while. People are often there for the first crucial couple of days or weeks, but as time passes, and as life goes on, eventually less people may be around and willing to provide support. It is important to remember a person will still be very much affected by a suicide in the months and years following, and they may still need and appreciate your help.

I hope this wraps things up nicely and gives you a direction of where to go and what steps to take next. The recovery process is just that – a process. Recovery doesn't happen overnight.

PART V

CONCLUSION: ADVERSITY MAKES US STRONGER

As authors, we have done our best to give you the tools to help you and those you love to prevent, and understand more fully, some of the major mental health challenges that affect us all throughout different times in our lives. We hope you've found each self-test and chapter useful and encouraging.

Life does not always provide us with unmitigated joy. Each season of our lives brings new challenges. As a young person, we may be bullied or misunderstood. During our teenage years, many of us will suffer through our first heartbreak while having to navigate hormonal changes that literally change us overnight. "Adulting" isn't easy. Sometimes we feel as if we're nailing it – seamlessly managing everything from financial to marriage stress. Other times, we feel like we're coming apart at the seams. And then there is aging. Getting physically older presents its own set of hurdles. Losing your vitality takes a physical and emotional toll. So does caring for elderly loved ones.

Life is both beautiful and brutal, "brutiful" as many of us like to say, which is why we want to drive one point home at the end of this mental health book. If you want to live a happy, healthy and fulfilling life, do not spend your time trying to avoid loss. First of all, it's impossible to do so. Secondly, loss and its cousin pain are two of your best teachers. Spend your time learning how to cope with loss and manage your pain. Denial is not your friend; sweeping any psychological symptoms or addictions you may be contending with "under the rug" will only make things harder for you in the end.

Remember your symptoms are messengers telling you something isn't quite right. Take a long look at what's causing those symptoms and then fully commit to taking care of your wellbeing – your emotional, spiritual and physical health – each and every day. As cliché as it sounds, surviving tough times makes us stronger people. Strive to be the person in the room who people describe as resilient and optimistic. Facing hard times sharpens are survival skills, makes us wiser and hopefully more empathic to those in need.

Know yourself, as the ancient teachers have been saying for over two thousand years. Assess your mental health, your intimate relationships and learn more about your personality type – so you have a better grasp on how you're doing right now, and if and where you need to heal. That way you can, with even more ease and grace, handle all the good and bad that naturally comes with living and loving in the modern world. *Test Your Self and Those You Love* provides you with easy tools to gain that self-knowledge. Use them. Enjoy them. Benefit from them.

Nell and I – as a psychotherapist and cultural anthropologist – have examined thousands of people and dozens of cultures. Every human being and every culture is unique. Every human being and every culture has specific challenges to overcome. One of the wonders of human existence is the variety of experiences each of us and each culture creates. Our wish for you is for you to use this book to manifest your best life – for you and those you love, and in so doing, contribute to creating the best world possible for all living creatures.

With the hope that all goes well in every aspect of your life,

Nell and Bill

Appendix A
Resource Directory

General Mental Health Resources

American Psychiatric Association – https://apafdn.org/

American Psychiatry Association – https://www.psychiatry.org/

American Psychological Association – https://www.apa.org/

Better Help Professional Counseling – https://www.betterhelp.com/

Brain & Behavior Research Foundation – https://www.bbrfoundation.org/

Breakthrough Mental Health Therapy – https://www.breakthrough.com/

Bring Change 2 Mind – https://bringchange2mind.org/

Center for Disease Control and Prevention (CDC): Division of Mental Health – https://www.cdc.gov/mentalhealth/index.htm

Diagnostic and Statistical Manual of Mental Disorders (DSM-5)

Good Therapy – https://www.goodtherapy.org/

Mayo Clinic – https://www.mayoclinic.org

MedlinePlus – https://medlineplus.gov/

Mental Health America – https://www.mentalhealthamerica.net/

Mental Health Resources, Inc. – http://www.mhresources.org/

MentalHealth.gov – https://www.mentalhealth.gov/

National Alliance on Mental Illness – https://www.nami.org/

National Council for Behavioral Health – https://www.thenationalcouncil.org/

National Empowerment Center – https://power2u.org/

National Institute on Mental Health – https://www.nimh.nih.gov/index.shtml

National Mental Health Consumers' Self-Help Clearinghouse – https://www.mhselfhelp.org/

One Mind – https://onemind.org/

Online Counseling Directory – https://www.onlinecounselling.com/

Online Therapy Institute – https://www.onlinetherapyinstitute.com/

PsychCentral – https://psychcentral.com/

Psychology Today – https://www.psychologytoday.com/

Recovery International – https://recoveryinternational.org/

Talkspace Online Therapy – https://www.talkspace.com/

Treatment Advocacy Center – https://www.treatmentadvocacycenter.org/

WebMD – https://www.webmd.com

World Health Organization (WHO)'s Department of Mental Health and Substance Abuse – https://www.who.int/nmh/about/msd/en/

General Resources for Children, Teens, & Families

Active Minds – https://www.activeminds.org/

Alateen – https://al-anon.org/for-members/group-resources/alateen/

American Academy of Child and Adolescent Psychiatry – https://www.aacap.org/

American School Counselor Association – https://www.schoolcounselor.org/

Association of Children's Residential Centers – https://togetherthevoice.org/

Bipolar Children – http://bipolarchild.com/

Born This Way Foundation – https://bornthisway.foundation/

Child Mind Institute – https://childmind.org/

Children's Health Council – https://www.chconline.org/

Half of Us – http://www.halfofus.com/

Juvenile Bipolar Research Foundation – https://www.jbrf.org/

LGBT National Help Center – https://www.glbthotline.org/

National Child Traumatic Stress Network – https://www.nctsn.org/

National Federation of Families for Children's Mental Health – https://www.ffcmh.org/

Office of Adolescent Health – https://www.hhs.gov/ash/oah/

Teen Health & Wellness – https://teenhealthandwellness.com/

The JED Foundation – https://www.jedfoundation.org/

The Trevor Project – https://www.thetrevorproject.org/

Worry Wise Kids – http://www.worrywisekids.org/

Personality

16 Personalities – https://www.16personalities.com/

Association for Research in Personality – https://www.personality-arp.org/

BPDWorld – https://www.bpdworld.org/

European Association of Personality Psychology – https://eapp.org/

Myers Briggs – https://www.myersbriggs.org/

National Education Alliance for Borderline Personality Disorder – https://www.borderlinepersonalitydisorder.org/

New England Personality Disorder Association, Inc. – http://www.nepda.org/

Personality Project – http://www.personality-project.org/

Personality Resources International – http://www.personalityresources.com/

Society for Personality and Social Psychology – http://www.spsp.org/

Depression & Mood Disorders

Anxiety and Depression Association of America – https://adaa.org/

Bipolar Disorder Research Network – http://bdrn.org/

Choices in Recovery *(Bipolar and Schizophrenia)* – http://www.choicesinrecovery.com/

Depression & Bipolar Support Alliance – https://www.dbsalliance.org/

Depression.org – https://www.depression.org/

Families for Depression Awareness – https://www.familyaware.org/

Freedom From Fear – http://www.freedomfromfear.org/

Hope For Depression Research Foundation – https://www.hopefordepression.org/

International Bipolar Foundation – https://ibpf.org/

International Society for Bipolar Disorders – https://www.isbd.org/
National Network of Depression Centers – https://nndc.org/
The Live Laugh Love Foundation – https://thelivelovelaughfoundation.org/
To Write Love On Her Arms – https://twloha.com/

Suicide
Alliance of Hope for Suicide Loss Survivors – https://allianceofhope.org/
American Association of Suicidology – https://www.suicidology.org/
American Foundation for Suicide Prevention – https://afsp.org/
International Association for Suicide Prevention – https://www.iasp.info/
Suicide Prevention Lifeline – https://suicidepreventionlifeline.org/
Suicide Prevention Resource Center – https://www.sprc.org/
Suicide.org – http://www.suicide.org/

Loss of Loved Ones / Grief Support
Alliance of Hope for Suicide Loss Survivors – https://allianceofhope.org/
Knights of Heroes Foundation – http://knightsofheroes.org/
Soaring Spirits International – https://www.soaringspirits.org/
The Compassionate Friends – https://www.compassionatefriends.org/

Anxiety
Anxiety and Depression Association of America – https://adaa.org/
Anxiety.org – https://www.anxiety.org/
Freedom from Fear – http://www.freedomfromfear.org/
National Anxiety Foundation – http://www.nationalanxietyfoundation.org/
The Anxiety Network – https://anxietynetwork.com/
The Child Anxiety Network – http://www.childanxiety.net/
The Live Laugh Love Foundation – https://thelivelovelaughfoundation.org/

Bullying
International Association on Workplace Bullying & Harassment – https://www.iawbh.org/
Megan Meier Foundation – https://meganmeierfoundation.org/
No Bully – https://www.nobully.org/
Pacer Center Kids Against Bullying – https://www.pacerkidsagainstbullying.org/
Pacer Center Teens Against Bullying – https://www.pacerteensagainstbullying.org/
STOMP Out Bullying™ – https://stompoutbullying.org/
Stop Bullying Now Foundation – http://www.stopbullyingnowfoundation.org/
StopBullying.gov – https://www.stopbullying.gov/
The Cybersmile Foundation – https://www.cybersmile.org/
Tyler Clementi Foundation – https://tylerclementi.org/
Workplace Bullying Institute – https://www.workplacebullying.org/

Gun Violence
Brady: United Against Gun Violence – https://www.bradyunited.org/

Everytown for Gun Safety – https://everytown.org/

Giffords: Courage to Fight Gun Violence – https://giffords.org/

Joyce Foundation – http://www.joycefdn.org/

Moms Demand Action for Gun Sense – https://momsdemandaction.org/

Sandy Hook Promise – https://www.sandyhookpromise.org/

The Coalition to Stop Gun Violence – https://www.csgv.org/

The Educational Fund to Stop Gun Violence – https://efsgv.org/

Eating Disorders

Eating Disorder Hope – https://www.eatingdisorderhope.com/

Eating Disorders Anonymous – http://eatingdisordersanonymous.org/

National Association of Anorexia Nervosa and Associated Disorders – https://anad.org/

National Eating Disorders Association – https://www.nationaleatingdisorders.org/

Overeaters Anonymous – https://oa.org/

The Eating Disorder Foundation – https://www.eatingdisorderfoundation.org/

Alcoholism

Alcoholics Anonymous – https://www.aa.org/

Dual Recovery Anonymous – http://www.draonline.org/

National Association for Children of Alcoholics – http://www.nacoa.net/

National Council on Alcoholism and Drug Dependence, Inc. – https://www.ncadd.org/

National Institute on Alcohol Abuse & Alcoholism – https://www.niaaa.nih.gov/

Drug / Substance Addiction

Addiction Center – https://www.addictioncenter.com/

Addiction Resource Center – https://www.addictionresourcecenter.org/

Addictions and Recovery – https://www.addictionsandrecovery.org/

Candle, Inc. – https://candleinc.org/

Dual Recovery Anonymous – http://www.draonline.org/

Narcotics Anonymous – https://www.na.org/

National Association for Children of Addiction – https://nacoa.org/

National Council on Alcoholism and Drug Dependence, Inc. – https://www.ncadd.org/

National Institute on Drug Abuse – https://www.drugabuse.gov/

Nicotine Anonymous – https://nicotine-anonymous.org/

reSET mobile application – https://www.resetforrecovery.com/

Start Your Recovery – https://startyourrecovery.org/

Substance Abuse and Mental Health Services Administration (SAMHSA) – https://www.samhsa.gov/

The National Association of Addiction Treatment Providers – https://www.naatp.org/

To Write Love On Her Arms – https://twloha.com/

Other Addictions

Addictions – https://www.addictions.com/

Gamblers Anonymous – http://www.gamblersanonymous.org/

Sex Addicts Anonymous – https://saa-recovery.org/

Relationships & Abuse

Allstate Foundation Purple Purse – https://www.purplepurse.com/

American Society for the Positive Care of Children – https://americanspcc.org/

Break the Cycle – https://www.breakthecycle.org/

Childhelp – https://www.childhelp.org/

Futures Without Violence – https://www.futureswithoutviolence.org/

Hope of Survivors – http://www.thehopeofsurvivors.com/

Joyful Heart Foundation – http://www.joyfulheartfoundation.org/

LoveIsRespect.org – https://www.loveisrespect.org/

National Center on Domestic and Sexual Violence – http://www.ncdsv.org/

National Center on Domestic Violence, Trauma & Mental Health – http://www.nationalcenterdvtraumamh.org/

National Center on Elder Abuse – https://ncea.acl.gov/

National Coalition Against Domestic Violence – http://www.ncadv.org/

National Network to End Domestic Violence – https://nnedv.org/

National Resource Center on Domestic Violence – https://nrcdv.org/

NO MORE – https://nomore.org/

One Love Foundation – https://www.joinonelove.org/

Prevent Child Abuse America – https://preventchildabuse.org/

Safe Horizon – https://www.safehorizon.org/

The 5 Love Languages – https://www.5lovelanguages.com/

Postpartum Depression and Other Illnesses

2020 Mom – https://www.2020mom.org/

Postpartum Men – http://postpartummen.com/

Postpartum Support International – https://www.postpartum.net/

PostpartumDepression.org – https://www.postpartumdepression.org

The International Marce Society – https://marcesociety.com/

PTSD

Department of Veterans Affairs – https://www.va.gov/

Make the Connection – https://maketheconnection.net/

Military OneSource – https://www.militaryonesource.mil/

National Center for PTSD – https://www.ptsd.va.gov/

National Veterans Foundation – https://nvf.org/

Psychology Health Center of Excellence – https://www.pdhealth.mil/

PTSD Alliance – http://www.ptsdalliance.org/

PTSD Foundation of America – https://ptsdusa.org/

Safe Call Now – https://www.safecallnow.org/

The Code Green Campaign – https://codegreencampaign.org/

VA Mental Health – https://www.mentalhealth.va.gov/

Veterans Families United – https://veteransfamiliesunited.org/

Alzheimer's & Aging

Aging In Place – https://www.aginginplace.org/

Alzheimer's Association – https://www.alz.org/
Alzheimer's Foundation of America – https://alzfdn.org/
Alzheimer's News Today – https://alzheimersnewstoday.com/
Alzheimers.Net – https://www.alzheimers.net/
CDC's Alzheimer's Disease and Healthy Aging – https://www.cdc.gov/aging/index.html
Children of Aging Parents – http://www.caps4caregivers.org/
Dementia Society of America – https://www.dementiasociety.org/
Family Caregiver Alliance – https://www.caregiver.org/
Forever My Home – http://www.forevermyhome.com
National Council on Aging – https://www.ncoa.org/
National Dementia Association – https://www.nationaldementia.org/
National Family Caregivers Association – https://caregiveraction.org/
National Institute on Aging – https://www.nia.nih.gov/

Spiritual Health

Spiritual Crisis Network – https://spiritualcrisisnetwork.uk/
Spiritual Emergence Service – http://spiritualemergence.net/
The International Spiritual Emergence Network – http://www.spiritualemergencenetwork.org/

Miscellaneous

Attention Deficit Disorder Association – https://add.org/
Clutterers Anonymous – https://clutterersanonymous.org/
International Obsessive Compulsive Disorder Foundation – https://iocdf.org/
NeedyMeds – https://www.needymeds.org/
One Recovery – http://1recovery.com/
Schizophrenia and Related Disorders Alliance of America – https://sardaa.org/
Schizophrenia International Research Society – https://schizophreniaresearchsociety.org/
Schizophrenia.com – http://schizophrenia.com/
The Institute for Functional Medicine – https://www.ifm.org/
The National Association of Social Workers – https://www.socialworkers.org/
Together Rx Access – http://trxaccess.org/
Well Spouse Association – https://wellspouse.org/

Appendix B
Book Recommendations

General Mental Health Resources

100 Interactive Activities for Mental Health and Substance Abuse Recovery by Carol A. Butler

12 Rules for Life: An Antidote to Chaos by Jordan B. Peterson

Becoming Whole: A Healing Companion to Ease Emotional Pain and Find Self-Love by Bruce Alan Kehr, M.D.

Cognitive Behavioral Therapy: 7 Ways to Freedom from Anxiety, Depression, and Intrusive Thoughts by Lawrence Wallace

Daring Greatly: How the Courage to Be Vulnerable Transforms the Way We Live, Love, Parent, and Lead by Brené Brown

Get Your Sh*t Together: How to Stop Worrying About What You Should Do So You Can Finish What You Need to Do and Start Doing What You Want to Do (A No F*cks Given Guide) by Sarah Knight

Girl, Wash Your Face: Stop Believing the Lies About Who You Are so You Can Become Who You Were Meant to Be by Rachel Hollis

How to Make Sh*t Happen: Make more money, get in better shape, create epic relationships and control your life! by Sean Whalen

I Thought It Was Just Me (but it isn't): Making the Journey from "What Will People Think?" to "I Am Enough" by Brené Brown

Maybe You Should Talk to Someone: A Therapist. HER Therapist, and Our Lives Revealed by Lori Gottlieb

No One Cares About Crazy People: The Chaos and Heartbreak of Mental Health in America by Ron Powers

Nutrition Essentials for Mental Health: A Complete Guide to the Food-Mood Connection by Leslie Korn

Rising Strong: How the Ability to Reset Transforms the Way We Live, Love, Parent, and Lead by Brené Brown

Start Here: Master the Lifelong Habit of Wellbeing by Eric Langshur

Supernormal: The Untold Story of Adversity and Resilience by Meg Jay

The Dialectical Behavior Therapy Skills Workbook: Practical DBT Exercises for Learning Mindfulness, Interpersonal Effectiveness, Emotion Regulation, and Distress Tolerance by Matthew McKay, Jeffrey C. Wood, & Jeffrey Brantley

The Gifts of Imperfection: Let Go of Who You Think You're Supposed to Be and Embrace Who You Are by Brené Brown

The Subtle Art of Not Giving a F*ck: A Counterintuitive Approach to Living a Good Life by Mark Manson

Type R: Transformative Resilience for Thriving in a Turbulent World by Ama Marston and Stephanie Martson

Unfu*ck Yourself: Get Out of Your Head and into Your Life by Gary John Bishop

What To Say When You Talk To Your Self by Shad Helmstetter

You Are a Badass®: How to Stop Doubting Your Greatness and Start Living an Awesome Life by Jen Sincero

Personality

Dangerous Personalities: An FBI Profiler Shows You How to Identify and Protect Yourself from Harmful People by Joe Navarro & Toni Sciarra Poynter

I Hate You–Don't Leave Me: Understanding the Borderline Personality by Jerold J. Kreisman, M.D & Hal Straus

Personality Plus: How to Understand Others by Understanding Yourself by Florence Littauer

Personality Types: Using the Enneagram for Self-Discovery by Don Richard Riso & Russ Hudson

Stop Walking on Eggshells: Taking Your Life Back When Someone You Care About Has Borderline Personality Disorder by Paul Mason & Randi Kreger

The 5 Personality Patterns: Your Guide to Understanding Yourself and Others and Developing Emotional Maturity by Steven Kessler

The Four Tendencies: The Indispensable Personality Profiles That Reveal How to Make Your Life Better (and Other People's Lives Better, Too) by Gretchen Rubin

The Road Back to You: An Enneagram Journey to Self-Discovery by Ian Morgan Cron & Suzanne Stabile

Type Talk: The 16 Personality Types That Determine How We Live, Love, and Work by Otto Kroeger & Janet M. Thuesen

Depression & Mood Disorders

10% Happier: How I Tamed the Voice in My Head, Reduced Stress Without Losing My Edge, and Found Self-Help That Actually Works–A True Story by Dan Harris

A Mind of Your Own: The Truth About Depression and How Women Can Heal Their Bodies to Reclaim Their Lives by Kelly Brogan, MD

An Unquiet Mind: A Memoir of Moods and Madness by Kay Redfield Jamison

Depression & Other Magic Tricks by Sabrina Benaim

Feeling Good: The New Mood Therapy by David D. Burns, M.D.

Hardcore Self Help: F**k Depression by Robert Duff, Ph.D

How to Be Happy (Or at Least Less Sad): A Creative Workbook by Lee Crutchley

I Want to Change My Life: How to Overcome Anxiety, Depression and Addiction by Steven Melemis

Retrain Your Brain: Cognitive Behavioral Therapy in 7 Weeks: A Workbook for Managing Depression and Anxiety by Seth J. Gillihan, Ph.D

Reviving Ophelia by Mary Pipher & Ruth Ross

The 10-Step Depression Relief Workbook: A Cognitive Behavioral Therapy Approach by Simon Rego, PsyD and Sarah Fader

The Archetype Diet: Reclaim Your Self-Worth and Change the Shape of Your Body by Dana James

The Bipolar Disorder Survival Guide, Second Edition: What You and Your Family Need to Know by David J. Miklowitz

The Depression Cure: The 6-Step Program to Beat Depression without Drugs by Stephen S. Ilardi

The Emotion Code: How to Release Your Trapped Emotions for Abundant Health, Love, and Happiness (Updated and Expanded Edition) by Bradley Nelson

The Happiness Advantage: How a Positive Brain Fuels Success in Work and Life by Shawn Achor

The Happiness Equation: Want Nothing + Do Anything = Have Everything by Neil Pasricha

The Happiness Trap: How to Stop Struggling and Start Living: A Guide to ACT by Russ Harris

The Mindful Way through Depression: Freeing Yourself from Chronic Unhappiness by Mark Williams

The Noonday Demon: An Atlas Of Depression by Andrew Solomon

The Upward Spiral: Using Neuroscience to Reverse the Course of Depression, One Small Change at a Time by Alex Korb

Undoing Depression: What Therapy Doesn't Teach You and Medication Can't Give You by Richard O'Connor

You Can Do All Things: Drawings, Affirmations and Mindfulness to Help With Anxiety and Depression by Kate Allan

Suicide

Dying to Be Free: A Healing Guide for Families after a Suicide by Beverly Cobain and Jean Larch

Grieving a Suicide: A Loved One's Search for Comfort, Answers & Hope by Albert Y. Hsu

How I Stayed Alive When My Brain Was Trying to Kill Me: One Person's Guide to Suicide Prevention by Susan Rose Blauner

Night Falls Fast: Understanding Suicide by Kay Redfield Jamison

No Time to Say Goodbye: Surviving The Suicide Of A Loved One by Carla Fine

Loss of Loved Ones / Grief Support

Healing After Loss: Daily Meditations For Working Through Grief by Martha W. Hickman

It's OK That You're Not OK: Meeting Grief and Loss in a Culture That Doesn't Understand by Megan Devine

The Grief Recovery Handbook, 20th Anniversary Expanded Edition: The Action Program for Moving Beyond Death, Divorce, and Other Losses including Health, Career, and Faith by John W. James & Russell Friedman

The Year of Magical Thinking by Joan Didion

Anxiety

Don't Feed the Monkey Mind: How to Stop the Cycle of Anxiety, Fear, and Worry by Jennifer Shannon

Feeling Good: The New Mood Therapy by David D. Burns, M.D.

Hardcore Self Help: F**k Anxiety by Robert Duff, Ph.D

Hope and Help For Your Nerves: End Anxiety Now by Claire Weekes

How to Be Happy (Or at Least Less Sad): A Creative Workbook by Lee Crutchley

I Want to Change My Life: How to Overcome Anxiety, Depression and Addiction by Steven Melemis

Real Happiness: The Power of Meditation by Sharon Salzberg

Retrain Your Brain: Cognitive Behavioral Therapy in 7 Weeks: A Workbook for Managing Depression and Anxiety by Seth J. Gillihan, Ph.D

The Worry Cure by Robert Leahy

When Panic Attacks: The New, Drug-Free Anxiety Therapy That Can Change Your Life by David D. Burns

Wherever You Go, There You Are: Mindfulness Meditation In Everyday Life by Jon Kabat-Zinn

You Can Do All Things: Drawings, Affirmations and Mindfulness to Help With Anxiety and Depression by Kate Allan

Bullying

Adult Bullying—A Nasty Piece of Work: Translating a Decade of Research on Non-Sexual Harassment, Psychological Terror, Mobbing, and Emotional Abuse on the Job by Pamela Lutgen-Sandvik

Bullying Beyond the Schoolyard: Preventing and Responding to Cyberbullying by Sameer K. Hinduja & Justin W. Patchin

Stick Up for Yourself: Every Kid's Guide to Personal Power & Positive Self-Esteem by Gershen Kaufman, Lev Raphael, & Pamela Espeland

Sticks and Stones: Defeating the Culture of Bullying and Rediscovering the Power of Character and Empathy by Emily Bazelon

The Bullying Breakthrough: Real Help for Parents and Teachers of the Bullied, Bystanders, and Bullies by Jonathan McKee

The Juice Box Bully: Empowering Kids to Stand Up for Others by Bob Sornson & Maria Dismondy

The Survival Guide To Bullying by Aija Mayrock

Gun Violence

A Mother's Reckoning: Living in the Aftermath of Tragedy by Sue Klebold

An Unseen Angel: A Mother's Story of Healing and Hope After Sandy Hook by Alissa Parker

Columbine by Dave Cullen

Confronting Gun Violence in America by Thomas Gabor

Fight Like a Mother: How a Grassroots Movement Took on the Gun Lobby and Why Women Will Change the World by Shannon Watts

The Gift of Fear by Gavin de Becker

Eating Disorders

8 Keys to Recovery from an Eating Disorder: Effective Strategies from Therapeutic Practice and Personal Experience (8 Keys to Mental Health) by Carolyn Costin & Gwen Schubert Grabb

Befriending Your Body: A Self-Compassionate Approach to Freeing Yourself from Disordered Eating by Ann Saffi Biasetti

Brain over Binge: Why I Was Bulimic, Why Conventional Therapy Didn't Work, and How I Recovered for Good by Kathryn Hansen

Decoding Anorexia by Carrie Arnold

Eating in the Light of the Moon: How Women Can Transform Their Relationship with Food Through Myths, Metaphors, and Storytelling by Anita A. Johnston, Ph.D

Help Your Teenager Beat an Eating Disorder, Second Edition by James Lock & Daniel Le Grange

Intuitive Eating: A Revolutionary Program that Works by Evelyn Tribole & Elyse Resch

Life Without Ed: How One Woman Declared Independence from Her Eating Disorder and How You Can Too by Jenni Schaefer

Never Binge Again: Reprogram Yourself to Think Like a Permanently Thin Person. Stop Overeating and Binge Eating and Stick to the Food Plan of Your Choice! By Glenn Livingston, Ph.D

The Bulimia Help Method: A Revolutionary New Approach That Works by Alison Kerr & Richard Kerr

The Rules of "Normal" Eating: A Commonsense Approach for Dieters, Overeaters, Undereaters, Emotional Eaters, and Everyone in Between! By Karen R. Koenig

Wasted: A Memoir of Anorexia and Bulimia by Marya Hornbacher

Alcoholism

Alcohol Explained by William Porter

Beyond the Influence: Understanding and Defeating Alcoholism by Katherine Ketcham, William F. Asbury, Mel Schulstad, & Arthur P. Ciaramicoli

Blackout: Remembering the Things I Drank to Forget by Sarah Hepola

Healing the Addicted Brain: The Revolutionary, Science-Based Alcoholism and Addiction Recovery Program by Harold Urschel

The 30-Day Sobriety Solution: How to Cut Back or Quit Drinking in the Privacy of Your Own Home by Jack Canfield & Dave Andrews

The Cure for Alcoholism: The Medically Proven Way to Eliminate Alcohol Addiction by Roy Eskapa

This Naked Mind: Control Alcohol, Find Freedom, Discover Happiness & Change Your Life by Annie Grace

Under the Influence: A Guide to the Myths and Realities of Alcoholism by James Robert Milam & Katherine Ketcham

Drug / Substance Addictions & Other Addictions

100 Interactive Activities for Mental Health and Substance Abuse Recovery by Carol A. Butler

Addiction and Grace: Love and Spirituality in the Healing of Addictions by Gerald G. May, M.D

Beautiful Boy: A Father's Journey Through His Son's Addiction by David Sheff

Beyond Addiction: How Science and Kindness Help People Change by Jeffrey Foote, Carrie Wilkens, Nicole Kosanke, & Stephanie Higgs

Healing the Addicted Brain: The Revolutionary, Science-Based Alcoholism and Addiction Recovery Program by Harold Urschel

I Want to Change My Life: How to Overcome Anxiety, Depression and Addiction by Steven Melemis

In the Realm of Hungry Ghosts: Close Encounters with Addiction by Gabor Mate, M.D

Recovery: Freedom from Our Addictions by Russell Brand

Rewired: A Bold New Approach To Addiction and Recovery by Erica Spiegelman

The Mindfulness Workbook for Addiction: A Guide to Coping with the Grief, Stress and Anger that Trigger Addictive Behaviors (A New Harbinger Self-Help Workbook) by Julie S. Kraft, MA

Unbroken Brain: A Revolutionary New Way of Understanding Addiction by Maia Szalavitz

Relationships & Abuse

Boundaries Updated and Expanded Edition: When to Say Yes, How to Say No To Take Control of Your Life by Henry Cloud & John Townsend

Healing from Hidden Abuse: A Journey Through the Stages of Recovery from Psychological Abuse by Shannon Thomas, LCSW

Healing the Trauma of Domestic Violence: A Workbook for Women by Mari McCaig, M.S.W & Edward S. Kubany, Ph.D ABPP

How to Be an Adult in Relationships: The Five Keys to Mindful Loving by David Richo

How to Talk so Kids Will Listen… And Listen So Kids Will Talk by Adele Faber & Elaine Mazlish

I Hear You: The Surprisingly Simple Skill Behind Extraordinary Relationships by Michael S. Sorensen

Love and Respect: The Love She Most Desires; The Respect He Desperately Needs by Emerson Eggerichs, Ph.D

Mending the Soul: Understanding and Healing Abuse by Steven R. Tracy

POWER: Surviving and Thriving After Narcissistic Abuse: A Collection of Essays on Malignant Narcissism and Recovery from Emotional Abuse by Shahida Arabi

Safe People: How to Find Relationships That Are Good for You and Avoid Those That Aren't by Henry Cloud & John Townsend

The 5 Love Languages: The Secret to Love that Lasts by Gary Chapman

The Language of Letting Go: Daily Meditations on Codependency by Melody Beattie

The Seven Principles for Making Marriage Work: A Practical Guide from the Country's Foremost Relationship Expert by John Gottman & Nah Silver

The Verbally Abusive Relationship, Expanded Third Edition: How to recognize it and how to respond by Patricia Evans

Why Does He Do That?: Inside the Minds of Angry and Controlling Men by Lundy Bancroft

Will I Ever Be Good Enough?: Healing the Daughters of Narcissistic Mothers by Karyl McBride

Wounds of the Father: A True Story of Child Abuse, Betrayal, and Redemption by Elizabeth Garrison

Postpartum Depression and Other Illnesses

A Mother's Climb Out Of Darkness: A Story about Overcoming Postpartum Psychosis by Jennifer Moyer

Beyond the Blues: A Guide to Understanding & Treating Prenatal and Postpartum Depression by Shoshana S. Bennett and Pec Indman

Down Came the Rain: My Journey Through Postpartum Depression by Brooke Shields

Good Moms Have Scary Thoughts: A Healing Guide to the Secret Fears of New Mothers by Karen Kleiman

Postpartum Survival Guide by Ann Dunnewold and Diane G. Sanford

Pregnant on Prozac: the essential guide to making the best decision for you and your baby by Soshana S. Bennett

The Fourth Trimester: A Postpartum Guide to Healing Your Body, Balancing Your Emotions, and Restoring Your Vitality by Kimberly Ann Johnson

The Mother-to-Mother Postpartum Depression Support Book by Sandra Poulin

The Postpartum Husband: Practical Solutions for Living with Postpartum Depression by Karen Kleiman

This Isn't What I Expected: Overcoming Postpartum Depression by Karen R. Kleiman and Valerie D. Raskin

What am I Thinking? Having a Baby After Postpartum Depression by Karen Kleiman

PTSD

Complex PTSD: From Surviving to Thriving: A GUIDE AND MAP FOR RECOVERING FROM CHILDHOOD TRAUMA by Pete Walker

Healing Developmental Trauma: How Early Trauma Affects Self-Regulation, Self-Image, and the Capacity for Relationship by Laurence Heller, Ph.D & Aline Lapierre, Psy.D

It Didn't Start with You: How Inherited Family Trauma Shapes Who We Are and How to End the Cycle by Mark Wolynn

Once a Warrior–Always a Warrior: Navigating the Transition from Combat to Home–Including Combat Stress, PTSD, and mTBI by Charles Hoge

The Body Keeps the Score: Brain, Mind, and Body in the Healing of Trauma by Bessel van der Kolk, MD

The PTSD Workbook for Teens: Simple, Effective Skills for Healing Trauma by Libbi Palmer

The PTSD Workbook: Simple, Effective Techniques for Overcoming Traumatic Stress Symptoms by Mary Beth Williams & Soili Poijula

Trauma and Recovery: The Aftermath of Violence–From Domestic Abuse to Political Terror by Judith L. Herman

When Someone You Love Suffers from Posttraumatic Stress: What to Expect and What You Can Do by Claudia Zayfert & Jason C. DeViva

Alzheimer's & Aging

Alzheimer's Disease: What If There Was a Cure?: The Story of Ketones by Mary T. Newport

Being Mortal: Medicine and What Matters in the End by Atul Gawande

Chicken Soup for the Soul: Living with Alzheimer's & Other Dementias: 101 Stories of Caregiving, Coping, and Compassion by Amy Newmark & Angela Timashenka Geiger

Creating Moments of Joy Along the Alzheimer's Journey: A Guide for Families and Caregivers by Jolene Brackey

Healthy Aging: A Lifelong Guide to Your Well-Being by Andrew Weil, M.D

Learning to Speak Alzheimer's: A Groundbreaking Approach for Everyone Dealing with the Disease by Joanne Koenig Coste

The 36-Hour Day: A Family Guide to Caring for People Who Have Alzheimer Disease, Other Dementias, and Memory Loss by Nancy L. Mace & Peter V. Rabins

The Alzheimer's Antidote: Using a Low-Carb, High-Fat Diet to Fight Alzheimer's Disease, Memory Loss, and Cognitive Decline by Amy Berger & David Perlmutter, M.D

The End of Alzheimer's: The First Program to Prevent and Reverse Cognitive Decline by Dale Bredesen

The Grace in Aging: Awaken as You Grow Older by Kathleen Dowling Singh

When Reasoning No Longer Works: A Practical Guide for Caregivers Dealing with Dementia & Alzheimer's Care by Angel Smits

You: Staying Young by Mehmet Oz, M.D & Michael Roizen, M.D

Spiritual Health

A Journey to Oneness: A Chronicle of Spiritual Emergence by Rasha

A More Excellent Way: Be in Health: Pathways of Wholeness, Spiritual Roots of Disease by Henry W. Wright

Broken Open: How Difficult Times Can Help Us Grow by Elizabeth Lesser

Emergence: Seven Steps for Radical Life Change by Derek Rydall

Emotionally Healthy Spirituality: It's Impossible to Be Spiritually Mature, While Remaining Emotionally Immature by Peter Scazzero

Going to Pieces Without Falling Apart: A Buddhist Perspective on Wholeness by Mark Epstein

Grace for the Afflicted: A Clinical and Biblical Perspective on Mental Illness by Matthew S. Stanford

Hidden Blessings: Midlife Crisis As a Spiritual Awakening by Jett Psaris PhD

It's Not Supposed to Be This Way: Finding Unexpected Strength When Disappointments Leave You Shattered by Lysa TerKeurst

Man's Search for Meaning by Viktor E. Frankl

Sacred Rhythms: Arranging Our Lives for Spiritual Transformation by Ruth Haley Barton

Spiritual Depression: Its Causes and Cures by David artyn Lloyd-Jones

Spiritual Emergency: When Personal Transformation Becomes a Crisis (New Consciousness Readers) by Stanislav Grof & Christina Grof

The Four Agreements: A Practical Guide to Personal Freedom (A Toltec Wisdom Book) by Don Miguel Ruiz & Janet Mills

The Power of Now: A Guide to Spiritual Enlightenment by Eckhart Tolle

The Seven Spiritual Laws of Success: A Practical Guide to the Fulfillment of Your Dreams by Deepak Chopra

The Untethered Soul: The Journey Beyond Yourself by Michael A. Singer

What is the Mother Wound? by Bethany Webster

When Spirit Leaps: Navigating the Process of Spiritual Awakening by Bonnie L. Greenwell

When Things Fall Apart: Heart Advice for Difficult Times by Pema Chodron

Miscellaneous

Becoming by Michelle Obama

Born for Love: Why Empathy Is Essential–and Endangered by Bruce D. Perry & Maia Szalavitz

Brain Lock: Free Yourself from Obsessive-Compulsive Behavior by Jeffrey M. Schwartz

Overcoming Unwanted Intrusive Thoughts: A CBT-Based Guide to Getting Over Frightening, Obsessive, or Disturbing Thoughts by Sally M. Winston & Martin N. Seif

Surviving Schizophrenia, 6th Edition: A Family Manual by E. Fuller Torrey

The Center Cannot Hold: My Journey Through Madness by Elyn R. Saks

Women's Bodies, Women's Wisdom: Creating Physical and Emotional Health and Healing by Christine Northrup, M.D

Appendix C
Hotlines

<u>*United States:*</u>
If you or a loved one is in immediate danger, call 911 now.
National Suicide Prevention Lifeline: 1-800-273-8255
Crisis Text Line: Text "START" to 741-741
Veterans: 1-800-273-8255, then press 1
Spanish: 1-800-273-8255, then press 2
Veterans Crisis Text Line: Text 838255
National Veterans Foundation Lifeline: 1-888-777-4443
PTSD Foundation of America Veteran Line: 1-877-717-7873
Military OneSource Hotline: 800-342-9647
LGBT Youth Hotline: 1-866-488-7386
Safe Call Now Public Safety Employee Crisis Line: 206-459-3020
National Volunteer Fire Council Fire/EMS Helpline: 1-888-731-3473
Copline International Law Enforcement Hotline: 1-800-267-5463
Frontline Responder Services Helpline: 1-866-676-7500
National Alliance on Mental Illness (NAMI) Helpline: 1-800-950-6264
Addiction Resource Center Helpline: (833) 301-4357
SAMHSA's National Helpline: 1-800-662-4357
Quit Smoking Helpline: 1-800-784-8669
National Domestic Violence Hotline: 1-800-799-7233
National Sexual Assault Hotline: 1-800-656-4673
Safe Horizon Domestic Violence Hotline: 1-800-621-4673
Love Is Respect Hotline: 1-866-331-9474
Love Is Respect Textline: Text "LOVEIS" to 22522
National Child Abuse Hotline: 1-800-422-4453
Office on Women's Health (OWN) Hotline: 1-800-994-9662
Postpartum Support International Hotline (English & Spanish): 1-800-944-4773
Postpartum Support International Textline: Text 503-894-9453
STOMP Out Bullying™ HelpChat Line: https://stompoutbullying.org/get-help/helpchat-line/
Alzheimer's Association Helpline: 800-272-3900
Suicide Prevention Online Chat: http://chat.suicidepreventionlifeline.org/GetHelp/LifelineChat.aspx
Boys' Town National Hotline (for teens): 1-800-448-3000
Boys' Town National Text Line: Text "VOICE" to 20121
IMAlive Crisis Chat Network: https://www.imalive.org/

Spiritual Emergence Service Phone Number: 604-917-0117
International Association of Fire Fighters PTSD Hotline (*members only*): 866-965-3074

International Suicide Hotlines:
Argentina: +5402234930430
Australia: 131114
Austria: 017133374
Belgium: 106
Bosnia & Herzegovina: 080 05 03 05
Botswana: 3911270
Brazil: 188 for the CVV National Association
Canada: 5147234000 (Montreal); 18662773553 (outside Montreal)
Croatia: 014833888
Denmark: +4570201201
Egypt: 7621602
Estonia: 3726558088; in Russian 3726555688
Finland: 010 195 202
France: 0145394000
Germany: 08001810771
Holland: 09000767
Hong Kong: +852 2382 0000
Hungary: 116123
India: 8888817666
Ireland: +4408457909090
Italy: 800860022
Japan: +810352869090
Mexico: 5255102550
New Zealand: 0800543354
Norway: +4781533300
Philippines: 028969191
Poland: 5270000
Portugal: 21 854 07 40/8 . 96 898 21 50
Russia: 0078202577577
Spain: 914590050
South Africa: 0514445691
Sweden: 46317112400
Switzerland: 143
United Kingdom: 08457909090

Notes

1 Weinberger, A., Gbedemah, M., Martinez, A., Nash, D., Galea, S., & Goodwin, R. (2018). Trends in depression prevalence in the USA from 2005 to 2015: Widening disparities in vulnerable groups. *Psychological Medicine, 48*(8), 1308-1315. doi:10.1017/S0033291717002781

2 https://www.nimh.nih.gov/health/statistics/suicide.shtml

3 https://everytownresearch.org/gun-violence-america/

4 Substance Abuse and Mental Health Services Administration. (2018). *Key substance use and mental health indicators in the United States: Results from the 2017 National Survey on Drug Use and Health* (HHS Publication No. SMA 18-5068, NSDUH Series H-53). Rockville, MD: Center for Behavioral Health Statistics and Quality, Substance Abuse and Mental Health Services Administration. Retrieved from https://www.samhsa.gov/data/

5 https://www.drugabuse.gov/related-topics/trends-statistics/overdose-death-rates

6 https://www.psychologytoday.com/us/basics/personality

7 https://qz.com/914002/youre-a-completely-different-person-at-14-and-77-the-longest-running-personality-study-ever-has-found/

8 True Colors Personality Test (freebie) – this version was made available to the public for free by Miss Johnson: https://www.teacherspayteachers.com/Product/True-Colors-Personality-Test-freebie-1309341

9 https://www.teacherspayteachers.com/Product/True-Colors-Personality-Test-freebie-1309341

10 https://truecolorsintl.com/the-four-color-personalities/

11 https://truecolorsintl.com/the-four-color-personalities/blue-personality-type/

12 T.H.Holmes and T.H. Rahe. "The Social Readjustment Rating Scale," Journal of Psychosomatic Research. 11:213, 1967.

13 https://dcf.psychiatry.ufl.edu/files/2011/05/HAMILTON-DEPRESSION.pdf

14 https://www.outcometracker.org/library/SDS.pdf

15 http://teenmentalhealth.org/wp-content/uploads/2015/12/TASR-A_Package.pdf

16 https://preventsuicidewv.org/wp-content/uploads/2014/03/ASAP-20.pdf

17 https://www.nimh.nih.gov/research/research-conducted-at-nimh/asq-toolkit-materials/index.shtml

18 Developed by Drs. Robert L. Spitzer, Janet B.W. Williams, Kurt Kroenke and colleagues, with an educational grant from Pfizer Inc. No permission required to reproduce, translate, display or distribute. Retrieved from https://www.phqscreeners.com/sites/g/files/g10049256/f/201412/PHQ-9_English.pdf

19 Copyright Adrian Angold & Elizabeth J. Costello, 1987; Developmental Epidemiology Program; Duke University

20 Copyright Adrian Angold & Elizabeth J. Costello, 1987; Developmental Epidemiology Program; Duke University

21 https://www.nimh.nih.gov/health/statistics/mental-illness.shtml

22 https://www.dosomething.org/us/facts/11-facts-about-depression

23 http://med.stanford.edu/depressiongenetics/mddandgenes.html

24 https://www.mayoclinic.org/diseases-conditions/depression/in-depth/depression/art-20047725

25 https://www.nimh.nih.gov/health/statistics/suicide.shtml

26 https://www.health.harvard.edu/mind-and-mood/what-causes-depression

27 https://www.mayoclinic.org/diseases-conditions/depression/symptoms-causes/syc-20356007

28 https://www.psycom.net/depression.central.women.html

29 https://www.mayoclinic.org/diseases-conditions/seasonal-affective-disorder/diagnosis-treatment/drc-20364722

30 https://www.apa.org/news/press/releases/2017/11/lowest-point

31 Mojtabai R, Olfson M, Han B. National Trends in the Prevalence and Treatment of Depression in Adolescents and Young Adults. Pediatrics. 2016;138(6): e20161878

32 https://www.johnshopkinshealthreview.com/issues/fall-winter-2017/articles/the-rise-of-teen-depression

33 https://www.cdc.gov/healthyyouth/data/yrbs/pdf/trendsreport.pdf

34 https://www.cdc.gov/healthyyouth/data/yrbs/pdf/trendsreport.pdf

35 http://www.childrenshospital.org/conditions-and-treatments/conditions/s/suicide-and-teens/symptoms-and-causes/

36 https://www.stanfordchildrens.org/en/topic/default?id=teen-suicide-90-P02584

37 http://www.myaccesshealth.org/news/anxiety-and-low-self-esteem-in-teens

38 https://yr.media/tech/only-smiling-on-the-outside-teens-hide-depression/

39 https://themighty.com/2018/04/how-to-hide-depression/

40 https://www.psychologytoday.com/us/blog/the-guest-room/201411/the-secret-life-people-smiling-depression

41 https://themighty.com/2016/10/why-people-are-afraid-to-recover-from-depression/

42 https://www.psychologytoday.com/us/blog/codes-joy/201405/is-fear-happiness-real

43 https://theconversation.com/half-of-teens-outgrow-depression-and-anxiety-22051

44 https://paradigmmalibu.com/teens-brain-fully-developed-age/

45 https://theconversation.com/half-of-teens-outgrow-depression-and-anxiety-22051

46 https://www.theguardian.com/science/2015/apr/10/psychology-empathy-distinguish-fake-genuine-smiles

47 https://psychcentral.com/blog/6-secret-signs-of-hidden-depression/

48 https://psychcentral.com/blog/6-secret-signs-of-hidden-depression/

49 https://psychcentral.com/blog/6-secret-signs-of-hidden-depression/

50 https://www.valleybehavioral.com/disorders/self-harm/signs-symptoms-causes/

51 https://www.villagebh.com/self-injury/symptoms-signs-effects/

52 https://www.cdc.gov/healthyyouth/data/yrbs/pdf/2017/ss6708.pdf

53 Stone DM, Simon TR, Fowler KA, et al. Vital Signs: Trends in State Suicide Rates – United States, 1999-2016 and Circumstances COntributing to Suicide – 27 States, 2015. MMWR Morb Mortal Wkly Rep 2018;67:617-624. DOI: http:/dx.doi.org/10.1558/mmwr.mm6722a1

54 https://afsp.org/about-suicide/suicide-statistics/

55 https://www.cdc.gov/healthyyouth/data/yrbs/pdf/2017/ss6708.pdf

56 http://prp.jasonfoundation.com/facts/youth-suicide-statistics/

57 https://www.nimh.nih.gov/health/publications/suicide-faq/index.shtml

58 https://www.stanfordchildrens.org/en/topic/default?id=teen-suicide-90-P02584

59 https://depression.org.nz/get-better/self-help/

60 https://www.helpguide.org/articles/depression/coping-with-depression.htm

61 http://1recovery.com/

62 https://butterfly-project.tumblr.com/

63 https://www.teenvogue.com/story/self-harm-alternatives

64 https://www.medicalnewstoday.com/articles/324515.php

65 https://depression.org.nz/get-better/self-help/

66 https://adaa.org/learn-from-us/from-the-experts/blog-posts/consumer/childhood-depression

67 https://www.ncbi.nlm.nih.gov/pmc/articles/PMC3184303/

68 https://www.ncbi.nlm.nih.gov/pmc/articles/PMC3184303/

69 https://www.everydayhealth.com/hs/major-depression-resource-center/how-nature-helps-depression/

70 https://adaa.org/about-adaa/press-room/facts-statistics

71 https://www.nami.org/NAMI/media/NAMI-Media/Infographics/GeneralMHFacts.pdf

72 https://blogs.scientificamerican.com/mind-guest-blog/the-growing-economic-burden-of-depression-in-the-u-s/

73 https://www.psychiatry.org/newsroom/apa-public-opinion-poll-annual-meeting-2018

74 Harder HG, Wagner SL, Rash JA. *Mental Illness in the Workplace: Psychological Disability Management.* Farnham, United Kingdom: Gower, 2014.

75 https://adaa.org/sites/default/files/Anxiety%20Disorders%20in%20Children.pdf

76 http://beyondocd.org/ocd-facts

77 https://www.anxiety.org/what-is-body-focused-repetitive-behavior-bfrb

78 https://www.psychiatry.org/patients-families/hoarding-disorder/what-is-hoarding-disorder

79 https://www.psychologicalscience.org/publications/observer/obsonline/neuroticism-predicts-anxiety-and-depression-disorders.html

80 https://adaa.org/about-adaa/press-room/facts-statistics

81 Spitzer RL, Kroenke K, Williams JB, Lowe B. A brief measure for assessing generalized anxiety disorder: the GAD-7. Archives of internal medicine. May 22 2006;166(10):1092–1097. PMID: 16717171

82 Hamilton M. The assessment of anxiety states by rating. Br J Med Psychol 1959; 32:50–55.

83 Mattick, R.P.; Clarke, J.C. (1998). "Development and validation of measures of social phobia scrutiny fear and social interaction anxiety". *Behaviour Research and Therapy*. 36 (4): 455–470. doi:10.1016/s0005-7967(97)10031-6

84 Stöber, J., & Joormann, J. (2001). A short form of the Worry Domains Questionnaire: Construction and factorial validation. Personality and Individual Differences, 31, 119-126.

85 https://www.apa.org/news/press/releases/2017/11/lowest-point

86 https://www.independent.co.uk/news/science/mindfulness-therapy-depression-anti-depressants-mental-health-research-meditation-a7003546.html

87 https://www.huffpost.com/entry/asmr-mental-health_n_5bb38283e4b0d1ebe0e51e38

88 https://www.medicalnewstoday.com/articles/322652.php

89 https://www.healthline.com/nutrition/7-health-benefits-of-water#section7

90 Huizen, J. (2018, June 28). "Can water help you lose weight?." *Medical News Today*. Retrieved from https://www.medicalnewstoday.com/articles/322296.php.

91 "6 Benefits of Staying Hydrated", Wright, Brierley, One Medical. Retrieved from https://www.onemedical.com/blog/live-well/6-benefits-of-staying-hydrated/

92 https://www.medexpress.com/blog/better-health/7-ways-to-stay-hydrated-that-dont-involve-drinking-water.html

93 https://americanspcc.org/our-voice/bullying/statistics-and-information/

94 https://nces.ed.gov/pubs2017/2017064.pdf

95 https://nces.ed.gov/pubs2012/2012314.pdf

96 https://www.pacer.org/bullying/resources/stats.asp

97 https://americanspcc.org/our-voice/bullying/statistics-and-information/

98 http://thenationshealth.aphapublications.org/content/47/7/E32

99 https://www.newsweek.com/bullied-victims-and-gun-violence-american-schools-worrying-relationship-629752

100 https://www.jahonline.org/article/S1054-139X(17)30195-7/abstract

101 https://www.thetrace.org/2018/12/gun-violence-facts-statistics-2018/

102 http://stopbullyingnowfoundation.org/main/

103 https://www.fbi.gov/file-repository/active-shooter-study-2000-2013-1.pdf/view

104 https://www.adl.org/murder-and-extremism-2018

105 https://www.cchrint.org/2017/10/10/another-mass-shooting-another-psychiatric-drug/

106 https://www.ncbi.nlm.nih.gov/pmc/articles/PMC4318286/

107 https://d3n8a8pro7vhmx.cloudfront.net/promise/pages/42/attachments/original/1524062511/SHP_Know_the_Signs_Guide_2018.pdf?1524062511

108 https://www.mentalhealthamerica.net/conditions/paranoia-and-delusional-disorders

109 https://www.mayoclinic.org/diseases-conditions/eating-disorders/symptoms-causes/syc-20353603

110 https://www.mirror-mirror.org/eating-disorders-statistics.htm

111 Arcelus, Mitchell, Wales, & Nielsen, 2011

112 February 2007 edition of Biological Psychiatry

113 Archives of General Psychiatry (Vol. 60, No. 2)

114 American Psychiatric Assoc. Diagnostic & Statistical Manual of Mental Disorders 4th Edition. Wash. DC, 1994.

115 Public Health Agency of Canada. Canadian Paediatric Surveillance Program, 2003 Results

116 LM, Irwin CE & Scully S: Disordered eating characteristics in girls: A survey of middle class children. Journal of the American Dietetic Association. 1992

117 Neumark-Sztainer, D. R., Wall, M. M., Haines, J. I., Story, M. T., Sherwood, N. E., van den Berg, P. A. (2007). Shared Risk and Protective Factors for Overweight and Disordered Eating in Adolescents. American Journal of Preventative Medicine.

118 https://www.eatright.org/health/diseases-and-conditions/eating-disorders/what-is-disordered-eating

119 www.psychiatry.org

120 https://www.mirror-mirror.org/eating-disorders-statistics.htm

121 The Renfrew Center Foundation for Eating Disorders.

122 https://www.mirror-mirror.org/eating-disorders-statistics.htm

123 https://www.mirror-mirror.org/eating-disorders-statistics.htm

124 https://www.mirror-mirror.org/eating-disorders-statistics.htm

125 Perry, L., Morgan, J. Reid, Brunton, J., O'Brien, A., Luck, A., & Lacey, H. (2002). Screening for symptoms of eating disorders: Reliability of the SCOFF Screening Tool with written compared to oral deliver. International Journal of Eating Disorders, 32, 466-472. https://www.marquette.edu/counseling/documents/AQuickAssessmentforEatingConcerns.pdf

126 http://media.samhsa.gov/data/spotlight/Spot061ChildrenOfAlcoholics2012.pdf

127 https://talbottcampus.com/alcoholism-statistics/

128 Bose, Jonaki, et al. *Key Substance Use and Mental Health Indicators in the United States: Results from the 2017 National Survey on Drug Use and Health.* Substance Abuse and Mental Health Services Administration, 2018, *Key Substance Use and Mental Health Indicators in the United States: Results from the 2017 National Survey on Drug Use and Health,* www.samhsa.gov/data/report/2017-nsduh-annual-national-report.

129 https://www.drugabuse.gov/related-topics/trends-statistics

130 https://www.drugabuse.gov/publications/drugfacts/understanding-drug-use-addiction

131 https://www.addictioncenter.com/addiction/addiction-statistics/

132 Substance Abuse and Mental Health Services Administration. (2018). Results from the 2017 National Survey on Drug Use and Health: Detailed Tables.

133 Bose, Jonaki, et al. Key Substance Use and Mental Health Indicators in the United States: Results from the 2017 National Survey on Drug Use and Health. Substance Abuse and Mental Health Services Administration, 2018, Key Substance Use and Mental Health Indicators in the United States: Results from the 2017 National Survey on Drug Use and Health. Retrieved from www.samhsa.gov/data/report/2017-nsduh-annual-national-report

134 https://www.addictioncenter.com/addiction/addiction-statistics/

135 https://www.drugabuse.gov/related-topics/trends-statistics/overdose-death-rates

136 https://www.cdc.gov/vitalsigns/painkilleroverdoses/index.html

137 Vivolo-Kantor, AM, Seth, P, Gladden, RM, et al. *Vital Signs: Trends in Emergency Department Visits for Suspected Opioid Overdoses–United States, July 2016-September 2017.* Centers for Disease Control and Prevention

138 Substance Abuse and Mental Health Services Administration. Center for Behavioral Health Statistics and Quality. Results From the 2015 National Survey on Drug Use and Health: Detailed Tables. https://www.samhsa.gov/data/sites/default/files/NSDUH-DetTabs-2015/NSDUH-DetTabs-2015/NSDUH-DetTabs-2015.pdf. Published September 2016. Accessed March 22, 2018.

139 Centers for Disease Control and Prevention: Opioid Overdose. https://www.cdc.gov/drugoverdose/index.html. Accessed March 22, 2018.

140 Hedegaard H, Warner M, Miniño AM. Drug Overdose Deaths in the United States, 1999-2016. https://www.cdc.gov/nchs/data/databriefs/db294.pdf. Accessed March 22, 2018.

141 https://www.drugabuse.gov/drugs-abuse/opioids/opioid-overdose-crisis

142 https://www.healthline.com/health/addiction/risk-factors

143 https://pubs.niaaa.nih.gov/publications/AA76/AA76.htm

144 https://pubs.niaaa.nih.gov/publications/AA76/AA76.htm

145 https://www.drugabuse.gov/publications/preventing-drug-abuse-among-children-adolescents/chapter-1-risk-factors-protective-factors/what-are-risk-factors

146 https://www.healthline.com/health/addiction/risk-factors

147 https://www.helpguide.org/articles/addictions/substance-abuse-and-mental-health.htm

148 https://pubs.niaaa.nih.gov/publications/AA76/AA76.htm

149 https://www.drugabuse.gov/publications/drugfacts/nationwide-trends

150 https://mchb.hrsa.gov/chusa11/hstat/hsa/pages/228sa.html

151 https://www.healthline.com/health/addiction/risk-factors#type-of-drug

152 https://www.medicalnewstoday.com/articles/323467.php

153 https://www.medicalnewstoday.com/articles/323467.php

154 Skinner HA (1982). The Drug Abuse Screening Test. Addict Behav 7(4):363-371. Yudko E, Lozhkina O, Fouts A (2007). A comprehensive review of the psychometric properties of the Drug Abuse Screening Test. J Subst Abuse Treatment 32:189-198.

155 https://www.statista.com/statistics/669037/share-of-americans-who-believe-in-love/

156 Locke, H. J., & Wallace, K. M. (1959). Short marital adjustment and prediction tests: Their reliability and validity. Marriage and Family Living, 21, 251–255. https://fetzer.org/sites/default/files/images/stories/pdf/selfmeasures/Self_Measures_for_Marital_Satisfaction_MARITAL_ADJUSTMENT_TEST.pdf

157 Rogge, R.D., Fincham, F.D., Crasta, D., Maniaci, M.R. (2017). Positive and negative evaluation of relationships: Development and validation of the Positive-Negative Relationship Quality (PN-RQ) Scale. Psychological Assessment, 29 (8), 1028 –1043. http://www.fincham.info/measures/pnrq.pdf

158 https://ncadv.org/statistics

159 http://www.domesticabuseshelter.org/InfoDomesticViolence.htm

160 https://www.apa.org/pi/women/resources/reports/postpartum-depression

161 https://www.apa.org/pi/women/resources/reports/postpartum-depression

162 https://www.apa.org/pi/women/resources/reports/postpartum-depression

163 https://americanpregnancy.org/pregnancy-health/depression-during-pregnancy/

164 https://www.lifespan.org/centers-services/multidisciplinary-obstetric-medicine-service-moms/common-conditions-during/anxiety

165 https://www.nhs.uk/conditions/post-partum-psychosis/

166 http://www.idph.state.il.us/about/womenshealth/factsheets/pdpress.htm

167 http://www.idph.state.il.us/about/womenshealth/factsheets/pdpress.htm

168 EDINBURGH POSTNATAL DEPRESSION SCALE (EPDS) J. L. Cox, J.M. Holden, R. Sagovsky, Department of Psychiatry, University of Edinburgh)

169 SUICIDE ASSESSMENT FOR A POSITIVE EPDS SCREEN (#10) Karen Kleiman THE POSTPARTUM STRESS CENTER, LLC

170 The Perinatal Anxiety Screening Scale: development and preliminary validation. Department of Health, State of Western Australia (2013)

171 https://www.goodreads.com/work/quotes/41758806-emerging-with-wings-a-true-story-of-lies-pain-and-the-love-that-heals

172 http://www.ptsdalliance.org/who-is-at-risk/

173 https://www.nimh.nih.gov/health/publications/post-traumatic-stress-disorder-ptsd/index.shtml#pub3

174 http://www.healmyptsd.com/education/post-traumatic-stress-disorder-statistics

175 https://maketheconnection.net/whats-new/ptsd-statistics

176 https://adaa.org/understanding-anxiety/posttraumatic-stress-disorder-ptsd

177 https://www.ptsd.va.gov/understand/common/common_veterans.asp

178 http://www.veteransandptsd.com/PTSD-statistics.html

179 https://www.ptsd.va.gov/understand/common/common_veterans.asp

180 https://nvf.org/veteran-mental-health-facts-statistics/

181 Abbot, C., Barber, E., Burke, B., Harvey, J., Newland, C., Rose, M., & Young, A. (2015). What's killing our medics? Ambulance Service Manager Program. Conifer, CO: Reviving Responders. Retrieved from http://www.revivingresponders.com/originalpaper

182 Peres, Julio F. P., Alexander Moreira-Almeida, Antonia Gladys Nasello, and Harold G. Koenig. "Spirituality and Resilience in Trauma Victims." *Journal of Religion and Health*46, no. 3 (2007): 343-50. Accessed July 1, 2019. doi:10.1007/s10943-006-9103-0.

183 https://www.verywellmind.com/ptsd-causes-and-risk-factors-2797397

184 https://www.verywellmind.com/ptsd-causes-and-risk-factors-2797397

185 http://www.traumacenter.org/resources/pdf_files/First_Responders.pdf

186 Brooks, S. K., Dunn, R., Amlot, R., Greenberg, N., & Rubin, G. J. (2016). Social and occupational factors associated with psychological distress and disorder among disaster responders: A systematic review. BMC Psychology, 4, 18. https://doi.org/10.1186/s40359-016-0120-9

187 https://maketheconnection.net/whats-new/ptsd-statistics

188 http://www.traumacenter.org/resources/pdf_files/First_Responders.pdf

189 Brooks, S. K., Dunn, R., Amlot, R., Greenberg, N., & Rubin, G. J. (2016). Social and occupational factors associated with psychological distress and disorder among disaster responders: A systematic review. BMC Psychology, 4, 18. https://doi.org/10.1186/s40359-016-0120-9

190 Weathers, F.W., Litz, B.T., Keane, T.M., Palmieri, P.A., Marx, B.P., & Schnurr, P.P. (2013). The PTSD Checklist for *DSM-5* (PCL-5). Scale available from the National Center for PTSD at www.ptsd.va.gov.

191 PCL-M for DSM-IV (11/1/94). Weathers, Litz, Huska, & Keane. National Center for PTSD – Behavioral Science Division. Retrieved from https://www.ptsd.va.gov/professional/assessment/adult-sr/ptsd-checklist.asp

192 Neugarten BL, Havighurst RJ, Tobin SS. The measurement of life satisfaction. J Gerontol 1961;16;134-143.

Life Satisfaction Index for the Third Age (LSITA-SF); (Barrett, A. J., & Murk, P. J. (2009). Life Satisfaction Index for the Third Age (LSITA): A measurement of successful aging. https://scholarworks.iupui.edu/handle/1805/1160)

193 Tool Reference: Jorm AF. A short form of the Informant Questionnaire on Cognitive Decline in the Elderly (IQCODE): development and cross-validation. Psychol Med 1994; 24: 145-153. https://www.alz.org/media/Documents/cognitive-assessment-toolkit.pdf

194 https://www.census.gov/newsroom/facts-for-features/2017/cb17-ff08.html

195 https://www.census.gov/newsroom/press-releases/2018/cb18-41-population-projections.html

196 https://www.cdc.gov/aging/pdf/mental_health.pdf

197 https://www.nimh.nih.gov/health/statistics/suicide.shtml

198 https://www.aginginplace.org/elderly-suicide-risks-detection-how-to-help/

199 https://www.alzheimers.net/resources/alzheimers-statistics/

200 https://www.alz.org/alzheimers-dementia/facts-figures

201 https://www.alz.org/alzheimers-dementia/facts-figures

202 https://www.alz.org/alzheimers-dementia/facts-figures

203 https://www.beingpatient.com/women-alzheimers/

204 https://alzheimersnewstoday.com/alzheimers-disease-statistics/

205 https://www.alzheimers.net/resources/alzheimers-statistics/

206 https://www.psychiary.org

207 https://www.medicalnewstoday.com/articles/323924.php

208 Adapted from American Psychiatric Association brochure, "Let's Talk Facts About – Alzheimer's Disease," 1992.

209 https://religionnews.com/2018/06/26/why-millennials-are-really-leaving-religion-its-not-just-politics-folks/

210 https://www.hindawi.com/journals/isrn/2012/278730/

211 http://www.fresnostate.edu/adminserv/learning/documents/Spiritual%20Wellness%20Assessment%2011_5_13.pdf

212 FACIT-Sp-Non-Illness: Functional Assessment of Chronic Illness Therapy – Spiritual Well-Being, a modified version for non-illness. English (Universal) 13 September 2010

Copyright 1987, 1997. Retrieved from https://www.facit.org/FACITOrg/Questionnaires

213 https://journals.sagepub.com/doi/pdf/10.1177/070674370905400502

214 Seirmarco, G., Neria, Y., Insel, B., Kiper, D., Doruk, A., Gross, R., & Litz, B. (2011, July 25). Religiosity and Mental Health: Changes in Religious Beliefs, Complicated Grief, Posttraumatic Stress Disorder, and Major Depression Following the September 11, 2001 Attacks. *Psychology of Religion and Spirituality.*

215 http://lifewayresearch.com/wp-content/uploads/2014/09/Acute-Mental-Illness-and-Christian-Faith-Research-Report-1.pdf

216 Pew Research Center. Survey Conducted April 25 – June 4, 2017.

217 Pew Research Center. Survey Conducted April 25 – June 4, 2017.

218 Gallup survey conducted by Frank Newport, Ph.D., 2017.

219 Gallup survey conducted by Frank Newport, Ph.D., 2017.

220 https://en.wikipedia.org/wiki/Spiritual_crisis

221 http://www.spiritofmaat.com/archive/sep2/truheart.htm

222 http://spiritualemergence.net/

223 From the back cover of *Spiritual Emergency: When Personal Transformation Becomes a Crisis (New Consciousness Readers)* by Stanislav Grof and Christina Grof, TarcherPerigee, 1989.

224 http://www.spiritualemergencenetwork.org/what-is-spiritual-emergency/

225 https://www.psychologytoday.com/us/blog/the-empowerment-diary/201507/is-it-psychosis-or-spiritual-emergency

226 https://www.encyclopedia.com/social-sciences/encyclopedias-almanacs-transcripts-and-maps/spiritual-crisis

227 http://spiritualemergence.net/

228 http://www.spiritofmaat.com/archive/sep2/truheart.htm

229 https://www.psychologytoday.com/us/blog/the-empowerment-diary/201507/is-it-psychosis-or-spiritual-emergency

230 https://www.iayt.org/page/SpiritualEmergence

231 https://blog.thewellnessuniverse.com/are-you-having-a-spiritual-crisis/

232 Levine, Madeline MPH. Jury, J. Nicolas, Ph.D., Mohseni, Kousha, MS., Srinivasan, MBBS., MPH., National Center for Health Research, 2010.

233 https://www.apa.org/news/press/releases/2017/11/lowest-point

234 https://www.healthline.com/nutrition/7-health-benefits-of-water#section7

235 Huizen, J. (2018, June 28). "Can water help you lose weight?." *Medical News Today*. Retrieved from https://www.medicalnewstoday.com/articles/322296.php.

236 "6 Benefits of Staying Hydrated", Wright, Brierley, One Medical. Retrieved from https://www.onemedical.com/blog/live-well/6-benefits-of-staying-hydrated/

237 https://www.medexpress.com/blog/better-health/7-ways-to-stay-hydrated-that-dont-involve-drinking-water.html

238 https://www.helpguide.org/articles/healthy-living/the-mental-health-benefits-of-exercise.htm

239 https://www.independent.co.uk/news/science/mindfulness-therapy-depression-anti-depressants-mental-health-research-meditation-a7003546.html

240 https://www.theguardian.com/theguardian/2000/apr/28/features11.g23

www.ingramcontent.com/pod-product-compliance
Lightning Source LLC
Chambersburg PA
CBHW081148270326
41930CB00014B/3083